# From Dualism to Oneness in Psychoanalysis

*From Dualism to Oneness in Psychoanalysis: A Zen Perspective on the Mind-Body Question* focuses on the shift in psychoanalytic thought, from a view of mind-body dualism to a contemporary non-dualistic perspective. Exploring this paradigm shift, Yorai Sella examines the impact of the work of psychoanalysts and researchers, such as Winnicott, Bion, Stern and Kohut, and delineates the contributions of three major schools of psychoanalytic thought in which the non-dualistic view is exemplified: (1) intersubjective; (2) neuro-psychoanalytic; and (3) mystically inclined psychoanalysis.

Reaching beyond the constraints of dualism, Sella delineates the interdisciplinary approaches leading to psychoanalysis's paradigm shift. Focusing on the unique contribution of Zen-Buddhism, the book draws on Ehei Dōgen's philosophy to substantiate the non-duality of subject and object, body and mind – ultimately leading from alienation and duality to what Bion has termed "at one-ment". The way in which psychoanalytic theory and practice may develop further along these lines is demonstrated throughout the book in a variety of clinical vignettes.

This book will inform the practice of all psychoanalysts, mental health professionals, psychotherapists and clinicians interested in body-mind issues in psychotherapy, in the philosophy of psychoanalysis, and in East–West dialogue.

**Yorai Sella, Ph.D.**, is a clinical psychologist, a psychoanalytic and Humanistic-integrative psychotherapist and a member of Tel Aviv Institute for Contemporary Psychoanalysis, Israel. He co-directs the East–West Integrative Psychotherapy training in the School of Social Work and teaches in the Faculty of Medicine, Tel Aviv University. He has practised Tai-Chi and martial arts for the past 30 years and is a student of Zen-Buddhism.

## Psyche and Soul: Psychoanalysis, Spirituality and Religion in Dialogue Book Series

Jill Salberg, Melanie Suchet and Marie Hoffman
Series Editors

The *Psyche and Soul: Psychoanalysis, Spirituality and Religion in Dialogue* series explores the intersection of psychoanalysis, spirituality and religion. By promoting dialogue, this series provides a platform for the vast and expanding interconnections, mutual influences and points of divergence amongst these disciplines. Extending beyond western religions of Judaism, Christianity and Islam, the series includes Eastern religions, contemplative studies, mysticism and philosophy. By bridging gaps, opening the vistas and responding to increasing societal yearnings for more spirituality in psychoanalysis, *Psyche and Soul* aims to cross these disciplines, fostering a more fluid interpenetration of ideas.

**Titles in this series:**

*Vol. 1: The Art of Jewish Pastoral Counseling: A Guide for All Faiths* by Michelle Friedman and Rachel Yehuda

*Vol. 2: Old and Dirty Gods: Religion, Antisemitism, and the Origins of Psychoanalysis* by Pamela Cooper-White

*Vol. 3: From Dualism to Oneness in Psychoanalysis: A Zen Perspective on the Mind-Body Question* by Yorai Sella

# From Dualism to Oneness in Psychoanalysis

A Zen Perspective on the Mind-Body Question

Yorai Sella

LONDON AND NEW YORK

First published 2018
by Routledge
2 Park Square, Milton Park, Abingdon, Oxon OX14 4RN

and by Routledge
711 Third Avenue, New York, NY 10017

*Routledge is an imprint of the Taylor & Francis Group, an informa business*

© 2018 Yorai Sella

The right of Yorai Sella to be identified as author of this work has been asserted by him in accordance with sections 77 and 78 of the Copyright, Designs and Patents Act 1988.

All rights reserved. No part of this book may be reprinted or reproduced or utilized in any form or by any electronic, mechanical, or other means, now known or hereafter invented, including photocopying and recording, or in any information storage or retrieval system, without permission in writing from the publishers.

*Trademark notice*: Product or corporate names may be trademarks or registered trademarks, and are used only for identification and explanation without intent to infringe.

*British Library Cataloguing in Publication Data*
A catalogue record for this book is available from the British Library

*Library of Congress Cataloging in Publication Data*
A catalog record for this book has been requested

ISBN: 978-1-138-57912-5 (hbk)
ISBN: 978-1-138-57913-2 (pbk)
ISBN: 978-1-351-26268-2 (ebk)

Typeset in Times New Roman
by Wearset Ltd, Boldon, Tyne and Wear

# Contents

Preface ix
Acknowledgements xii

**Introduction** 1

Intention and aims: unitive experience and the unitary turn 3
Conceptual guidelines and methodology 5
Structure of the book 8
Languages and translation 11
Notes 11

## PART I
## The quest: embodied minds and mindful bodies in psychoanalysis 13

### 1 A mysterious leap 15

Introduction 15
The body-mind problem 18
Body-mind dualism, the psyche-soma and psychoanalysis 22
In search of a theory: the psyche-soma and body-mind relations in psychoanalysis 28
Reframing paradigms 32
Conclusion and dialogue 38
Notes 41

## 2 Mysterious leaps: from psychosomatics to the psyche-soma    42

*Theory and meta-theory 42*
*Psyche-somatic meta-theories 43*
*The psyche-soma in object-relations 48*
*Psyche-somatic theory as a pivot of theoretical reformulation 54*
*Conclusion and dialogue 55*
*Notes 59*

## 3 The ascension of the body: representation and presentation    60

*The body 61*
*A new "ordering structure" 64*
*The soma's role in clinical theory and technique: the clinical body and the reflexive mind 72*
*Conclusion and dialogue 73*
*Notes 77*

## 4 Unitive experience and a unitary turn    79

*Unitive experience and unitary epistemology 80*
*The unitary turn: a hypothesized paradigm shift 83*
*Conclusion and dialogue 95*
*Notes 98*

## 5 The unitary turn: overarching conceptual structures    99

*Concepts 100*
*Traversing the "leaps": preliminary outlines for unitary formulations 108*
*Conclusion and dialogue 113*
*Notes 116*

## PART II
## 'Body-mind-one': the psychoanalytic riddle and the Zen response                117

*Introduction 117*
*Buddhism, Zen and psychoanalysis: an introduction 121*
*Contours of the psychoanalytic-Buddhist discourse:*
  *a brief history 123*
*Notes 126*

### 6 Non-duality in Zen-Buddhism: implications for the mind-body question in contemporary psychoanalysis                127

*Non-duality: Mahāyāna roots 128*
*Non-duality in Zen-Buddhism 131*
*Potentiality and the 'pre' of pre-ontology 139*
*Conclusion and dialogue 142*
*Notes 146*

### 7 The body of the Buddhist 'body-mind'                148

*Early Buddhist models of the 'body-mind' 149*
*Zen body and non-duality in Dōgen's* Shōbōgenzō *154*
*The clinical body 158*
*Conclusion and dialogue 163*
*Notes 167*

### 8 Embodiment and interpretation – not two                168

*Discursive thinking, language and body in*
  *psychoanalysis 172*
*Zen non-duality and an embodied language 176*
*Zen language 182*
*Conclusion and dialogue 187*
*Notes 191*

### 9 A non-dualistic body-mind-set in psychoanalysis?                192

*Meditative practice and contemporary*
  *psychoanalysis 194*

*In dialogue 195*
*Attunement 200*
*A Zen-minded attuned presence: the practice-wisdom of
    empathy 204*
*Conclusion and dialogue 211*
*Notes 215*

**10 From duality to oneness: Zen contributions to
psyche-soma meta-theory in contemporary
psychoanalysis**   216

*Point of departure 216*
*A unitary turn 219*
*The reformation of language and categories 220*
*The Zen of 'body-mind' 222*
*Conclusion and future directions 230*

*References*   234
*Index*   257

# Preface

Stationed in compulsory army training duty in the dust-draped, sandy hills of the Judea Desert in the midst of summer, nothing could prepare me for the formative experience I was about to witness. Our company leader suffered severe sunstroke. He was agitated, his face was flushed and his headache seemed agonizing. Standing by him was a newly arrived recruit, holding his hand. Slowly and intently he held some pressure points, continuously asking "What's happening now?" Gradually the Zen-Shiatsu procedure he was following gave my company leader – whose initial response was reluctance – great relief.

While some of my friends were interested in the technicalities of this curative procedure, I was observing the new recruit's face, his movements and his body language. I felt that, somehow, the key to the relief of suffering lay in his composed, yet intent and compassionate, features; that the way in which the young soldier held the pressure points, positioned his hand and timed the gentle intensity of his questions was a mindful extension of his psyche; that the physical headache had somehow relented to a mental disposition.

But was it a "physical" headache? Was the agitation physical? And was the aetiology really "sunstroke"? Or was it, rather, the price of leading a recalcitrant company in impossible conditions after – it had turned out – a separation from his erstwhile girl-friend? Only years later would I learn of Daniel Stern's *Forms of Vitality* and of Ehei Dōgen's contention that 'mind' and 'mindfulness' are as inseparable from pebbles and mountains as they are from skin, flesh, bones and marrow. But, already, naïvely free from preconceived categorizations, I could hardly fail to register the common denominators between desert heat, a warm, aching heart and the suppression of a heated, internal, emotional milieu. Hence, what had begun to intrigue me then was the intuition that suffering was caused by a synergy of physical, emotional and mental factors, compounding to form a physio-mental conglomerate.

I have been interested in the embodied mind and the mindful body since then. In Zen meditation, I learnt embodied composure. Through Zen-Shiatsu, I learnt that, in order to sense physical flow, I had to rest my mind; I also learnt that in order to rest my mind I had to allow for the full impetus of free flow: the two are inextricably intertwined. As Dōgen preaches, the concrete and the abstract, the practical and the mental are indivisible. When describing the meditative posture, he thus portrays it as a physio-mental state which is, contemporaneously, indivisibly, a spiritual "realization of practice" and a physical "practice of realization".

Zen taught me embodiment; Zen-shiatsu and Tai-Chi taught me the inter-corporeality of intersubjectivity, the constant, embodied, immanently intertwined dance of two seemingly disparate psyche-somas. Inextricably connected – body-mind immanently in relation to an-other's body-mind – these practices provided me with constant reminders of non-duality; constant reminders of the fact that – in Dōgen's words – the state wherein "your body-mind as well as the bodies and minds of others drop away", is prerequisite to the study of oneself and of other selves: this is performed through what Buddhism terms the 'Three Jewels' of 'body', 'mind' and 'speech'.

Being a student of clinical psychology in the 1980s meant a thorough study and internship based on classical psychoanalysis. My own analysis showed me that psychoanalysis worked. Moreover, it worked because of features I had already identified as healing: the mysterious leap from the mind to the body was definitely there, but the definitive categorizations of mind versus body were altering, had altered. This shift was seemingly going unnoticed. I was intent on finding how, what and where the psychoanalytic canon provided the configuration necessary for bridging what I perceived to be two artificial – body to mind, psyche-soma to psyche-soma – breaches. This book is the outcome of this research.

The following manuscript is thus a psychoanalytic foray beyond the constraints of dualism into unitive experiences and unitary formulations. Contemporary psychoanalysis, we know, is no longer an arena in which "nothing takes place … but an interchange of words between the patient and the analyst" (Freud, 1916, p. 17). Often it is an interactive setting wherein one watches – in consternation, awe and often in silence – the unfolding of creation and creativity from within deep psyche-somatic, incommunicado body-mind sets.

Silently interacting we, as therapists – consciously and unconsciously – provide 'silent' and 'procedural' interpretations. Their fecundity, their richness and their ultimate success in the provision of meaning are dependent on the integrity of our body-mind presence, a presence tantamount to what Durban (2011) terms "total interpretations"; within this conceptual trajectory, the totality of our presence is directly related to the totality of the patient's psyche-soma. Meaning is thus embedded in certain paralogical modes of body-mind presence, in a mystery of 'being' which is neither strictly physical nor strictly mental. Daniel Stern – in his last book before his death – termed these multifaceted mysteries "forms of vitality": experientially, ontologically and – ultimately – clinically, they transcend the 'body' to 'mind', psyche-soma to psyche-soma, divide. They thus stand as what Thomas Kuhn (2012) has termed "a new kind of fact" leading to a "paradigm shift", with a meta-theoretical – rather than a solely theoretical – status.

Inspired by my unusual desert army experience I commenced study and work as a therapist over 30 years ago. I spent both fervent and tranquil hours engulfed in the austerity of Zendos, the gravity of psychoanalytical consulting rooms and in sweat-washed martial arts *dojos*. I have worked with hundreds of patients in public, national health and private settings in Zen-Shiatsu, acupuncture, meditation, movement and body-oriented psychotherapy. Gradually integrating what I learnt from these practices into my psychoanalytic psychotherapy practice I feel now that I have come to befriend what Occidental philosophers term the 'hard question' – i.e. the 'body-mind question' – enough to acknowledge new kinds of facts, thus formulating new meta-theoretical, theoretical and clinical working-hypotheses.

With this in mind, I hope this book may accompany and aid others in forging their own path towards meaning formation and alleviation of suffering from within a cohesive theoretical framework and a vital psychesomatic being.

# Acknowledgements

I would like to begin by acknowledging my indebtedness to all my tutors of the Hermeneutics and Culture track in Bar Ilan University's Interdisciplinary Studies Department. They taught me more than I could ever have hoped for concerning thorough and critical textual probing and intercultural analysis. Without them the interdisciplinary research required for this text could not have come to be. Especially, I would like to express my gratitude to Dr Aner Govrin, who created a unique environment for the integration and cross-fertilization between the psychoanalytic and hermeneutic disciplines.

This book would never have come to be without the Psyche and Soul series editors: Jill Salberg, Melanie Suchet, and Marie Hoffman. Their patience, encouragement and trust throughout long months of reworking were indispensable in turning this text from a somewhat esoteric philosophical manuscript to a much friendlier and more useful one. Thank you!

I would like to extend my gratitude to Professor Yolanda Gampel from Tel-Aviv University's Psychology Department, who stood by my side with perfect trust at the final stages of this work. Yolanda's wisdom, courage and open-mindedness have long been an inspiration. Her support helped me retain faith in the value of this book in times of doubt.

I thank Professor Jacob Raz, former head of the Department of East Asian Studies in Tel Aviv University, for accompanying the initial stages of this conceptual foray. Professor Raz helped me separate the wheat from the chaff and concentrate on the writings of Ehei Dōgen as a constant stabilizing landmark.

My warm gratitude to Professor Galia Patt-Shamir, head of the Department of East Asian Studies in Tel Aviv University, for her patience, encouragement and sagacious advice.

I extend my heartfelt thanks to Raanan Kulka – a true teacher and guide – for his unqualified support for this project and for the inspiration he gave me in the course of writing this book. With a rare blend of compassionate involvement and scholarly equanimity, Raanan's example enlightened me as to the manner in which the psychoanalytic process and Buddhist practice may converge to form a complementary and life-sustaining stream of 'practice realization'.

I would like to thank my colleague and friend, Naomi Urbach-Shvili of the Dmut Institute, Jerusalem, for accompanying the initiation and progress of this project in numerous informal conversations, in our joint clinic and in a variety of Jerusalem's coffee shops. Naomi helped me fathom essential facets of the Zen-Daoist interface as relates to energy, vitality and the realities of constant flux and 'un-integration'. Our joint work and her long-standing support over the years have had an important influence on formulating and structuring this conceptual work.

I thank my colleague and friend Dr Ester Pelled for helping me think out some aspects of this work and for standing by me at significant landmarks during the writing of this book.

I wish to thank my colleague and friend Dr Eitan Bolokan from the Department of East Asian Studies in Tel Aviv University, for collegially aiding me and for tutoring me in my first hesitant steps of studying both Japanese language and Dōgen's *Shōbōgenzō*. With his profound commitment to elucidating Dōgen's mystical-realistic heritage, Eitan constantly inspired me and consistently provided me with a road map of immaculate precision.

I extend my thanks to my friends and colleagues, Dr Alon Reshef, Einat Drucker and Tamar Eshel-Bialer of HaEmek Hospital's Integrative Psychiatry Unit, Afula, for their sincere interest in my work, for their helpful remarks and for their companionship and support along the way.

My thanks to Rami Yulzari, Aviv Tatarsky, Eilat Zuckerman, Idit Yunis, Yaniv Pesso and their students of the Maga School of Zen-Shiatsu. Their unqualified trust provided this book with the 'without thinking' embodiment required for a 'body-mind study of the way', leading to a 'moulting of body and mind'.

This work would never have come to be without hours spent in psychoanalytic processes and in training of long duration under the guidance of the following therapists and teachers of psychotherapy, martial arts, medical practice and meditation: Helen Davis of the Minster Center for Integrative-Humanistic Psychotherapy, Maura Sills and Ian Rees of the Karuna Institute for Buddhist-informed Core Process Psychotherapy, Ken Waight, founder of the Seishin-Kitaido system and Dokyo San Roshi of the Jerusalem and London Zendos. Asi Ben-Porat, Benyamin Davidesko and Master Michiko Nitobe – Tai Chi, Chi-Kong and martial arts instructors. Last but not least: my friend, colleague and Zen-shiatsu instructor, Nigel Dawes, and my tutors and supervisors, Stephen Russel, Dr Judith Issroff and Mati ben-Zur. I am greatly indebted to all of them for hours spent in study, in silent analysis, in movement and in heartfelt sobs and laughter which arise from deeply abiding in an atmosphere of sincerity and companionship.

My heartfelt thanks to my patients and clients. Their unwavering trust enabled me to follow our intertwined paths in faith and to reciprocate by facilitating the – often hazardous and painful – joint process of dependent co-arising in and of body, speech and mind.

My students over the years have been a source of support and inspiration. I have learnt much of what I now know through years of experimenting, sharing in their experimentations and listening to their formulations. This book is born of our shared psychotherapeutic work, meditative contemplations and expressive movements; ultimately these have led us to rare moments of revelation, allowing us to experience 'body and mind as one'.

And, finally: my most heartfelt and deepest thanks to my beloved wife, friend and partner, Tali, and to my lovely daughters, Liel and Suf, who unhesitatingly supported me. Without their patience and endless love throughout the long years of writing, this book would never have come to be.

Bless you all.

# Introduction

Historically, Freud's incomprehensible "leap from a mental process to a somatic [one]" (Freud, 1909, p. 157) – the "mysterious leap from the mind to the body" – provided the blueprint for the psychoanalytic theory of psychotherapy: it has shown that body and mind interact; it has also shown that – where a cohesive body-mind meta-theory is lacking – mystery, inconsistency and confusion prevail: psychoanalytic prehistory supported the use of physical treatments to treat mental ailments; psychoanalytic history – spawned by the 'mind to body leap' – rendered physical interventions taboo. With such drastic pendular swings in the meta-theory of psyche-soma theorization, it is not surprising that concrete-physical aspects of clinical methodology are circumspect: British analyst Graeme Galton (2006) faced harsh criticism when researching the use of touch in psychoanalytic psychotherapy; psyche-somatic convergence – a bridging of the 'mysterious leap' – is considered a theoretical misnomer: discussing *Bodies in Treatment*, relational analyst Frances Anderson (2008) describes being "at a loss for words and feelings" (p. 22) that might enable her to approach and describe the non-dual nature of her own experience of a joint, non-dual psyche-somatic core.

Personally, I was fortunate to have escaped their predicament. My first therapist – a psychoanalyst, Zen student and long-time supervisee of Donald Winnicott's – used to give me a big burly hug at the end of our sessions, often complementing this gesture by commenting: "You are much more present here, now." What I could not avoid – as a psychology graduate – was puzzling over the experience, analysing its components and attempting a formulation of what she meant when she referred to my "presence": I could not but attempt to determine, define and delineate the physiological-sensual and mental-psychological contours of this elusive experience and its conceptualization. And – reflecting on our sessions and feeling the undulating emotional residues of this physical holding – could not but wonder: is this appropriate psychoanalytic procedure? Where and under what rubric does it fit in? Where does it enter the syllabus?

Inspired by such experiences and driven by accounts such as Galton's and Anderson's, this book was conceived of as an intuition as to the developing proclivity towards non-dual formulations in contemporary psychoanalysis (see Black, 2011, and Stolorow, 2011, for some examples). Emerging from this intuition is the conviction that non-dualistic philosophies may contribute to the formulation of a novel theoretical substrate for a comprehensive model of body-mind relations within psychoanalysis. Inevitably, this intuition must contend with a competing one, of long standing:

> That man is made up of mind and body seems so self-evident that we cannot readily imagine what it would be like to be without such a hypothesis; indeed, this concept is not considered a hypothesis linked to a particular philosophical model at all, but an indisputable fact of nature.
>
> (Basch, 1976, p. 388)

The psychoanalytic credo is reiterated in linguistic and philosophical models: Johnson (1993, p. 2) stipulates that "mind body dualism is so deeply embedded in our philosophical and religious traditions, in our shared conceptual systems and in our language, that it can be seen to be an inescapable fact of our human nature".

It has thus seemed to be a potentially promising conjecture that – since "in the absence of *external feedback*, the language and conceptualization of a discipline grow increasingly arcane and splintered" (Sawyier, 1973, p. 216, my italics) – alternative theories be drawn upon, from outside the habitual ken of psychoanalysis. Early instances of East–West dialogue have provided a fertile field for such cross-fertilization, particularly since the point of departure for "equations ... between Eastern and Western ideas is that the two worlds do not start with the same assumptions and premises ... [or] ... categorizations of experience" (Watts, 1957, p. 93). This is extremely pertinent to the emerging field of interdisciplinary dialogue in the history of medicine (Kuriyama, 1999).

Epistemology lagging behind ontology is a feature that psychoanalysis shares with other fields of applied knowledge: even when rethinking the ontology of dualistically based clinical practice in regard to body and mind (as suggested in Lazar, 2001; Reis, 2007) it has taken little heed of the epistemological implications of this practice. Moreover, it has – to date – failed to produce a coherent theory regarding the complexity of reciprocal body-mind connections within subject–object matrices: despite the fact that, even today, "most clinical practitioners today know (although often in a non-theoretical and intuitive way) that mind and body are inseparable ... they are without the vocabulary and concepts to address – let alone the tools to probe – this mindful body" (Scheper-Hughes & Lock, 1987). It is thus my contention that ontological and epistemological cohesion regarding all these issues may benefit tremendously from discourse with an indigenously non-dualistic philosophical culture. Therefore, I would suggest that Eastern theoretical formulations may serve as a potential theoretical infrastructure for stating alternative categories, leading to non-dualistic configurations for body-mind relations in psychoanalysis.

## Intention and aims: unitive experience and the unitary turn

It is thus my intention to examine the ontological and epistemological assumptions and presumptions underlying contemporary psychoanalytic theory, in regard to the 'body-mind' question. I will endeavour to chart the evolution of psychoanalysis in this regard and to survey the pathways of both implicit theoretical developments and explicit theories, regarding 'psyche-soma'[1] relations. I suggest that major strands in contemporary theory and practice pertaining to 'psyche-soma' relations rely, at times inadvertently, on presuppositions, assumptions, presumptions and theoretical terminology which lie outside the scope of explicit psychoanalytical convention. These often lead – implicitly or explicitly – to the espousal of non-dualistic terminology. More particularly, I focus on major tenets of contemporary psychoanalytic practice, emerging from the following premises:

1  Intersubjectivity presupposes the effect of the analyst's state of mind on the analysand's somatic experience and somatic state (see Frie, 2007; and Knoblauch 2011, 2014, for contemporary examples).

2 Neuro-psychoanalytic theory and developmental research recognize the continuity and persistence – throughout life – of physio-mental states that developmentally pre-date and preclude verbal communicability, but are communicable semiotically (Stern, 1985; Beebe & Lachmann, 1994, 1998; Trevarthen, 2005).
3 Mystical-religious terminology within psychoanalytic theory suggests the existence of an overarching framework that circumvents conventional categorization of body-mind and psyche-soma into exclusive and discrete substances or functions (Eigen, 1981, 1983; Lawner, 2001; Black, 2006a).
4 Insights from Object Relations and Independent School theories allude to a potential state, prior to psychosomatic differentiation, both temporally, i.e. developmentally, and ontologically (Milner, 1969; Meltzer, 1986; De Bianchedi, 2002).

I stipulate that these innovative paradigm shifts regarding psyche-somatic unitive experiences are not lodged in parsimonious, cohesive and coherent philosophical statements to support their research and clinical findings. I shall consequently assert that, owing to the lack of both coherent theoretical support and attendant terminology within psychoanalytic theory, conceptual and terminological lacunae have evolved. Consequently, I propose that – "as there currently exists no overarching framework that can conceptually connect the basic terms of psychoanalytical theory in regard to the 'body-mind question', the conceptual framework itself becomes an ultimate goal of research" (Opatow, 1999, p. 97). All of the above are accompanied by examples and vignettes from my personal and clinical experience.

The book will therefore review and survey the underpinnings of explanatory frameworks regarding psyche-soma relations in psychoanalysis. It will then demonstrate the manner in which their blind spots are potentially illumined by concepts, terminology and methodologies borrowed from Eastern paradigms. More specifically, I seek to substantiate the potential contributions and applicability of Zen-Buddhist philosophical tenets to the question of psyche-soma relations within psychoanalysis. The text will outline these tenets, focusing on the specific contributions of Eihei Dōgen, the founder of Japanese Soto-Zen, as explicated in his magnum opus, *Shōbōgenzō*,[2] with particular attention given to exegesis of body-mind relations in his work. I will argue that a conceptual mesh derived from Zen-Buddhism provides a potential world-view and overarching infrastructure for the perception, conceptualization and implementation of a 'unitary turn' as regards 'unitive' body-mind relations within psychoanalysis. This and the preceding observations will be organized along four axis:

1 Potentiality of existence as a predicate which precedes substantial manifestation.
2 Constant change as a foundational position.
3 Inevitable limitations and constraints on language, as a valid means of construing and recognizing reality.
4 The meditative state as enabling a presence within, and a non-judgemental recognition of, a non-dualistic psyche-somatic state.

I shall endeavour to show how the convergence of these attributes serves to create a conceptual explanatory framework, which enriches and validates nascent and established paradigms regarding body-mind relations in contemporary psychoanalysis. In doing so, it furthers the cohesion and integration of seemingly discrete psychoanalytic paradigms. It thus serves to substantiate a congruent 'unitary turn' in the perception and conceptualization of body-mind relations in psychoanalysis.

## Conceptual guidelines and methodology

According to the framework charted above, the book proceeds in the following steps:

1 Outlines the evolution and current status of philosophical and theoretical presuppositions regarding body-mind relations underlying orthodox psychoanalytic theories.
2 Points out the tendency of these presuppositions and theories to gradually shift from paradigms relating to discrete structures to paradigms inclusive of psycho-somatic unity.
3 Examines the proposition of a 'unitary turn' in the conceptualization of psyche and soma relations within intersubjective, neuro-psychoanalytic and mystical-religious trends within psychoanalysis.
4 Implements insights gained from these strands in examining the assumption that, in significant fields within contemporary psychoanalysis, 'body' and 'mind' are regarded as a compound unitary structure.

5 Examines Zen-Buddhist philosophical concepts as potential contributions and alternatives for conceptualizing unitary models and unitive experiences in contemporary psychoanalysis.

In taking these steps the text will draw most particularly on four major sources:

1 Canonical psychoanalytic literature specifically pertaining to body-mind and psyche-soma relations, such as Donald Winnicott's "Mind and its relation to the psyche-soma" (1954), or Didier Anzieu's *The Skin Ego* (1989). Through these texts I shall demonstrate the existence of salient features – shared by otherwise divergent and competing schools of psychoanalysis – pertaining to unitive experiences and unitary formulations of body and mind.
2 Psychoanalytic texts explicitly or implicitly presenting unitary formulations or nomenclature, such as Winnicott's "psyche-soma" (1956), Bion's "at-one-ment" (1970), or Daniel Stern's *Forms of Vitality* (2010). The psychoanalytic papers used and cited will be drawn from the Psychoanalytic Electronic Publishing's (P.E.P.) virtual library. I regard journals published in this format as representing the *Zeitgeist* prevalent at the time of their issue. Cumulatively I shall show them to represent particular conceptual *Weltanschauungen* (world-views).
3 Buddhist texts implicitly or explicitly relating to body-mind relations. I favour Zen-Buddhist texts over Theravadin texts owing to Zen's foundationally non-dualistic outlook. I focus particularly on Eihei Dōgen's canonical *Shōbōgenzō*, due to its cohesive contributions to a 'body-mind' compound predication. The varied contexts in which the term 'body-mind' is employed in this text amalgamate to enable the hermeneutic reading of the 'body-mind' as a composite structure and a compound epistemological and semiotic vehicle. Dōgen's unique contributions to the understanding of non-duality as cited in psychoanalytic texts support this approach (see Adams, 1995; Rubin, 1996; Magid, 2000; Alfano, 2005; Safran, 2006; Kulka, 2012).
4 Regarding the *Shōbōgenzō*, I draw on both general interpretations and commentaries (such as Tanahashi, 1985, 2010; Cook, 1989; Stambough, 1990; Heine, 1994; Kim, 2004, 2007) and on interpretations and commentaries pertaining *specifically* to mind-body relations

within the *Shōbōgenzō* (such as Shaner, 1985a, 1985b; Kasulis, 1989, 1993; Nagatomo, 1992; Yuasa, 1987, 1993).

Additionally, I shall use the ongoing conceptual dialogue between psychoanalysis and Buddhism as a supportive scaffolding throughout the book. Within this dialogue, psychoanalytical literature has historically concentrated on issues such as Buddhist meditative practice as an altered state of mind, as enhancing perception, or as a spiritual extension of psychoanalytic thinking. It is, however, my contention that, though this fertile and long-standing dialogue has contributed much to psychoanalysis, its specific potential contribution to the question of 'body-mind' or 'psyche-soma' relations has gone largely unnoticed. This is in stark contrast to the richness of literature pertaining to Buddhist-based 'body-mind' theory in cognitive psychology (Varela, Thompson & Rosch, 1993; Nauriyal, Drummond & Lal, 2006) or cognitive psychotherapy (Siegel, 2010).

Throughout the book – and especially in Part I – a number of eminent Occidental philosophers are mentioned, viewed through a restricted prism: Plato and Aristotle are briefly presented as the founding fathers of Occidental philosophical orthodoxy and – Plato especially – as the forebears of Cartesian dualism. Otherwise, the various philosophers mentioned are those whose concepts are used in psychoanalytic papers – cited in the text – in support of psychoanalytic theorizing, with two qualifications:

1 The particular value of phenomenology – Merleau-Ponty's work in particular – in supporting contemporary psychoanalytic body-mind theories warrants a somewhat deeper survey of its contributions. This is underscored by the obvious affinity of the phenomenological outlook with Buddhist theorizing (see Parkes, 1987; Abe, 1992; Park & Kopf, 2009), which lends particular weight to its argumentation regarding the 'body-mind' experience in the present text.
2 Lakoff and Johnson's – together and separately – monumental philosophical-linguistic project provides an invaluable testimony to the intertwining of body, mind, culture and language; it thus provides an invaluable infrastructure for analysing and deciphering the connections between them in the inter-cultural context of this book.

## Structure of the book

The book is divided into two Parts. Part I considers the progression, within psychoanalysis, from a dualistic vantage point, through interactionist models to some unitary formulations. It considers some proposed resolutions to the mysterious leap from the psyche to the soma, pointing out their limitations. The point of departure for Part II is that conceptual, philosophical and cultural aspects of non-dualistic Eastern philosophies – particularly Zen-Buddhism – potentially provide an alternative ordering to body-mind relations. This enables the accommodation of unitive experiences and unitary formulations and language, potentially providing a revised framework for body-mind meta-theory in psychoanalysis.

## Part I: the quest: embodied minds and mindful bodies in psychoanalysis

Chapter 1 shows how psychoanalysis replicates the classical philosophical 'body-mind' debate, adhering to categorical, evaluative and developmental fissures between psyche and soma. With contemporary psychoanalysis displaying a growing recognition of psyche and soma non-duality, the need arises for extra-disciplinary theorems to escape from these engrained presuppositions: phenomenology is shown to provide some support for a co-joint psyche-soma unit. The potential advantages of Eastern non-dual formulations – free of Platonic and Cartesian heritages – to provide these alternative meta-theoretical paradigms are discussed.

Chapter 2 traces the legacy of the energetic and psychosomatic models. It focuses on the need to formulate a theory accommodating multiple 'leaps' between the patient's and analyst's 'psyche' and 'soma', suggesting intricate and reciprocal interactive psyche-somatic functioning. It explores the manner in which recognition of non-verbal modes of interaction within specific psychoanalytic schools upsets the conventional division between biologistic and hermeneutic meta-theories. It further demonstrates 'psyche-somatic' theory to be a pivot of theoretical reformulation: direct *presentation* – as opposed to symbolic representation – and the analyst's psyche-somatic predisposition and physical demeanour are seen to be determining factors in the analytic process.

Chapter 3 traces the ascension of the 'soma' and body-determined subjectivity. Drawing on Merleau-Ponty's phenomenological theory, it suggests that psychoanalysis has come to acknowledge the enacted and performative aspects of interaction as intersubjectively determining subjectivity. This partly semiotic communication is cast against the aspirations – and perceived limitations – of linguistic interpretation. Consciousness and subjectivity are thus redefined to include a somatic component: unconventionally, they are not seen as limited to cognitive capacities, and are not located in the head; rather, they are seen as suffusing the whole body.

Chapter 4 considers specific strands within psychoanalysis which have embraced unitive experience and/or unitary formulations. This espousal is displayed in the use of terminology alluding to joint psyche-somatic 'pre-reflective', structures and processes, leading to experiential 'oneness', 'fusion' or 'undifferentiation'. This is followed by a critical appraisal of the positions taken by intersubjective, mystical-religious, neuro-psychoanalytic and some developmental thinkers. Overarching linguistic categories – such as 'aliveness', 'vitality' and 'rhythm' – are shown to straddle and override 'psyche' to 'soma' divisions. In a similar vein, it is suggested that overarching categories referring to 'proto', 'pre' or 'supra' ordering structures may converge to form the seminal basis for innovative 'connectionist' meta-theoretical propositions.

Chapter 5 examines whether conceptualizations in earlier chapters converge to form cohesive theories of non-duality. The point of departure is that novel categories of experience or an ultra-experiential framework are required in order to substantiate the theoretical findings cited in previous chapters. 'Paradox', 'complementarity', 'mysterious undercurrents' and 'systems/connectionist' models are considered as potential resolutions for the dilemmas posed in the preceding chapters. The perceived limitations of the above explanatory models emphasize the need for a meta-theoretical framework bringing together ontological considerations and epistemological ones. The chapter consequently sets the stage for the introduction of Eastern paradigms as alternative paradigmatic explanatory models.

## Part II: 'body-mind-one': the psychoanalytic riddle and the Zen response

Part II is largely a mirror image of Part I, returning to the same themes through a Zen-Buddhist perspective. The Introduction comprises two sections: the first is a revision reiterating the basic tenets of Part I, listing inadequacies and contradictions in extant body-mind configurations. The second provides a summary of psychoanalytic-Buddhist dialogue, showing the contribution of Buddhist approaches in providing a wide existential matrix within a non-dualistic framework. It is stressed that *the purpose of the present work is not comparative or dialogical*: it uses the Buddhist terminology provocatively, in order to potentially enhance, enrich, modify or substitute extant terminology, where psychoanalytic non-dualistic propositions fall short.

Chapter 6 focuses on Nāgārjuna's philosophy of 'emptiness' of substantiality and of intrinsic meanings as the foundation and precursor to Zen-Buddhist notions of non-duality. The non-plurality of the world and the non-difference of subject and object are shown to be inextricably co-determined by an embodied, participatory, "without-thinking", active cognizance. Additionally, configurations of the potentiality of existence continuously subsisting substantial manifestation, and the substantiality of constant change are shown to nullify orthodox 'body' to 'mind' dichotomies. Rather, they adhere to connectionist and systems theorems deferring to emergent non-discriminate properties.

Chapter 7 follows three discrete trajectories of body-mind relations: examining early Buddhist concepts, the body-mind is presented as a stringently interactive system, mutually and reciprocally constituted. The outcome is a fluctuation of body-mind impromptu selfhoods, described as a series of continuous 'events'. Next, Dōgen's radical view as to the indivisibility of the body-mind system is evaluated in light of its phenomenological, ontological and epistemological implications. Finally, the issue of the "clinical body" is conceptualized as an intricate physical-mental-emotional network, defined and organized by the liminal concept of 'qi'.

Chapter 8 examines 'discursive' versus 'embodied' thinking and seeks to counter two supposedly veridical propositions: the proposition as to the ineffable nature of reality, and the proposition as to the inherent limitations of language. Dōgen's unique epistemological approach is introduced, stressing his concepts pertaining to a joint physio-mental posture (in meditative practice) and to the "moulting" of body and mind. Seeking to bridge the gap between 'presentation' and 'representation' and the 'sign-signified' breach, the category of 'expression' is introduced. Within this category, language and practice are indivisible, welding verbal utterances with an embodied cognizance, thus creating "live words".

Chapter 9 negotiates the challenge of outlining an embodied therapeutic disposition, conducive to furthering body-mind integration. Initially, it discusses Buddhist meditative practice as enhancing the therapist's introspective, perceptual and empathetic capabilities. It then focuses on Zen's particular contribution to mutual psyche-somatic 'attunement' and its relation to the concepts of 'attunement' and 'interpretation' in contemporary psychoanalysis. The terms 'intercorporeality' and 'interpenetration' between analyst and patient further refine these concepts. Finally, the notion of the therapist's embodied empathic-compassionate role as *constitutive of the patient's body-mind integration and transmutation* is introduced.

Chapter 10 re-examines the point of departure and the basic premises on which the entire manuscript rests. Initially it charts out the route from duality to oneness in psyche-soma relations implicitly taken by specific strands of contemporary psychoanalysis, exposing some of the conceptual lacunae along this route. The culmination of this chapter is in outlining the epistemological, ontological, phenomenological and linguistic contributions of Zen-Buddhism to the view of the psyche-soma according to psychoanalysis. These converge in the re-contextualization of 'potentiality', 'change', 'meditative states' and 'constraints on language' as comprising an infrastructure enabling the reappraisal of unresolved dilemmas and paradoxes presented in Part I. A brief outline for future research and its potential implications are then presented.

## Languages and translation

For convenience sake, citation of Buddhist texts defers to the nosology and transliteration most prevalent within psychoanalytic texts, which is, by and large, Sanskrit (designated Skt.): thus "sūtra" and not "sutta", for example. The only exceptions are quotations wherein other transliterations form part of the text, or on rare occasions when convenience (readers' familiarity with specific terms) dictates otherwise. The prevalent abbreviation accompanying Zen texts is Jap. (Japanese). In using Chinese terms, the modern Pinyin transliteration is used. For Dōgen's opus magnum, the *Shōbōgenzō*, I rely mainly on Kazuaki Tanahashi's (1985) and (2010) compilations.

## Notes

1 The differences between the terms 'psychosoma/tics', 'psyche-soma' and 'psychesoma' will be discussed in Chapters 1, 2 and 3.
2 Literally meaning "Treasury of the True Dharma Eye" (Tanahashi, 1985, 2010).

Part I
# The quest
Embodied minds and mindful bodies in psychoanalysis

# Chapter 1

# A mysterious leap

## Introduction

It's Monday morning. As the hours pass, they define themselves by 50-minute lots, by ten-minute slots for tidying up, opening the window, airing, noting the transference, the resonance, the ambience, the counter-transference, jotting down a few words, looking at messages, WhatsApps, emails, stretching, going to the toilet.

The first patient sits on the couch. He originally approached me regarding intimacy issues. He is forlorn, subdued. His monotonous drone numbs us both; he sinks and stoops as he goes on...

The second patient approached me years ago for unexplained dissociative episodes. She hides her chest and breasts by hunching her shoulders. As she lies down, her eyes close as if dreaming, blinking rapidly. She yawns and exhales heavily, frustrated at being unable to sob.

The third patient originally sought therapy in order to resolve a marital crisis. He comes in briskly, exuding a fresh odour which I identify with his overall Hassidic appearance. His throat is tight and at times – his jovial attitude notwithstanding – he seems to be literally choking. He had sought therapy fearing breakdown yet yearns for a "big bang" – a radical new beginning to his current life as an established family man living in hypocrisy.

It's almost lunch time and I have a moment to take mental note – and some written notes – of what has transpired. I write: the first patient leaves the room holding his head differently, and there is more brusqueness in his gait; the second has some more softness in her chest and has stopped sighing. The third is speaking more openly and his voice is less tense.

They have all experienced some psyche-somatic change as an outcome of a psychoanalytic therapy hour.

Over the past century or so, the aims and scope of psychoanalysis have changed so radically that its initial imperative, the treatment of bodily symptomatology via the 'talking cure', is easily forgotten. The theoretical seeds underlying this imperative were sown by Freud. So were its theoretical shortcomings.

> Freud spoke of an enigmatic leap from the psyche to the soma: in suggesting a "leap" Freud reaffirmed at once the existence of the psyche and the soma as two different entities, as well as the mysteriousness of the interaction between the two.
> (Arieti, 1981, p. 181)

Although striving to discover the common ground the convergence of physical and mental disorder (Wallace, 1992), within the constraints of then-contemporary conceptualizations, Freud gradually resigned himself to the fact that the "leap" "can never be fully comprehensible to us" (Freud, 1909, p. 157).

Freud was a scientist and his puzzlement rested on scientific premises: given that body and mind are two distinct entities, how does one explain the fact that bodily symptomatology reflects mental-psychic issues? Moreover, Freudian theory represented another seeming paradox. Recapitulating the transfiguration of "the Word was made flesh" (John, 1:14), it relied on the transformative capacity of words: without conceptually spelling it out, Freud suggested that the mental contents of the psychoanalyst's mind – verbally transmitted – could affect the body of the patient. He termed this transformative vehicle "interpretation". The mysterious leap from the mind to the body represented an intra-personal enigma; the leap encapsulated in interpretation reflected an interpersonal mystery, a miraculous leap from one person's 'psyche' to another person's 'soma' within the dyadic matrix of psychoanalytic interactions. Both intrapsychic and interpersonal leaps have pervaded psychoanalytic thinking ever since, creating the blueprint for psychoanalytical world-views.

Contending with these paradoxical "leaps", contemporary praxis and methodology have done much towards eliding the dualistic positioning of body and mind, subject and object, gradually embracing non-dualistic formulations (see Black, 2011; Stolorow, 2011). However, despite having reformulated clinical practice, it has taken little heed of the implications of these reformulations on orthodox, dualistically based, theory and meta-theory. Over and above all, it has all but overlooked its far-reaching impact on the reformation of the psychoanalytic world-view: as opposed to Freud's (1933a) original one, which repudiated philosophical, religious and aesthetic contributions, the contemporary world-view cherishes philosophical and mystical inputs. It incorporates both Western phenomenological propositions and Eastern philosophies' seemingly mystical contributions. Together they converge to present "new kinds of facts", leading to what Kuhn (2012) terms a "paradigm shift", reflected in non-dualistic attitudes to psyche-soma relations.

Freud eventually replaced his original energetic economic model with later topographical and structural models. The gradual decline of physiologically based theories went hand in hand with the elision in meta-theoretical statements based on the centrality of instincts, drives and energy. While acknowledging that the ego "is first and foremost a body ego" (Freud, 1923, p. 26), Freud made it clear that direct attention to physical attributes of experience was circumspect, was considered regressive, and was to be suspended during analysis. Over the years it has become more and more the narrated associations and thoughts – the *representations* of the body – and not the *presence* of 'body qua body' that are dealt with by the therapist, defining psychoanalysis "in terms that tend to disregard, minimize, ignore, or prescind from ... bodily involvement" (Meissner, 2003b, p. 280). Having forsaken the physiologically based "Project for a Scientific Psychology" in 1895, Freud himself described the discipline he fathered as "characterized not by the material it treats but by the technique it uses" (Ammon, 1979, p. 15). As the body's role in later theory declined, body-mind theory has converged – across psychoanalytic schools – around the following premises:

1 *The developmental standpoint*: the view of the body as the primitive aspect of selfhood, within an epigenetic model wherein the symbolical contents of the mind gradually supersede the bodily-based primary processes.
2 *The evaluative standpoint:* the view of the body as inferior and the psyche as the superior counterpart within the 'psyche-soma'.
3 *The categorical standpoint*: the view of the body and mind as comprising substantially different contents and belonging to mutually exclusive categories, thereby substantiating the body-mind dualism.

On what conceptual, cultural and philosophical grounds do these presuppositions rest? What subsists them and how do the Freudian inexplicable "leaps" reflect them? In order to respond to these questions I would like to uncover some of the philosophical substrate from which psychoanalysis emerged.

## The body-mind problem

Long anticipating Freud's paradoxes, the body-mind problem has widely been held to be a – if not 'the' – central issue in Western philosophy of mind, regarded by some as insoluble. Consequently, the implications of sought-after resolutions to the mind-body question are seen by some thinkers to be sublimely significant: little wonder that Thomas Nagel – the renowned author of *Mind and Cosmos*– has suggested that "a solution to the mind-body problem will alter our conception of the universe as anything has, to date" (1986, p. 51).

## *Western classical philosophical heritage and the 'body-mind' question*

What makes this question so essentially important and its resolution so paradoxical? Put in a nutshell, the inherent paradox – as viewed within the Western philosophical-cultural heritage – is as follows:

1  The human body is a material thing.
2  The human mind is a spiritual thing.
3  Mind and body interact.
4  Spirit and matter do not interact (Campbell, 1970, p. 14).

The Western history of philosophy ascribes the foundations of the body-mind debate to Plato's dualism. Platonic depictions of the soul as "using the body", "being available for the body", "donning the body as a cloak in such a way that it may be shed", as featured in the *Phaedo* (see Rist, 1970/1988), have been the blueprint for Western body-mind dualism. It is due to this depiction that "the truth of the idea that human beings consist of a material body and an immaterial soul or spirit" (Cooper, 1989, p. 36) is so deeply ingrained. The same configurations were later transposed onto metaphysical terms more applicable to early psychoanalytic theory or psychological research, such as 'motive' or 'impulse' (Klein, 1970) or onto the concept of the 'mind' itself.

The hold of Platonism was further reinforced via the influential thrust of "Christian Platonism" (Cooper, 1989) wherein "dualism of body and soul, matter and mind, god and the world was grafted on to Greek thought" (Zeller, 1955, p. 314). Accordingly, debate as to the role and function of the immaterial aspects of the 'psyche-soma' has been relegated to the realm of theology rather than philosophy. The soul's sovereignty over the body was attributed to its transcendental origin; since it was universally accepted that "the human soul is immaterial and immortal, that it is the form of the body and that ... it is directly created by god" (James, 2000, p. 112), alternative views were declared heresy, and accordingly, punishable.

Inherent within this position we find the seemingly indubitable prejudice that has accompanied Western conceptual traditions in various forms: since 'Genesis creation' was initiated by the "Word of God", it carried within it the supremacy of a "word-divinity" duo. The value-laden prejudice of this duo suggests the intrinsic precedence of the immaterial over the material, manifest in the sanctity of the 'word' when transmuting the somatic 'flesh', denying the somatic faculty an equally essential-substantial status. Models of psychosomatic relations embedded within the Platonic-Christian philosophical tradition therefore carry the seeds of both a developmental and an evaluative bias, favouring the immaterial over the material-phenomenal.

## Aristotle

Platonic and Aristotelian views converge in equating the uniqueness of human subjectivity with immateriality.[1] However, for Aristotle, the mind's independent function, as a reflective apparatus, defines human personhood, in contradistinction to the animation of *all* living beings by a 'soul'. Implicit within this proposition we find the claim that "the greatest happiness and the greatest good for man [are] ... realized ... in the contemplative life" (Aristotle, *Nicomachean Ethics*, x, 7, quoted in Armstrong, 1999, p. 12). Aristotelian theory thus anticipates the European Enlightenment in stressing the *intellectual component of the immaterial aspect of human personhood*, it – and not the 'soul' as such – is described as immortal.

Equally relevant is Aristotle's emphasis on logical reasoning as the superior form of rhetoric: 'logos' shares its Greek etymology with 'the spoken word', on the one hand, and, significantly, is equated with the divinity of Christ incarnate, on the other. This suggests a triune welding of rationality, divinity and verbal communication. Thus, it has become culturally embedded within Western culture that a higher self-postulate (the rational part) "must seek to control the lower self (body, desire, emotion) [and] ... that each of us has an inner core (... true self or a 'soul') that transcends our bodily, situated self" (Johnson, 1993, p. 2). Hanna and Maiese (2009) argue that psychoanalysis's long-standing formulation of the drive-instinct-based unconscious, as the locus wherein "according to the 'reason versus emotions' dichotomy, emotions are taken to be inherently disruptive and overwhelming, psychic compulsions, or forces not under our direct control" (p. 239) reflects this.

Referring to Freud's allusions to Burckhardt's (1999 reprint) *The Greeks and Greek Civilization*, Klein (1970) notes finding some unexpected parallels between the classicists' and Freud's thinking. Freud's structural model – for one – is highly reminiscent of Plato's allusions to the soul as a tripartite formation comprising a human charioteer driving two steeds (Babakin, 1978, p. 52). Similarly, Freud's diagnosis of Hans's phobia, wherein "horses" metonymically parade as "instincts" (Frank, 1983), and Freud's allusions to a "master" of the "ship" seem to echo both Plato's and Aristotle's metaphors for 'soul' and 'reason' versus 'body' and 'instincts' (Kirsner, 1986). Thus, Freud's original theory – suggesting a hierarchy of brain functions – resonates with Greek philosophy: the highest brain function is attributed to the pre-frontal cortex, responsible for voluntary – i.e. conscious – control (Meissner, 2003a). Implicit is the prejudiced position, favouring conscious (cortically determined) volition.

In the modern era, Cartesian dualism has carried this line of philosophical thinking forward, seeking to "prov[e] *the real difference between man's body and soul*" (Descartes, 1641/1989, the subtitle of Descartes's sixth Meditation): Cartesian dualism features in more psychoanalytical papers than any other philosophical approach,[2] and a direct line connects it with Greek classical philosophy (Broadie, 2007). Due to Cartesianism, "mind body dualism ... is so deeply embedded in our philosophical and religious traditions, ... conceptual systems and ... language, that it can be *seen to be an inescapable fact of our human nature*" (Johnson, 1993, p. 2, my italics); it is due to Cartesianism that the hypothesis that "man is made up of mind and body" (Basch, 1976, pp. 387–388), is "so self-evident that [it] ... *is not considered a hypothesis linked to a particular philosophical model at all, but an indisputable fact of nature*" (ibid., my italics); and, largely due to the pervasive influence of Cartesianism, the modern human subject has, for centuries, been identified with the reflecting cogito – the 'res cogitans' – and not with the corporeality of the bodily 'res extensa'.

It is Cartesian dualism – with its scientific aspirations – which thus subverts the issue of body-mind relations, reframing it as the body-mind 'problem', a conceptual blind spot or lacuna. This blind spot is then grafted onto Western therapeutic theories: as Voss (2002) pointedly phrases it when discussing Descartes's contributions to medicine: "we [would] have to [radically] transform Descartes's conception of heart and soul in order to fill the lacunae he bequeaths to the physicians who are his heirs" (p. 196). The question then arises: having been bequeathed this heritage, how far – and in what alternative intellectual domain – need we conceptually wander in order to escape its constraints and encounter the nemesis of Cartesian dualism: the possibility of an "embodied mind" (Lakoff & Johnson, 1999)?

Some years ago I was invited to lecture on Eastern mind-body medicine in a national mental health clinic in the city of Ramat-Gan. The lecture hall was somewhat of an improvised affair and, as such, seemed to reflect the – not unusual – professional stratification: psychiatrists and head clinical psychologists occupying the front benches, interns and various therapists further back, nurses and auxiliary staff at the very back. I lectured on the idea of non-duality in Eastern medical models and noticed some of the younger interns and the more experienced psychotherapists attentive and engaged. Some of the people occupying the front seats, however, were shifting uneasily in their seats.

After a while, one of them, a senior psychiatrist – engaged and interested – offered: "What you are suggesting, then, is that we substitute one theoretical model for another?"

I was taken aback at this, but it took me time to realize why and recognize the depth of the misunderstanding: I sought to represent an alternative world-view, within which the model I was presenting was an obvious facet, a natural extension thereof. I thus felt that according with the interlocutor's well-meant attempt at reconciliation would constitute an internal contradiction: what I was trying to put across was not an alternative theoretical model within a shared world-view; rather, it was a particular representation of the world-view itself.

I took a deep breath and began again, aware of the immensity of this conceptual divide. In need of external support, I started out by quoting psychologist and Zen-shiatsu therapist Shizuto Masunaga:

> Would you say that the following statement – a 'sensation of life is ... the sensation of two as one-ness' since 'when you feel oneness there is life' (Masunaga, 1976, p. 50) is a valid alternative theoretical model for psychiatric practice?

I asked.

Predicated so particularly on Western cultural axioms, the status of body-mind relations thus provides a fertile ground for comparative cultural-philosophical study. In a radical and provocative portrayal of this comparative field of study, Kuang-Ming (1997) maintains that, within Western philosophical traditions the prominent positions regarding the mind-body problem have been either monistic – reducing one to the other – or dualistic, hence searching for a connecting agent. Conversely – claims Kuang-Ming, the so-called 'hard problem' of Western philosophy – wherein the discrete existence of 'mind' and 'body' as differentiable categories is axiomatically accepted – does not exist as a core issue within the Asian philosophies. In fact, the position represented *by problematizing the question itself reflects an intrinsic cultural norm*, with concomitant philosophical-linguistic ramifications. These subtend medical theory, with implications for therapeutic practice. The East, he insinuates, may provide a meta-theoretical perspective; consequently, I suggest, promoting *a radically different view of the basic strata of the theory on which psychoanalysis stands.*

## Body-mind dualism, the psyche-soma and psychoanalysis

In their exhaustive study, *Psyche and Soma: Physicians and Metaphysicians on the Mind-Body Problem from Antiquity to Enlightenment*, Wright and Potter (2000) consider the "Functions of Psyche and Soma" to be one of the crucial issues of the mind-body debate. This is congruent with psychoanalytic attempts at meta-theoretical formulations (see Rubinstein, 1965; Wallace, 1992; Holt, 1997, for some examples). True to its philosophical heritage, the 'psyche-somatic' question puzzles psychoanalysis, having long presented a challenge that was beyond the scope of psychoanalytic theoretical resources. Contemporary psychoanalysis, however, is making preliminary attempts at clarification from within its own conceptual premises. Seeking to step beyond the a priori confines of 'the body-mind *problem*', psychoanalytically minded theorists provide "explanation[s] that include the tension of *ambivalence-polarity*" (Hutten, 1961, p. 276), thus seeking to elucidate the "mind-body *continuum*" (Wrye, 1996, p. 283, my italics). In its attempts to bridge the gap between these unitary proposals and psychoanalytic convention, psychoanalysis contends with its own philosophical assumptions, presuppositions and prejudice.

## Psyche and soma

Thus far, I have argued that – based on the principle of immanent and substantial difference between the spiritual and the material, it must be accepted that – with regard to psyche and soma – "[the] two worlds are defined by the disparate nature of the facts comprising them" (Leibowitz, 2005, p. 23). Reis spells out the intellectual conundrum:

> Arising from Descartes's bifurcation of people into two distinct parts, mind and body, a philosophical problem was created.... Because of this strict dualism ... we cannot infer from the mere presence of the body of the other ... that a mind is "housed" within.
> 
> (1999, p. 374)

Hence we see and sense a body; we speak to and analyse the contents of a mind; physicians attend to the physical body; psychotherapists and psychoanalysts to the psyche. The extent to which we relate to the patient's body and speak to his "embodied mind" does not rest on a cohesive theory: there is only sparse meta-theory to support us when intuitively recognizing the "bodily thinking" subject sitting across from us and commissioning our professional aid.

The same holds for our use of language. The theories held by clinicians define, dictate and delimit professional language; the 'talking cure' functions within the constraints carved out and delimited by language. Rhees (Wittgenstein & Rhees, 1968) reminds us of the corollary in the Wittgensteinian postulation: the conscious mind cannot, by definition, entertain linguistic attributes that transcend limitations imposed on it by the limits of conventional language: "Our ordinary language ... which pervades all our life, holds our mind rigidly in one position" (Wittgenstein, quoted in Blomfield, 1982, p. 296). The implication, as pertains to psyche and soma relations, is that norms as to 'body-mind' relations dictate the use of language and metaphor that, in a dialectic fashion, define and cement the 'psyche' and 'soma' and 'body' and 'mind' relations, according to accepted conventions within a given cultural milieu. These, Wittgenstein might say, are the rules of the psychoanalytic 'language game'.

What resolutions do contemporary schools of body-mind relations have to offer? What are their limitations and how do they stand within the psychoanalytic body-mind dilemma?

Let me begin by a short foray into four psychoanalytic clinics, reporting in italics on their patients' predicament in relation to the specific somatic condition of menstruation and uterine bleeding:

> The second patient'[s] problem was gynecologic: she suffered, prior to her analysis, from amenorrhea and vicarious menstruation ... apart from the menstrual problem the patient suffered from depression, headaches, various conversion symptoms, and stubborn constipation.... Her mother's interest in children was not limited to her own [:] ... there was always someone pregnant or giving birth.... The patient reacted to these events with horror and fantasies.... It will be easily understood that her chronic constipation was in accordance with an anal pregnancy fantasy.
> 
> (Deutsche, 1959)

*In this description bodily symptomatology is seen as a 'conversion' of specific mental "fantasies".*

When I reported that my patient's uterine bleeding stopped after a psychotherapy session with me, following many years of analyst-patient bonding in treatment, and that allowed the patient to avoid a hysterectomy and to heal, Joyce interpreted the bleeding as the

30-something year old patient just reaching her psychological readiness for her adolescent pubescence in the bleeding of the monthly menses.

(Kavaler-Adler, 2011)

*In this depiction the bodily achievement is representative of a psychological-mental developmental step forward.*

My supervisor wanted to illustrate what was meant by "attacks on linking" using a clinical vignette: a young patient related to him that she was in the habit of sniffing her menstrual blood from her underwear. The supervisor was extremely repulsed and found himself unable to go on paying attention: "You see, in this way, she attacked thinking and the links between us."

In my reading the opposite was true. The patient courageously shared her interest – and perhaps her pleasure – in the odour of primeval fertile femininity issuing forth from her. Rather than an "attack" – perhaps there was here an invitation to form a link.

(R.F., 2016, pers. comm.)

*This illustrates how dwelling on somatic issues is cast as a 'resistance' – a defence against confronting conflictual mental content.*

As she describes the ebbs and flows of her menstrual cycle over the years I notice both the ebbs and flows of my attention in the session and what seems to be a near halting and a rapidly-pushing-on lilt in her own speech. As I draw her attention to this her expression notably changes.

(Sella, 2013)

*In this clinical vignette, I outline similarities between seemingly disparate phenomenon, pointing out overarching 'body' and 'mind' categories, one of which is "flow".*

Far from representing the magnitude of psychoanalytical theorizing, the above examples point out the confusion and inconsistency in psychoanalytical theory as regards the body-mind question. Proposed resolutions lie on both sides of the 'dualistic-monistic' divide, each side of the divide again subdivided into a number of proposed resolutions. In a series of papers published through 2003, Meissner (2003a, 2003b, 2003c) unravels the conceptual underpinnings underlying psychoanalytically oriented dualistic and monistic approaches to the question. Meissner (2003a) starts out by delineating four stages of pendular swings in the evolution of these proposed resolutions:

1 An attempt to make the distinction between mind and body one of distinction in kind or substance, i.e. substantial dualism.
2 An attempt to show that there is no second substance to be distinguished, i.e. monism.
3 An attempt to draw a distinction of degree, i.e. epiphenomenalism.
4 The conclusion that it is really a distinction in kind after all, but in 'kind of concept', not 'kind of substance', i.e. linguistic parallelism.

Using these distinctions as a rough guide, I shall list major conceptual models of 'psyche-soma' relations in psychoanalysis, commenting in italics on some of their shortcomings when relevant to the present discussion.

## Dualistic solutions

1 *Classical dualism* suggests that body and mind constitute different substances and exist on different planes (i.e. material versus spiritual or transcendental). *Its seemingly clear-cut distinctions defy the "experience near" psychoanalytic experience of a unified bodily-mental phenomenology.*
2 *Interactionism* points to a relationship between two distinct entities. *The age-old body-mind conundrum is intrinsic to this position: whereas it may describe hypothesized body-mind interactions, it fails to suggest the agent responsible for the mutual confluence between the material and the immaterial.*
3 *Epiphenomenalism*, postulating the primacy of neural activity in mental activity, suggests that mental occurrences, be they conscious or unconscious, are illusions. *This postulation lacks a mechanism explaining the effect of the immaterial on neural activity: positing subjectivity as an "epiphenomenon" of a material substrate is*

*incongruent with the evident efficacy of psychoanalytic verbal interpretations.*
4  *Parallelism* denotes that no direct causality exists between psyche and soma, *thereby questioning the validity of the unconscious as a causal determinant in psycho-somatic symptomatology.*
5  *Linguistic parallelism* postulates that it is the language relating to the body and to the mind as discrete referents – rather than the mind or body as such – that maintains an inherent and insurmountable separation. *The proposed resolution consciously ignores the experience and phenomenology of 'psyche-somatic' states, replacing them by their symbolic signifiers, thus embracing a hermeneutic theoretical proposition.*

## Monistic solutions

Monistic solutions reflect the traditional idealist-materialist divide, reducing the body-mind phenomena, and the corollary psyche-soma relations, to either the immaterial psychic, or the material, somatic, pole. These approaches include:

1  *Panpsychism* maintains that all reality, including what appear to be exclusively material phenomena, are an expression of an overarching 'psyche'. Panpsychism is easily allied with mystical-religious approaches within psychoanalysis. *However, it seems unable to account fully for psychoanalysis's emphasis on the unique individuality of personal subjectivity.*
2  *Neutral monism* reverses the argument of linguistic parallelism, promoting a view of reality which is in itself neutral, but describable in terms of either physical or mental terms. *Espousal of this approach would necessitate the consolidation of a comprehensive unitary language, in addition to proposing a unitary view of reality.*
3  *Embodiment*, according to which, mind is the product of bodily processes but not reducible to them. This approach regards the mental, immaterial aspects of psychic reality, as 'emergent properties' of the body. Embodiment has been championed by both humanistic psychotherapy and branches of psychotherapy influenced by Eastern approaches, as a frame of reference that seeks to counterbalance the Occidental mentalistic-immaterial bias. *This approach carries a*

*distinct materialist undercurrent, dove-tailing with neuropsychoanalytic monistic resolutions.*

4 *Identity theory* – widely accepted as one of the most convincing current paradigms – acknowledges the different manifestations of the mental and the physical, but proposes that they are but two ways of designating the same physical process: "mental phenomena are not epiphenomena, but are acknowledged as real; but they are nonetheless regarded as identical with certain brain processes" (Meissner, 2003a, p. 305). Identity theory appears to be validated, by current research bridging the dualistic and parallelistic divides, showing that verbal psychotherapy affects neural synapses in a way which correlates with behavioural, cognitive and emotional changes (Schore, 2003). *My only qualification is that it currently seems impossible to create a definitive experimental test to resolve whether the underlying mechanism behind these changes is epiphenomenal, parallelistic or otherwise.*

In adopting an interactive philosophical paradigm of functional dualism, Freud was guided by pragmatic considerations: the "talking cure" – the standard psychoanalytic interpretative-verbal procedure – was found beneficial in treating physiological symptomatology (paralysis and anaesthesia in Anna O's case). Conceptually this meant that a "not-physical" – i.e. metaphysical-verbal – intervention could affect bodily symptomatology: the foundations were laid for *the conceptual paradox of a philosophically dualistic philosophy acknowledging a one-way interactive methodology* of ameliorating physical suffering through metaphysical interventions. Beginning with Freud's irresolute (and fluctuating) formulations as to the 'body-mind question', the body-mind breach is often regarded as the evasive unconscious of the psychoanalytic discipline itself (see Elisha, 2011). The above array of incomplete resolutions bears testimony both to the intellectual challenge of the "hard problem" itself, and to the incumbent shortcomings of the psychoanalytic theoretical engagement with it.

## In search of a theory: the psyche-soma and body-mind relations in psychoanalysis

With the progression in psychoanalytic theorizing, the heritage of incomplete resolutions was seen more clearly to be at odds with clinical knowhow pointing to "the various 'leaps' from mind to body, from body to mind, from mind to mind, and from body to body" (Gates, 1959, p. 15) within the psychotherapeutic relationship. The sine qua non of *a mutually constitutive relationship* between patients' and therapists' psyche-somatic aspects – prevalent in contemporary object-relations, intersubjective and developmental theory – gradually made the need for a parsimonious theory more pressing than ever. This entails formulating a philosophical infrastructure that supports a unified, personal 'psyche-soma' and a mutual, dual, interactive-constitutive apparatus.

Since "psychoanalysis itself does not have the resources to resolve the mind-body problem" (Loewald & Meissner, 1976, p. 173), it has tended to borrow concepts from related disciplines. The paradigmatic shift is such that psychoanalysis now turns to those very disciplines disparaged by Freud (1933b) in his seminal lecture, "The question of a Weltanschauung", as unscientific: philosophy, religion and art aesthetics. However, the introduction of terminology borrowed from such disciplines does not, in itself, provide the sought-after conceptual infrastructure. Notably, in the case of concepts borrowed from Eastern philosophy, their instrumental implementation often fails to do justice to their original terminology's full explanatory and theoretical potential (see Nauriyal et al., 2006, pp. xxi–20, for an elaboration). Thus, while retaining an instrumental value, these extra-disciplinary concepts have – to date – remained unintegrated into psychoanalytic theory and fail to provide the sought-after conceptual framework.

## *Weltanschauung and the mind-body question*

Earlier, I mentioned that when I gave my lecture on Eastern mind-body medicine it was assumed that I was merely replacing one theoretical model for another. My unconscious response reflected the destabilization I experienced when I felt that it was the 'world-view' – my world-view – the framework that provided the very underpinnings of the theoretical model, that was being challenged. Hence my somewhat adamant reply regarding "life [as] ... the sensation of two as one-ness". From an integrative philosophical neuro-psychoanalytical perspective, Opatow (1999) takes these same conceptual queries regarding duality to task: "as there currently exists no overarching framework ... [for a] psychoanalytical theory in regard to the 'body-mind question', the conceptual framework itself becomes an ultimate goal of research" (p. 97).

Accordingly – against the pervasive hypostasis of body-mind dualism – some strains within contemporary psychoanalysis seek to reconsider the "framework itself". Broadly speaking, this includes incorporating meta-theoretical structures of a paradigmatic stature such as intersubjectivity, systems and complexity theories. Typically, these developments represent explicit and implicit presuppositions that diverge from orthodox psychoanalysis. In their stead they stipulate that – as monistic and dualistic philosophical solutions are insufficient – a "middle ground of ... *mind–body unity*" (Meissner, 2003b, p. 339) is required. The ensuing emergence of new hypotheses and formulations regarding psyche-somatic relations in psychoanalysis is especially evident in three major fields within contemporary practice and theory:

1   Theories reliant on intersubjective formulations, such as relational psychoanalysis and self-psychology (Atwood & Stolorow, 1984).
2   Theories reliant on neuro-psychological research, such as Attachment and contemporary developmental theories, supporting the idea of both intrapsychic and inter-subjective psyche-soma regulatory "loops" (Schore, 2001, 2003; Beebe & Lachmann, 2002).
3   Theories and clinical formulations stemming from a mystical-religious frame of reference, such as is evident in the psychoanalytic theories of Wilfred Bion (1970) and Michael Eigen (1981). These have gradually attained a place well within mainstream psychoanalytic thinking (see Sorenson, 2004; Sperry & Shafranske, 2005; Black, 2006b).

## Methodological issues and the mind-body question

Freudian methodological theory, and its derivative technical injunctions, maintain that verbal – thus *metaphysical* – interventions comprise the sole media of therapeutic intervention. The bracketing of the body and the bodily was signified by the passive posture. With the patient lying on the couch, the psychotherapeutic interaction was to be "conducted by two adults, [the patient] refraining from any muscular effort and ... perceptual stimulus that might distract him from his mental activity" (Freud, 1904, p. 56).

Implicit within Freud's technical instruction of abstinence (Freud, 1912) and neutrality (Freud, 1915) were the following:

1. Refrain from physical touch or contact in analyst-patient interactions. The underlying supposition being that psychoanalytic technique is purely a verbal-metaphysical event.
2. The patient's psychic effects on the analyst (counter-transference) is a confabulatory factor, to be analysed and neutralized.
3. The patient's bodily presence and the way in which it registers in the psychoanalyst's consciousness or unconscious are not psychoanalytically relevant material.
4. While the analyst's bodily *presence* might influence the patient's psyche – thereby necessitating abstinence and even lack of eye contact – the perceived absence of his bodily presence is regarded as an indifferent fact (or rather, disregarded).
5. Free association was to include what came into the patient's mind, i.e. *the cognitive contents of consciousness* in the form of "ideas" (Freud, 1900, for example).[3]

Increasingly, over the years, it has become clear that Freud's dual ideal – of insulating the psychic from the somatic and postulating the "objective analyst" as neutrally attending to the patient's subjectivity – is fraught with at least three substantial inconsistencies:

1. Never having disposed of a positivistic disposition and an underlying materialistic theoretical position, the initial "mysterious leap" was never accounted for.
2. The somatic components of subjectivity – i.e. "what the analyst senses from his own ... somatic reactions to the patient's conscious and unconscious communications..." (Twemlow, 2001 p. 24) were not taken into account.
3. Incorporating somatic aspects of subjectivity within the construct of *inter-subjectivity* brought home the need to contend with multiple "leaps" between both the therapist's and the patient's bodies and minds (see Gates, 1959).

The initial rift appeared already in Kleinian theory, as the discrepancy between the methodological and theoretical propositions started to emerge: whereas psychoanalytic technical instructions remained relatively stable, methodological theory gradually came to regard countertransference and projective-identification and their attendant emotional and sensual impressions, as part and parcel of analytic theory. Consequently, the orthodox subject–object predication as isolable psyche-somatic entities came under closer scrutiny and criticism. Almost concurrently, Attachment, developmental and Object Relations theories came to acknowledge *pre-verbal psychic structures* as relevant content matter with high explanatory value, constituent of both neonate and adult subjectivity. All the above strains thus converge in taking issue with dualistic presuppositions, inasmuch as they implicitly contest their basic premises.

## Reframing paradigms

### Subjectivity and the psyche-soma

In his "Philosophical paradigms in psychoanalysis", Rendon (1986) suggests that paradigmatic shifts within psychoanalysis reflect a gradual movement from the Cartesian, subjectivist-intra-psychic discipline, to a Hegelian paradigm, ascribing normative health, development and psychopathology to the concrete inter-personal reality of external environment and social structures. He regards Fairbairn's rendering of libidinal processes as "object-seeking" and "object-dependent" and Sullivan's reframing of libidinal body zones as "social contact zones" as representing the tendency of movement from an objectivist-biologically determined portrayal of the psychic, to a subjectivist, socially contrived view.

The enquiry initiated by Rendon may be developed thus:

1 If body and mind are seen to mutually, synthetically, affect each other.

And

2 Analyst's and analysand's existences and relationships are perceived as real as opposed to comprising a sum of transferentially determined verbal associations and interpretations.

And

3   Each of them is possessed of what appears to be a somatic and what appears to be a mental component.

Then

4   A reformulation of the multiple effects of the quadruple interactions between one psyche-soma duo and the other is required in order to further the efficacy of therapeutic procedure.

Berger (1996) situates the same dilemma within the context of the Cartesian–Lockean–Kantian subject.[4] Kantian subjectivism suggests that the sensory 'how' is closely linked to the subjectivity of 'how one sees' (metaphorically) since – after being sensorially absorbed – objects are cognitively placed according to pre-determined 'categories' (Kant, 1787/1999): it is this "*intellectual* intuition" that is the substrate of shared communication since *only the ideas that provide the conceptual mesh* are "the publicly shareable ... hence objective..." (Hannay, 1979, p. 35) communication. The 'truth' of interpretations lies, therefore, in the feasibility of a shared "categorical" conceptualization of its contents, a truth with which the analyst is familiar, and that is recognizable as a "truism" by the analysand.

Together Rendon's (1986) and Berger's (1996) discomfort with Freud's dualistic legacy, carrying within it a dual deference of objectivity (the analyst's) to subjectivity (the patient's), and psychic to somatic implies a punishing choice: since somatic inter-subjectivity is subordinated to its communicability "*as language*, as construction, as process, *as representation*" (Dimen, 1996, p. 386, my italics), one acknowledges either the solipsistic somatic aspects of subjectivity, or upholds the shared supremacy of language and linguistic communication. This account – most obviously – does not account for the emerging "middle ground of ... *mind–body unity*" (Meissner, 2003b, p. 339) towards which non-Cartesian psychoanalysis is veering. Within this latter philosophical position – often tinged with theistic sentiments – human beings evince an "unacknowledged unity at the basis of all human experience..." (Thandeka, 1995): a pre-representational potentiality embraces both conceptuality and being, thinking and embodiment – as appears, for example, in Bion's (1952) 'proto-mental' capacities, in Kohut's (1984) 'experience-near' sphere, in Stern's (1985) 'core self' or in Damasio's (1999) 'background sensations and emotions'.

I shall return to the potential for an embodied-hermeneutic disposition from Occidental and Eastern perspective in Chapters 3 and 9, respectively.

## *Internal and external influences*

Throughout its history the psychoanalytic movement has confronted internal challenges to its world-view regarding the psyche-soma. Jung's and Reich's expulsions from the Psychoanalytic Society in 1912 and 1936, respectively, signified, among other things, a response to their challenge to psychoanalytic dualistic orthodoxy. Humanistic psychotherapy, incorporating phenomenological and existential contributions, has posed a parallel challenge, from without. Formative essays such as "The human body" (Mahrer, 1978) thoroughly examined and reviewed the basic premises of psychoanalytical philosophy of science from a phenomenological perspective. Acknowledging a psychic panorama that emphasizes primary processes, their phenomenological enquiry questioned the validity of a psyche-somatic split, encouraging and eliciting research regarding the body's crucial role in giving rise to sensations and inchoate emotions. As was made clear within this investigation, it is impossible to demarcate the 'bodily', the 'psychical' and the 'external world' as distinct within a given phenomenological "experience" (Boss, 1979). In investigating the phenomenology of "dasein[5] in its bodiliness" (ibid., p. 21) Binswanger's (1962) and Boss's "dasein psychotherapy" paid tribute to unified psyche-somatic manifestations as being "neither psychical nor somatic" (1979, p. 21). Thus formulated, subjectivity was reframed as reflecting experiential aspects of a 'present-time' human state, denoting a unified psyche-somatic state qualitatively different from the dualistic Cartesian 'body' and 'mind' dichotomy.

## *Philosophical-phenomenological influences*

The phenomenological-existential stance in humanistic psychotherapeutic modalities regarding body-manifestations as a substantial foundational phenomena was supported and punctuated by Merleau-Ponty. Incorporating phenomenology and Gestalt psychology, Merleau-Ponty asserts that meaning is not derived from cogitation. Rather, "meaning emerges already at the level of the 'expressive' relationship of body and the world", while the "body expresses total existence not because it is an external accompaniment to that existence [but because] … this incarnate significance is the external phenomenon of which body and mind, sign and significance are abstract moments" (quoted in Besmer, 2007, p. 32). The radical conclusion of these assertions coalesces in the formulation of an existential epitaph, Sartre's "existence, preceding essence": if, underlying 'body' and 'mind' are 'being' and 'existence', the axiom of the body and mind as two essentially and substantially different forms or substances is rebutted.

## Zen contributions

A major external influence on the re-evaluation and reformulation of psyche-soma relations within psychoanalysis has been the dialogue with Eastern disciplines. Despite initial apprehension, Eastern perspectives infiltrated analytic thinking relatively early, having originally influenced the analytic-psychoanalytic corpus through the pioneering work of Jung in the 1930s. Jung went as far as to declare that Daoist texts were the first external source of validation for theories he had developed for over 15 years (Wilhelm, 1984).

In the 1960s it was Fromm et al.'s (1974) pioneering text *Zen-Buddhism and Psychoanalysis* that highlighted Zen-Buddhism's "stimulating and refreshing influence…" (Molino, 1998, p. vii) on psychoanalysis. The inadequacy of Western dualistic philosophical substrata to substantiate a new outlook on "embodied subjectivity" (Kelman, 1960/1998, p. 77) underscored its ingrained "affective contaminations" and "false intellectualizations" (Fromm, 1960/1998, p. 70): Fromm saw both – affective and intellectual distortions – as reflecting a dualistic prejudice "based on a subject–object split" (ibid.).

Owing to its influence, Zen-Buddhism, in particular, attained the status of a "privileged vehicle and terrain for the dialogue…" with psychoanalysis (Molino, 1998, p. xiii). D. T. Suzuki's and Fromm's contributions came to the fore as a resource that, while challenging axiomatic presuppositions, facilitated the introduction of *nouvelle* strains of thought, potentially conducive to developing non-dualistic models of mind-body connections. One such innovation was the notion of the clinical and theoretical potency of a spiritual world-view. Couched within this notion was a non-reductive reconceptualization of 'primary' sensations. Whereas Freud (1930) had viewed "oceanic sentiments" as pathological regression, Zen's welding with Fromm's humanistic world-view embraced "oceanic feelings" as potentially representing an existential answer to "finding union within ourselves ... and with nature" (Fromm, Suzuki, & de Martino, 1974, p. 87): the stage was set for a reappraisal of the relations between the primary somatic and mental-spiritual attributes.

In contemporary psychoanalytic psychotherapy, one often finds it difficult to distinguish between experience and its categorization, between affect and thought and between present time interaction and its interpretative elaboration. Often we find patients – unsolicited – beginning a psychotherapeutic session by declaring "it is my mother's influence", or "of course, I am unconsciously evading this issue", or – even more pertinently – "I realize that it is not my body at all" as if internal objects, the unconscious and Western psychosomatic theory constitute their personal categories of experience. Conversely, the evolving Zen-psychoanalytic dialogue paved the way for a thorough reassessment of body-mind relations in therapeutic practice, within a new subject–object conceptual framework: unfettered by Occidental a priori categorical differentiations, Zen-Buddhist teachings helped review, and at times revoke, the normative Occidental position, wherein the body is seen as the contingent – often inferior – counterpart in the psyche-somatic duo. Devoid of a developmental psychological scheme, Zen's alternative psychological conceptual framework helped revise the seemingly axiomatic building-stones of progression: "body-to-mind", "primary-to-secondary" and "sensual-to-cognitive" (see Yuasa, 1987; Kasulis, Ames, & Dissanayake, 1993). Whereas value-laden terminology was initially used to devalue meditative practice, models of unmediated, silent, embodied modes of being within psychoanalytic interaction gradually gained acceptance and validation (see 'Introduction' in Molino, 1998; Alfano, 2005).[6]

In addition, Zen helped mould a viable and robust alternative, based on a cultural vantage point in which

> not only ... [is] ... the substantial opposition between the soul and the body ... unknown ... so [is] the distinction between the sensible and the rational ... [since] ... the 'purity' of mind abstracted from context ... cannot be maintained:
>
> (Kasulis et al., 1998, p. 163)

adopting Zen-Buddhist terminology afforded a view of an a-intellectual psyche-somatic modus which saw the mind as housed and contextualized within the body, and the body and mind as a unitary given. With its gradual infiltration into mainstream psychoanalytic thought, the way was set for recognizing that an a priori dichotomy between body and mind may possibly be a cultural bias – reinforced by linguistic and conceptual convention – rather than a 'fact' *sui generis*.

The above has a direct bearing on the underpinnings and presuppositions typical of the *therapeutic traditions* conversant with Zen terminologies: therapeutic disciplines emergent from the wedding of Daoist and Zen philosophies adhere to the notion that "medicine ... [is] ... a part of philosophy and religion, both of which propound oneness with nature, i.e. the universe" (Veith, 1972, p. 10). Consequently "traditional ... doctors apply a single conceptual mode to both physical and mental illness" (Eisenberg & Wright, 1995, p. 169). This relates to both the medical findings and the means of acquiring knowledge. Thus:

1 Owing to their rigorous and foundational non-duality, Eastern medical formulations repudiate the validity and necessity of "classifying the [physical and psychological] symptoms into two groups, or saying which group of symptoms are primary or secondary" (Ng, 1985, p. 449).
2 "In opposition to the Western cultural tradition of 'knowing' by '...thinking over things and abstracting forms from them...'", intuitive-unmediated experience is paramount since "we know by experiencing things at the-heart-of our-body (*hsin*)" (Kuang-Ming, 1997, p. 93).

Contemporary psychoanalytic conceptualizations of non-duality in regard to the body-mind relationship informed by Zen-Buddhism (see Magid, 2000, 2002; Safran, 2006) are an obvious extension of the above; taken together, they provide a potential *Weltanschauung* and overarching infrastructure for the perception, conceptualization and implementation of a proposed 'unitary turn' as regards body-mind relations within psychoanalysis. This is particularly so in four respects:

1 Potentiality of existence as a predicate bearing a discrete existence which precedes substantial manifestation (countering the position

that a manifestation of either 'body' or 'mind' carries a foundational significance).
2. Constant change as a substantial position (countering the position that a thing is either 'bodily' or 'mentally' manifested or determined).
3. Inevitable limitations and constraints on language and of intellectual-discursive knowledge in construing reality (rebutting the notion that 'we know by thinking' and that 'factually true verbal statements indicate knowledge').
4. The meditative state as enabling a presence within – and a non-judgemental recognition of – a non-dualistic psyche-somatic state (i.e. the potential of engagement with reality without preconceived categorizations).

A survey of the psychoanalytic literature will uncover the fact that these propositions are already used as conceptual addenda and as a fertile source for comparative cross-referencing for numerous clinical observations and theoretical conceptualizations (Fromm et al., 1974; Rubin, 1996; Molino, 1998; Magid, 2002; Epstein, 2005; Cooper, 2010, for some examples). In the following chapters I shall show how their convergence creates a cohesive conceptual mesh which enriches and validates paradigm shifts regarding psyche-soma relations in contemporary psychoanalysis: in providing them with a cohesive *Weltanschauung*, it serves to substantiate a congruent 'unitary turn' in the perception and conceptualization of body-mind relations in psychoanalysis.

## Conclusion and dialogue

In this chapter I have suggested that classical philosophical models embracing body-mind dichotomies, ramified by theological prejudice, persist in influencing cultural presuppositions. These have carried through from Platonic to Cartesian paradigms which persistently pervade psychoanalysis. Accordingly, psychoanalytic views as to body-mind relations replicate cultural convention: proposed dualistic resolutions suggest an obvious dichotomy; monistic resolutions inevitably fall on one or the other side of the debate, i.e. they are materialistic or idealistic, empirical or transcendental, mentalistic or behaviouristic, and so forth. Within these conventions 'psychic-cognitive-intellectual-verbal-metaphysical' attributes are traditionally given precedence over the 'motional-sensual-emotional-enacted-physical' categories of experience; thus the persistent and pervasive classical body-mind debate, in its seemingly immutable, dichotomous, categorical, evaluative and developmental distinctions, is retained.

The fact that body and mind psyche-somatic interaction is the original sine qua non of psychoanalysis stands at odds with these ingrained distinctions, creating the conceptual conundrum of the "*mysterious* leap from mind to body". Having forsaken the "Project for a Scientific Psychology" in 1895, Freud failed to establish a parsimonious argument for psyche-somatic interaction. Following the decline of the energetic economic meta-theory, the role of the body in the theory of the unconscious was marginalized, underscoring the evaluative and developmental supremacy of the mental-psychic components within the psyche-soma duo. Establishing and representing a vicious circle, these hierarchies affect the nomenclature and terminology used in psychoanalysis, which inevitably perpetuates its perceived presuppositions.

I contextualized the advent of Kleinian, Attachment and Object Relations theories within a philosophical shift from the Cartesian and Kantian subject to a Hegelian paradigm. Within this latter trajectory, the enigma of interpersonal "leaps" between analysts' and analysands' bodies and minds was added to the original mystery of the "mysterious leap from mind to body". Extending beyond the bounds delineated by Freud's world-view, I have, accordingly, suggested that three different strains within psychoanalysis converge in introducing competing non-dualistic paradigms: inter-subjective, neuro-psychoanalytic and mystical-religious trends reflect a "change of disciplinary matrix" (Phillips, 1991, p. 404). Brought together, these propositions indicate a 'unitary turn' creating what Kuhn (2012) terms a "paradigm shift" as regards psyche and soma relations, wherein a formerly non-existent 'psyche-soma unit' is implicitly indicated. Perceived non-dualistically the psyche-soma proclaims its phenomenological and factual existence, constituting a composite entity in its own right: 'psyche' and 'soma' as discrete entities require a "leap" to bridge them; psyche-soma, as a composite entity, requires none. The psyche-soma thus perceived conforms to what Kuhn defines as "a new *sort* of fact" (ibid., p. 53). Kuhn warns that declaring a "new sort of fact" as such – thereby stimulating the need to assimilate it within existing structures – sets a "scientific crisis" in motion (ibid.).

Seeking to resolve this crisis and stepping beyond the bounds of "Cartesianism" and Kantian subjectivism, the age-old problem of 'psyche and soma relations' now resurfaces as a study inclusive of *somatic aspects of subjectivity and of intersubjectivity*. Alternative conceptualizations of the very "structures of subjectivity" (Atwood & Stolorow, 1984) mark the substrate of this innovative conceptualization. According to these alternative postulations, subjectivity includes developmentally pre-verbal and pre-symbolical aspects of psyche and soma, contributing to a "two body" embodied psychology (Aron, 1998, p. xix); the dyadic relationship represents complex "leaps" from one psyche-soma entity to another, leading to a rich contextual interaction; the methodological implication is that unconscious modes of sensual-bodily aspects of the analyst's reverie (a concept coined by Ogden, 1989) have significant repercussions on psychoanalytic procedure and outcome. As an outcome, psychoanalysis's world-view is changing so as to espouse a paradigm of "two as oneness".

A proposed non-dualistic framework of the body-mind requires its distinct nomenclature and terminology. Novel terminology and embodied language may enable descriptive construal and technical innovations accommodating individual and reciprocal "leaps" "from mind to body, from body to mind, from mind to mind, and from body to body" (Gates, 1959). The current reformation of language in regard to body-mind relations in psychoanalysis (compare Smith 1986 or Irwin, 1996, with Stern, 1985 or Knoblauch, 2001) is one of the omens pointing to a departure from orthodox paradigms, enabling an embodied analytic hermeneutic stance, both theoretically and methodologically.

Changes in the disciplinary matrix have been in sync with confluent influences on psychoanalytic propositions both from within and without its habitual ken: phenomenological-existential-humanistic theories have emphasized the body's primary role in defining existence and subjectivity. Supportive of these views, Zen-Buddhism's role – as a compatible and enriching discipline championing the concept of a "life-oneness" (Masunaga, 1976, p. 19) – has been paramount in challenging psychoanalytic formulations regarding duality in general, and 'body' to 'mind' duality in particular. This is especially pronounced in regard to the notions of potentiality of existence preceding substantial manifestation, constant change as a substantial position, limitations on linguistic 'sign-signified' fit and recognizing meditative states as furthering non-discriminative dispositions. In conceptually substantiating these propositions, Zen-Buddhism provides a conceptual framework to accommodate the complex matrix of mutual perceived leaps from and between the analyst's and analysand's 'psyches' and 'somas'.

## Notes

1 This notwithstanding, some aspects of Aristotle's dualism seem to be antecedent to later, interactionist, Cartesian-like models, the soul acting interdependently with sense-perception and the imaginal capacities.
2 Data based on a comparative search-screening of all articles and major texts appearing in the P.E.P. – Psychoanalytic Electronic Publishing – inventory.
3 This has been the case despite Freud's later recapitulation of his injunctions: these include sensations as valid content matter for free association (Freud, 1912).
4 See Ricouer (1970) and Stolorow (2005), on Kant's relevance to contemporary theory.
5 From German, often translated as 'presence', 'existence' or 'being'.
6 See Balint (1968/1979) for an early example.

Chapter 2

# Mysterious leaps
## From psychosomatics to the psyche-soma

In Chapter 1, I argued that positing psyche-somatic relations as a problem is intrinsic to the dualistic Western cultural and philosophical heritage. Despite Freud's seeming theoretical flexibility,[1] Freudian meta-theory failed to conceptually avoid the limitations imposed by this dualistic heritage. From within them, Freud sought to theoretically substantiate the manner in which a one-way interaction between mind and body resulted in mental events being etched upon the somatic arena in the form of symptoms. Keeping in step with the scientific aspirations which motivated Freud, later thinkers sought to establish a fit between mental-unconscious motivations and physiological pathological manifestations.

The present chapter will explore the theoretical underpinnings of these efforts. It will also establish their shortcomings, ultimately demonstrating that developments in theoretical conceptualizations often reversed the convention of a one-directional interaction leading from mind to body: rather than pointing to a direct explanatory pattern, these findings indicate a two-way interaction; rather than forming linear explanations, these interactions point to a diffuse web of multiple causations and correlations. Instead of "psychosomatics", the mesh of somatic involvement in forming the "structures of subjectivity" (Atwood & Stolorow, 1984) ultimately implicates a compound psyche-soma.

### Theory and meta-theory

Theories flourish, meta-theory is sparse: psychoanalysts concur as to the necessity for a "theory of therapy" for psychoanalysis (Friedman, 1988); what they consistently differ on are the constituents of its meta-theoretical underpinnings. The original bulwarks of psychoanalytic meta-theory was its solemn belief in the existence of a theory of mind; propounding it "has

... led the whole psychoanalytic parade into history" (ibid., p. 149). This, claims Friedman, is faded glory: surveying psychoanalytic meta-theory and ingrained theoretical methodological stances, Friedman argues that a theory of mind is now considered "a professional dinosaur – awesome, ungainly and useless" (ibid.). The downfall of a coherent psychoanalytic 'theory of mind' threatens the validity of its kindred, derivative theory: to date, there exists no canonical theory of body-mind or psyche-soma relations within psychoanalysis.

In his study, *The Foundations of Psychoanalysis*, Grunbaum (1984) contends that "for all the fundamental defects of Freud's clinical arguments, their caliber and amenity to scrutiny [are] mind-boggling, as compared to the reasoning of ... neo-revisionist epigone..." (p. 247). In an incremental work entitled *The Anatomy of Psychotherapy*, Friedman (1988) concurs, maintaining that, after Freud (granting the possible exception of Kohut), no coherent theory of mind has been put forward; consequently, no derivative or contingent model of body-mind and of psyche-soma relations has assumed supremacy or taken hold as *the* psychoanalytic model. The embarrassing result is that psychoanalytical literature referring to 'theory' or 'meta-theory' of mind still focuses on Freudian theory (Mackay, 1986; Holt, 1997; Scalzone, 2005 demonstrate this) to the marginalization of all other theorists.

## Psyche-somatic meta-theories

### Freud's energetic proposition as an overarching meta-theory

Freud's original meta-theory aspired to scientific status based on positivistic assumptions current at the turn of the 20th century. His materialism guided him towards positing the "mind or psychical apparatus ... [as] a certain physical system rather than something mental, which stood to the human body in a parallel, epiphenomenal, or interactive relation" (Natsoulas, 1984, p. 196). Consequently, Freud's original formulations of "psychic energy" as the determinant of instinctual and emotional expression, were modelled after physicalist conceptualizations, such as the concept of electrical currents and he "often use[d] examples from physics to illustrate and justify the methods of psychoanalysis.... Implicit in this approach is the idea that they are both essentially the same: they are both sciences" (Freud's model, explicated in Mackay, 1986, pp. 376–377).

'Scientific physicalism', as it appears in Freud's writing, is the view that the human organism is an integral part of the physical universe, natural and pre-determined in its behaviour. Within this context the human mind is not anything over and above the physical aspects of this organism, with mental life a "function of an apparatus ... extended in space"[2] (Freud, 1940, p. 145) and that its "bodily organ, and scene of action, [is] the brain" (ibid., p. 144). Thus, the mind is equated with brain and both stand within Freud's materialistic monism or interactive dualism: in this model, *energy is a concrete-physical* active force, binding sensations and ideas. Metapsychology, resting on these empirical foundations, reflects the notion that ideas are issued forth into the realm of the conscious and, through it, reality, by being bound with energy (see Scharff & Birtles, 1997). Schafer artfully shows how, within the psychoanalytic movement as a whole, this is part and parcel of a "penchant for dualism" (1970, p. 428), manifest in the preponderance of binary postulations: conscious-unconscious, libido-aggression, and so forth.

## *The rise and fall of psychosomatics*

Herself suffering from mental malaise, renowned author Virginia Woolf – speaking on behalf of a "generation of young men decimated in ... war" (Sellers, 2010, p. 42) – captures the tragic implications of this call for scientific objectivity. In her novel, *Mrs Dallaway*, Septimus – one of an array of protagonists – returns from the fighting in the First World War, suffering from a mental breakdown; since no physical signs are apparent and no obvious psychological explanation is offered, his doctor declares there is *"nothing the matter* with him" (Woolf, 1925, p. 75, my italics). Septimus feels "his body ... macerated till only the nerve fibres ... [are] left", experiencing his fear as a "weight on his eyes" (ibid., p. 77). Yet, victim to the call for objectification – the *esprit du temps* – Septimus's malady is aggravated by his own merciless self-criticism: from within his suffering – in a delusional state – he himself still insists that "one must be scientific above all things" (ibid., p. 76).

The scientific monistic-energetic viewpoint provided a relatively coherent and parsimonious basis for the economic model in psychoanalysis. Simply put: the libidinal causation of symptomatology seemed congruous with an experience of repression of energy and with its symbolical underpinnings. In philosophical terms: what the patient had – the ontology (his condition) – could be explained by the epistemological tools of physically-based science. However, with its emphasis on drives, instincts, libido, cathexes, charge and discharge, this model became embarrassingly irrelevant in the later topographical, structural and more contemporary models. Moreover, it has gradually instated a long-standing caesura between epistemology and ontology: the former a seemingly monistic 'energetic' theoretical model; the latter, an apparently dualistic theory relating to a differentiated 'psyche' and 'soma', and their diagnostic counterparts in the form of a psychological evaluation and a physical check-up; as Septimus's condition demonstrates, within this schism *the subjectivity of a compound psyche-somatic state* could not be accounted for.

Following Freud, the theory and science of "psychosomatics" were – unsurprisingly – the first differentiated effort in response to the challenge of a psyche-soma conceptualization in psychoanalysis: seeking to establish a direct link between unconscious conflicts and specific bodily manifestations, psychosomatics sought to dispel the "mystery" of the "mysterious leap": it was consequently investigated within a monistic explanatory model, aspiring to medical validity, or striving to achieve symbolical univocal reliability. Studies conducted at the Chicago Psychoanalytical Institute in the 1960s seemed to validate this approach, supposedly establishing that the aetiology of particular disease entities – such as peptic ulceration, ulcerative colitis and asthma – was psychologically unconsciously determined (Alexander et al., 1968). An attempt was made to bring even compound psyche-somatic phenomena such as shell-shock – as experienced by Septimus – into the fold of 'science'. In historical reality, the force of scientific prevalence had dismal implications: in instances in which a scientific explanation – i.e. valid unconscious aetiology – was provided, the psychosomatic symptoms were considered a bona fide malady; diagnosed otherwise, they were considered feigned, judged to be a mark of cowardice, often leading to execution by a firing squad (Hallett et al., 2006, p. 73).

The case of 'shell-shocked' patients had become the Occam's razor in the history of Western psychological science since it inevitably reflects the distance between psychosomatic explanatory theory and its ineptitude in conferring meaning upon experience: within this schism, somatic aspects and the subjectivity of 'meaning-formation' within psychoanalytic theory have become irreconcilably sundered, as the following case study illustrates.

Eitan is a young man who was referred to me by a colleague. He had sought therapy following exposure to a near-death experience in a bombing in a pedestrian walkway in the heart of Jerusalem, from which he emerged physically unscathed. However, since then, he had experienced a lowering of hearing, spurts of dizziness and a sensation of "discontinuity of movement" which he experiences as "being like an old man". His interest in his habitual pastimes has dulled. He has gradually become incommunicative, spurting out at times with explosive rage. He was diagnosed with posttraumatic stress disorder (PTSD) and attended regular psycho-dynamically oriented therapy sessions.

Eitan is short, and – although ordinarily soft-spoken – seems to be recalcitrant in communication, as if the slightest indication of interest in something constitutes a violation of self-integrity. His body seems dense and inflexible. He often describes his only problem as being "a hollow, cold feeling in my lower back. This is where my lack of energy begins, and from there it rises through my spine to my head." Despondently – but still remote and with a cynical tinge – he often asks me: "Do you, with your Eastern knowledge, understand what I am saying? No one else does. Is it something mental? Am I normal? It's not psychological because I am fine ... but the physical check-ups show no abnormalities either." Plaintively Eitan reiterates a question so often felt and expressed at times of crisis: "Can you tell me what it means?"

As psycho-dynamically oriented clinicians we are often faced by similar issues. Attempting to decipher Eitan's predicament, I reverted to classical psychosomatic psychoanalysis. I discovered it to be enticing reading; I found the idea a captivating one that

> endosomatic perceptions – worsen ... the effect of the radical unbinding of the defused death drives ... putting into place ... this enigmatic system of survival we call mechanical thinking ... cut off from the roots of its drives and disembodied.
>
> (Aisenstein, 2006, p. 678)

It was obvious, however, that Aisenstein's terminology was incompatible with Eitan's experience and failed to help him in his search for meaning in our sessions. My thwarted attempts served only to highlight the distance that currently prevails between experience and theory and between symptomatology and the urge towards meaning formation: while cogent and intellectually consistent, orthodox psychosomatics lies outside the purview of contemporary perceptions of subjectivity and, accordingly, does not carry the persuasive power that the monopoly of scientific argumentation had a century ago. In plain words, my interpretations along those lines did not represent any 'common sense' and consequently did not make sense.

True: psychosomatics' evolution reflected a transition from the formulation of "symptom as instinct vicissitude", to the concept of "body as symbol" and, eventually, to the interpersonal notion of "body language as conversion stream" (Ammon, 1979). Its days of glory, however, were short-lived: What began as a purist aspiration of elucidating Freudian theory ended up in a multiplicity of "many meanings and approaches ... that can hardly agree among themselves, beyond posing the problem, determining the area of research, and methodology" (ibid., p. 1). Ironically, psychosomatic theory has thus gradually complied with Freud's fear that his psychoanalytic model would become the "handmaiden to psychiatry". Apart from a specific lineage within French psychoanalysis, psychosomatic theory has largely transformed into a study of 'stress' and 'social medicine research', with correlational rather than explanatory investigations predominating research. Wittkower sadly sums up: "the hopes bound up with psychoanalytic psychosomatics have not been fulfilled ... either in the aetiological and the therapeutic area..." (cited in Ammon, 1979, p. 2).

## *Proposed alternatives*

Shortly after Freud's death, the marginalization or outright rebuttal of the 'psychic energy' model within psychoanalysis was an established fact (Kubie, 1947); hand in hand with it went the decline of psychosomatic theorizing. However, psychosomatic theorizing left its traces in the wake of alternative models: these models – of meta-theoretical stature – used the Freudian unconscious and attendant energetic model as a point of departure, setting two clear-cut competing patterns for future strains of psyche-somatic theorizing:

1 *Energetic legacy*: some theoreticians and clinically-oriented psychoanalysts consider Freud's insistence on a meta-psychology, within

which "mind must be understood in terms of concepts such as force, energy, structure, matter, and so on" (Mackay, 1986) as a legacy that has still not been satisfactorily replaced. This line of thought highlights "recent psychobiological and neurobiological studies [that] ... strongly indicate that the concept of the drive, devalued over the last twenty years, must be reintroduced as a central construct of psychoanalytic theory" (Schore, 1997, p. 827). Thus, an objective, monistic, body-based meta-psychology – the return of psychoanalytic theory "from the precincts of philosophy and theology into the purview of standard empirical science" (Opatow, 1999) – is proposed.

2   *Hermeneutic (re-)constructivist theories* critique the equation of 'brain' with 'consciousness'. These theories regard the return to a neurophysiological version of drive-theory as leading to the reification of a supposedly objective theory of causation and meaning formation, providing "an illusion of safety at the cost of dynamic range and flexibility" (Shapiro, 2003, p. 559). Within this approach, causative factors pertaining to the body's primary role in psyche-soma relationships make way for a meta-psychological model emphasizing subjective meaning-formation and intentionality. Freud's earlier insistence on the validity of the idea of 'psychic energy' as a construct within the natural sciences is *reframed, ipso facto, so as to suggest that Freud's initial intention was to present seemingly physical forces as metaphorical representations.*[3] Within this strain, the primacy of text and language is pronounced and energetic propositions are contingent upon their narrative representation.

## The psyche-soma in object-relations

### From 'intra-psyche-somatic' subject to 'psyche-somatic' leaps

Freudian theory is predominantly intra-psychic and its developmental model is epigenetic: emerging from a somatic substrate it maintains that the ego "is first and foremost a body ego" (Freud, 1923, p. 26). More particularly, consciousness arises at *'the border'* of the body: since the organism is determined by its bodily borders, the ego is derived from bodily sensations springing from the surface of the body. The ego thus comes to form "a *mental projection* of the surface of the body, ... *representing* the superficies of the mental apparatus" (footnote, ibid., p. 26 of English edition, my italics).

Reis (2006) extrapolates on the notion of the 'border' between the 'intra' psychic and outside world. He proposes that, in adhering to a Kantian notion of subjectivity, Freudian hypotheses indicate a mentalization of bodily experiencing, the mind separated from the external world and from others via the construct of mental *representation* of sense-data. Evidently this formulation carries within it the legacy of Cartesianism, wherein reflection is equated with 'being' and subjectivity is defined by the 'res cogitans' (ibid.), residing in the brain-mind, "with the 'head' of the ideal-observer ... incorporeal and detached" (Sawyier 1973, p. 226). This contention echoes the traditionally positivistic conception, in which reality is seen as 'out there': "being 'in there' means residing in the certitude of the intra-psychic world, ... existing as a knowable, certifiable essence..." (Schafer, quoted in Mitchell, 1993, p. 58), i.e. "existing in the mind". In a similar vein, claims Reis (2006), Klein's and Bion's models have "elevated the contents of the mind to a privileged status over perception, making what is in the mind even more 'real' than the world as experienced, or relations with others" (ibid., p. 185). Their definition of "in thereness" does not – naturally – include non-cognitive attributes of perceptual subjectivity, such as proprioception, introception and kinaesthetic capacities.

Against the backdrop of these perspectives, Rendon (1986) equates the transition from Freudian to Object Relations theory with the transition from Kantian to Hegelian determination of the contents of consciousness. Rendon maintains that the orthodox Freudian and Kleinian views are in sync with Reis's (2006) critique (discussed above): the "other's" subjectivity is not apperceived via a psyche-somatic intercourse with its psyche-somatic being; instead he is cast as "[an]other human being ... known ... [by] ... the internal image (phantasmal or symbolic) that indicates him or her and that mediates our relationship to him or her" (Grotstein, quoted in Reis, 2006, p. 184). This claim is congruent with the Kantian position of a "pure" subjectivity, which does not defer to the body, to the senses and to the perceptual apparatus, but to the isolable 'mind' itself. Object Relations theory, he argues, displays a radically different – Hegelian – framework, manifesting in the dialectic of an *independent "pure" consciousness and a "dependent consciousness*, whose essential nature is ... to live or to be for another..." (Hegel, 1807/1977, p. 115, my italics).

Scharff and Birtles (1997) strike the last nail, suggesting Hegel's contention, that "the 'originative' source of change ... is one thing in relation to another" (pp. 292–293), stands in contradiction to body-mind dualism. The conceptual base for Object Relations interactive framework, they suggest, lies in an intrinsic dual-track inter-dependence of body and mind, subject and object.

The far-reaching implications of this conceptual shift stand in stark contradistinction to both Platonic-Cartesian dualism and Kantian subjectivity, as:

1 Relocating the arena of conflict and the frictional borders, from a solipsistic intra-psychic sphere to a relational inter-personal one.
2 Providing the theoretical substrata for a 'theory of mind' which takes dialectical synthesis into account, and provides the basis for a unified body-mind matrix, embedded in the perceptual-physical body.
3 The synthesis, relating to reality as *interactively presented and inextricably intertwined with the mind* rather than as solely *represented within it*, is applicable to the mother-baby matrix (and – by extension – analyst-analysand) and to the body-mind dialectics, alike.

Extrapolating on these two basic positions lends clarity to hitherto "mysterious leaps" since they focus directly on the intricate *quadruple matrix, emergent in the interaction between the two nuclear matrices: the infant-mother dyad and the psyche-soma matrix*, with each discrete aspect of the matrices relating to all three others.

## Dialectics of 'res cogitans' and 'res extensa'

Going beyond the constraints of orthodox psychosomatics, one of the most influential theories has been that of Joyce McDougal. In a theoretical welding of psychosomatic theorizing and Object Relations psychoanalytic theory, McDougal (1989) makes it clear that *somatic symptoms constitute a substitute for reflection* and for its articulation in the form of verbal communication, in both intra-psychic reaction to emotional pain, and in inter-personal communication of emotional pain (p. 9). For McDougal, somaticizing – a form of *archaic pre-verbal communication* – reflects a circumscription of neurosis, resembling psychotic failures of symbolic function (ibid., pp. 28–29). Stepping beyond the bounds of orthodox psychosomatics, her portrayal is thus a dual intra-psychic/inter-psychic one, redefining the intrinsic connection between somaticity and meaning formation.

The British Independent and Object Relations school went even further and, within them, Donald Winnicott's approach to the question of psyche and soma is germane. Winnicott asserts that the 'mind' constitutes a specific part of a 'psyche' which, in its turn, inhabits a unique and particular space along the *psyche-somatic continuum*. In Winnicott's model, the 'psyche' is an "imaginative elaboration of somatic parts, feelings, and functions, ... of physical aliveness" (Winnicott, 1975, p. 244).

In a paradoxical twist, typical of his theorizing, Winnicott flips over the convention that the psyche-mind is the determinant of meaning and metaphysical perception. For Winnicott (1960), it is the physiological, involuntary, rhythmic, somatic patterns of breath, heart-beat and heart-rate that give rise to and determine supposedly psychic attributes, such as temporal perception and conceptualization: meaning-formation is dependent on the body itself.

As an example, I reflect back to Eitan, supposedly lost in psycho-somaticity, apparently bereft of symbolic functions, frustrated by loss of representational meaning. Eitan had asked, poignantly, cynically, hopefully if I, "with my Eastern knowledge", understood what he was saying. In retrospect, I think I can respond in the affirmative: in line with Winnicott's conceptualizations "Eastern knowledge" confirms that internal "gestures" (energy rising up his spine, etc.) intrinsically carry their own meaning not in "representing" well-being but – as 'embodied meaning' – i.e. they *meant* his well-being. When I suggested this to Eitan, his tension noticeably relaxed.

Winnicott's repeated contention that "there is no such thing as an infant", connotes the inherent significance of *concrete* maternal/environmental provision. The postulate of an axiomatic 'infant-mother' dyad highlights the inclusion of somatic, concrete, dependent relationality in psychoanalytic research. More particularly, it underlies the investigation of how psyche-somatic apparatuses of dyads – infant-mother, and, by inference analyst-analysand – interact. Winnicott's portrayal exemplifies the transition from the construal of a solipsistic constitution of the mind's contents, to a formulation stressing 'object-subject' and 'mind-soma' dialectical positions. This new formulation brings in its wake a reformulation of body-mind relations within psychoanalysis.

Further down the line, Ogden (1989) postulates a third major ontological 'position', designated "the autistic-contiguous position", in addition to Melanie Klein's "schizoid-paranoid" and "depressive" positions. The "autistic-contiguous position", as outlined by Ogden (1992), supports the proposition that archaic mental and psychic states emerge from the phenomenology of perceptual-sensual states: they enrich symbolic-metaphorical underlying structures within the unconscious, but also *reside as specific, determinant structures within it, benignly persevering throughout life*. They thus become the basis of what is progressively acknowledged in psychoanalysis as "embodied cognition" (Bucci, 2012).

Ogden (1992) writes: "sensations and words like 'comfort' ... 'safety', 'connectedness' ... *will be attached to the experience of shapes...*" (p. 55, my italics) as *unmediated derivatives* of sensual perception. In this context, the soma's perceptual role is therefore not to be superseded by more refined psychic systems. Rather, it provides a continuous archaeological substratum, benignly manifesting in psychical life and aliveness. Ogden's (1989, 1992) propositions enrich Winnicott's in proposing that the 'soma' acts both as substrata for metaphor (symbolical meaning) *and* as a persistent, crucial determinant of actual meaningful psychical contents, compiling to form an ontological position, crucial to psychological well-being.

## The mind-set of the analyst and the psyche-soma: implications of the dual 'subject–object' and 'psyche-soma' reformulations

Technique and clinical demeanour, as defined by the rules of abstinence and of neutrality (Freud, 1915), were initially modelled upon the "surgeon, who 'puts under' all his feelings, even his human sympathy, and concentrates his mental forces on ... performing the operation as skillfully as possible" (Freud, 1912, p. 115). These injunctions strictly retained medical protocol, seeking to objectify the patient's subjectivity. Conversely, in Object Relations theory, the tools of psychoanalytic examination have transformed from reliance on *cognitive appraisal of objectified content* to an explicitly psyche-somatic interactive grid of communication. Whereas the Kleinian position maintains that "projective identification is an operation that the solipsistic infant performs internally..." (Reis, 2006, p. 179), Object Relations theory revises this position, explicitly acknowledging projections as communications. Admitting the interactive capacity of contents of mind-consciousness to traverse the space between two individuals without the mediation of physical action *or* verbal communication (see Grotstein, 2002; Schore, 2002) inevitably validates the notion of a non-dualistic modus of interaction.

The gradual reformulation in clinical understanding of Object Relations theory is mirrored and emphasized by a shift in methodology and technique. Radically diverging from injunctions of neutrality, it introduces terms such as "facilitation" (Winnicott) and "reverie" (Bion) into psychoanalytic methodology. Winnicott went so far as to describe psychotherapy as an overlap between the *therapist's and the patient's ability to play* (Winnicott, 1982); the Winnicottian-style "direct presentation of reality" (Little, 1993) necessitated a re-evaluation of physical-sensual experience in psychoanalytic technique. This is modelled on what "presentation" of objects, and concrete "holding" and "handling" of the infant by the mother contribute to his psychical well-being (see Winnicott, 1986). The theoretical shift is mirrored in psychoanalytic disposition and reflected in the analyst's mind-set and demeanour. Masud Khan, Winnicott's protégé, describes in his Preface Winnicott's "relaxed physicality ... [as he] listened with the whole of his body ... a childlike spontaneity imbued his movements" (Winnicott, 1975, p. ix); his biographers Clancier and Kalmanovitz (1987) describe him as "reminiscent of a circus clown" (p. 64) – a far cry from Freud's injunctions for surgical comportment!

In sync with this, Winnicott critiques conventional psychosomatics, suggesting that it easily objectifies the psyche-soma as "a subject ... theoretical survey..." (1966, p. 510). Winnicott goes on to portray the therapist's detached, theory-oriented focus on psychic-somatic contents as a dissociated state. Accordingly, rather than relying on an objectified and solipsistic *cognitive appraisal of content* dependent on the analyst's surgical demeanour, he considered a state of mind in which *the sensual and perceiving body* participates to be crucial for furthering the analytic process. This is supported by current clinical research suggesting that "subsymbolic modes of communication themselves may be sufficient in some cases to bring about therapeutic change..." (Bucci, 2012, pp. 282–283).[4] In meta-theoretical terms, this is revolutionary: the body – in its emotional, spontaneous and involved interaction – has attained a unique and specific *psychical* status.

To summarize: emotional life as conceived in Object Relations theory is deeply connected to both the *intra-somatic* sphere, and to leaps between psyche-somatic entities – manifest in the transferential relationship via "different levels of mental elaboration, from discharge to abstraction" (Lombardi, 2002, p. 363): bodily *corollaries of the contents of such communications* – projections currently acknowledged as "somatic counter-transference" (Rick, 2013) – are recognized as valid communications. Concurrent methodological-technical corollaries imply that analysts appear less "caught up in the content of words and the insight and incisiveness of their paradigms" and more aware of "the *texture or feeling of the gestural communication* or the need it is expressing" (Reis, 1999, p. 411, italics in the original).

## Psyche-somatic theory as a pivot of theoretical reformulation

In 1959, Gates proposed that the distinction between 'mind' and 'body', that had functioned as the Occam's razor in psychoanalytic observation and theory formation, was an irrelevant issue, camouflaging an evidently much more intricate relationship: intertwining "leaps" "from mind to body, from body to mind, from mind to mind, and from body to body" (quoted in Deutsche, 1959, p. 15). Congruent with Gates's proposition as to the multiple 'psyche' 'soma' 'leaps', the importance of the 'body qua body' – the body as such – in interaction, alongside representational aspects of the body, body image and bodily schemas is gradually recognized.

The sway of Winnicott's enterprise, in particular – though hesitant in its aspirations for meta-theoretical-paradigmatic status – points towards a partial reversal of evaluative priorities; conceptually it leads to a mutually constitutive, hyphenated 'psyche-soma' instead of the 'substantial-psyche-contingent-soma', of orthodox 'psychosomatics'. Winnicott's conceptualization of the "psyche-soma" unit and his insistence on the substantiality of benign "unintegration" and of "chaos" as unitive experiences, are seminal to his profound influence on psychoanalytic theory. Following Winnicott, the picture of psyche and soma relations upholds the body's contribution to psychic reality and body-mind relations.

Freud's original "mysterious leap" related to the mystery of psychical events affecting the body. Transposed into psychoanalytic technique, it meant that psychical events – linguistically mediated through interpretations – could affect physical symptomatology. The present chapter traced the opposite trajectory, showing that physical "handling" and even physical "objects" and "shapes" determine psychical contents, providing the substrate for 'psyche-soma' in a way that endures throughout life. A two-way tangent is thus established: The mother/therapist's psychic state is constituent of the infant/patient's soma; somatic 'handling' and 'holding' are constitutive of the infant/patient's psyche, in particular in its attribute of "indwelling" in the soma.

Substance and psychical processes are shown to interact within these configurations. How is this so?

Proposing a "lingua franca" connecting unitary neuro-psychological and psychoanalytic formulations, Scalzone (2005) maintains that the seemingly incompatible categories of 'structural-material' and 'procedural-psychic' co-exist in that "*structures* are stable processes at a low speed of change, whereas *processes* are structures in rapid movement ..." (p. 1411, italics in the original). Scalzone suggests:

> they are in some way very similar things that belong to a continuum: two faces of the same coin: We can ... say that they belong 'contemporaneously' to the res cogitans and to the res extensa and that they can be both symbolic and sub-symbolic.
>
> (Ibid.)

As I shall point out in the following chapters, "continuum", "interchangeability" and "complementarity" represent common denominators, germane to any non-dualistic solution: a unified mode of categorization, a unifying agent and a unified nomenclature. They consequently approximate foundational notions of non-dualistic Eastern body-mind disciplines.

## Conclusion and dialogue

Friedman (1988) portrays contemporary psychoanalytic meta-theory of mind as a misnomer, a dinosaur; Winnicott (1966) argues that the theory and practice of psyche-somatic integration in psychoanalysis fall prey to the inevitability of dissociation, in therapist and patient alike, moulded by what Roos (1982, p. 195) has termed disciplinary "hidden presuppositions". Grunbaum (1984) argues that contemporary meta-theory "is so

Babel-like as to defy the derivation of sensible deductions that can be put to ... test". Major psychoanalytical theorists, such as Holt (1967), Gill (1976), and Schafer (1975), have made an appeal for a complete rejection of meta-psychology!

The inconsistency and ineptitude of post-Freudian theorizing regarding the 'mind' and – consequently – the 'psyche-soma' are evident. In the present chapter I introduced the potential substrate for some alternative meta-theoretical paradigms, tracing two explicatory progressions:

1   Arising from the shortcomings of the energetic proposal of a differentiated 'psyche' and 'soma' and of 'psychosomatics': a substantiality of the 'psyche-soma' as a subjective entity.
2   Arising from relational and developmental perspectives of pre-verbal interactions: an innovative perspective as to the 'psyche' and 'soma' within quadruple reciprocal matrices.

Put together, these two progressions alter the field of inquiry, highlighting key meta-theoretical questions as to the 'extension' of the psyche and the 'subjectivity' of the soma. These are developed in the Object Relations School.

Lawner (2001) suggests that, due to Object Relations theory's emphasis on a psyche-soma continuum, "metaphors for ... mental life [are derived] from ... [the] ... body and ... material ... world, and metaphors for the doings of the ... material world, from [the] mind" (pp. 531–532). The insinuation is that subjectivity does not defer to cognition but to a compound 'psyche-soma', and that it connotes a reciprocal interpenetrative system with the outside world. Symbolical representation is still awarded primacy, but "direct presentation of reality" (Little, 1993), is seen as invaluable for accessing and exploring the mind, and – what's more – is considered crucial to technique and to the amelioration of symptomatology. Since primary mental concepts such as temporality and spatiality[5] are conceived of as being derived from the soma – two pillars of conventional theory are shaken: the theory of epigenetic developmental progress from body to mind, and the evaluative preference for the conscious mind over the body's involuntary and voluntary somatic expressions. Based on these notions I would speculate that – following the bombing raids – both Virginia Woolf's Septimus and my patient Eitan suffered a crisis largely mediated by distortions in the parameters of space, audio-thresholds and inappropriate holding in its most concrete sense.

Stretching beyond the bounds of given a priori categories – neither solipsistically internal nor exclusively external – the system I wish to present is a relational and reciprocal one. The transition from 'psychosomatics' to the 'psyche-soma' is consequently couched within a psychoanalytical analysis of transitions from a perceived Cartesian and Kantian analytic approach to a Hegelian-synthetic one. In their independent, dependent and interdependent aspects, other bodies and one's own body, in interaction, are seen to have a concrete function in the evolution and existential experience of consciousness and psychic life (see Anzieu, 1989, 1990). From these perspectives the psychoanalytic project itself is recast as an arena addressing the mind-body relationship, and "attempting to overcome any *dualism* by proposing a unitary picture of the human being..." (Mancia, 1994, p. 1284, my italics); this is mediated by the analyst's psyche-somatic clinical demeanour.

Object Relations theory in general, and Winnicott's epistemology in particular, have gone a long way towards ablating the border between the physical and the meta-physical, responding to the queries implicated in Chapter 1:

1 Does a hyphenated 'psyche-soma' constitute a new category circumventing Cartesianism?
2 If such a new category is implicated, what is the agent that evades or supersedes dualism, circumventing apparently apodictic categorical distinctions?

And, keeping in mind the opposing 'energetic' to 'hermeneutic' configurations:

3 To what extent is the amalgamated 'psyche-soma' a linguistic metaphorical formulation, or a substantial one?

Humanistic strands of psychoanalysis have long rebutted the categorical delineation of discrete "physical, psychical, and spiritual layers..." since it may fallaciously "appear ... that the layers could be separated from one another" (Frankl, quoted in Pytell, 2006, p. 492). Substantiating the aspiration for inseparability, however, necessitates a conceptualization of an overarching psyche-somatic reality. Philosophically, this requires reframing the categorical-evaluative hierarchy of mind and body, and providing a cohesive language for this reformulation. I have mentioned that Scalzone (2005) suggests that one such proposition would be to envisage a *continuum* of interchangeable 'structures' and 'processes': these would belong "'contemporaneously' *to the res cogitans and to the res extensa* ... be[ing] both symbolic and sub-symbolic" (p. 1411, my italics).

I mentioned two patients in this chapter, a fictional character and one of my own patients. What torments Woolf's Septimus is that scientism is objective, surgically analytical, remorselessly divisive of his subjective psyche-somatic experience; what upsets Eitan is the consistent failure of the contemporary Western paradigm to consolidate meaning formation with somatic manifestations. In these contexts, concepts such as the Winnicottian "paradox" (1975), Balint's "area of creation" (1979), Ogden's (1989) "autistic-contiguous position" and Bion's "proto-mind" (in Van Buren, 2002) will be considered in the following chapters; I shall suggest that attempts at creating overarching categorizations benefit from reaching beyond conventional Occidental epistemology and ontology bound by its "penchant for dualism" (Schafer, 1970, p. 428). In Chapters 6–9 I shall establish the advantages of including Zen-Buddhist conceptualizations, terminology and nomenclature in the portrayal of such emerging unitary propositions within contemporary psychoanalysis. In this review, I shall examine the feasibility of a "realm of mental experiences that ... make assaults on the sense of time, space and other conditions of limitation" (Van Buren, 2002, p. 150).

Where scientism and modernism sought to analyse and define, a deconstruction of psyche-soma renders the two entities inherently intertwined: one cannot speak of a body without evoking the thought or memory of its binary 'trace' – the 'mind' or 'psyche'. The configuration of unitary propositions rests on interdependence and contextuality: "There is no such thing as a baby" demonstrates the inseparability of environment and subject, of somatic interaction and subjectivity. Hence mind and body no longer stand as discrete entities but are co-extensive and co-dependent: no longer 'psyche' and 'soma' leading to the contingency of 'psychosomatics' but rather, a hyphenated 'psyche-soma', interconnected and "inter-defined". However, before I follow this line of reasoning through, it is necessary to investigate the manner in which the soma has gained in status so as to assume an equivalent foundational role in the 'psyche-soma' duo within contemporary psychoanalysis: in Chapter 3, I shall consequently relate the way in which the soma has come into its own.

## Notes

1 Wallace (1992, p. 233) lists "methodically interactive-dualist", "parallelist", "epiphenomenalist", and "noninteractionally dualist" as some of the theoretical stances attributed to Freud in different bodies of research.
2 Freud is implicitly alluding to Descartes's canonical distinction of the body – the corporal substance – as 'res extensa' – the "extended domain", as opposed to the 'res cogitans' as that of the mind.
3 That is, "'force' (i.e. 'I feel forced to do something'), [which] is elevated to the status of an objective phenomenon in physical terms, and then used to postulate, as an axiom, the existence of another phenomenon ('energy'), which was originally metaphoric" (Rapaport & Gill, 1959).
4 Winnicott (1987) himself went so far as to stipulate that, in some instances, concretely somatic interventions – *including touching the patient (!)* – were invaluable. Thus, Winnicott's revolutionary technical contributions also represent the return of the "body qua body" to the psychoanalytic realm; its suppression has had perilous implications on the practice and relevance of psychoanalysis (Anzieu, 1990).
5 Considered a priori by Kant, i.e. primary, uncaused.

Chapter 3

# The ascension of the body
Representation and presentation

Chapter 2 focused on the reformation of psychoanalytic theory in regard to psyche-somatic relations. In particular, I stressed the revolutionary implications of Object Relations theory, in which interactive-dialectic formulations redefine the 'psyche-soma': a dual pathway was shown to lead from an isolatable 'mind' to a progressively integrated 'psyche-soma', and from an isolated ego to 'object relations'. In this context I suggested that the body – alive, breathing, handling, holding, gazing – is a determinant entity rather than the mere biological substratum of consciousness: in contradistinction to Freud's original model, I proposed an intertwined 'psyche-soma' unit, which develops through interaction with other 'psyche-somas', with obvious implications for psychotherapeutic methodology.

In a recent symposium entitled "Ordinary Psychosis", Bichowsky – a Lacanian psychoanalyst (and colleague) – lamented the fact that in contemporary practice physical symptoms rarely relent to interpretation. Interested in this notion I entered an e-mail correspondence with him in which he stressed the fact that currently he finds that the body no longer stands as a 'sign' for the mind: quoting Brousse (2007), he suggested that "we are no longer in a world of metaphor. We are at best in a world of metonymy ..." (p. 13). Meaning, therefore, is drawn from the juxtaposition of entities "parallel[ing] the transition from modern art to installation art" (ibid.). The metaphor is clear: body symptomatology has ceased to symbolically signify the mind's conflicts; instead significance is drawn from relationships within "relational" installations, meaning emerging from the way in which objects stand in relationship to each other. Similarly, the body and mind gain their significance from their relationship, within a psyche-somatic arena which recognizes the body as a substantial phenomenon within psychic life and the body's participation in performative, present-time communication; implied is the fact that embodied resonance, gestures and enactments are part and parcel of the psychotherapeutic interaction.

In the present chapter I shall follow these themes through. I shall begin with the conceptual progression that has made the ascendance of the body so pronounced, within which the 'body qua body' gained in status: within this altered cultural environment a heightened interest in reality as 'present' and 'presented' – rather than as 'reconstructed' and 'represented' – paved the way for a phenomenological psychoanalytic inquiry. I shall show how the soma's newly-gained status and foundational role – binding cognition with the body, reconciling hermeneutics and energetic paradigm – has informed the hypothesized 'unitary turn' in psychoanalysis, both methodologically and philosophically.

## The body

In the 17th and 18th centuries, Western Europe revelled in the bodily presentations of the grotesque. Cohen-Shabot (2008) demonstrates the manner in which theatrical performances, such as Molière's *Le Malade Imaginaire* – welding the grotesque with the bodily-concrete – reflect these anti-rationalist cultural paradigms. In order to instate its rationalist credo, psychoanalysis – emerging but a century later – long shied away from the 'concrete' – historically identified with the 'grotesque' – seeking to incorporate the bodily within the purview of the symbolic and the imagined: 20th-century French novelist Marie Cardinal (1983) recounts her shock when her account of incessant uterine bleeding evoked a response of total indifference from her analyst; Freud himself referred to his own body with mock-compassion as "poor Konrad", thereby distancing himself from its concreteness, which – due to his long-standing illness – caused him much anguish.

Composite studies show the body and 'embodiment' to be primary motivational and cultural forces, forming the basis of subjective and intersubjective lived experience (Kohavi, 2009); as such, they serve as an ideal fulcrum for comparative-cultural studies (Hall & Ames, 1998). The ambivalence regarding the soma's controversial role is acknowledged in disparate fields: it stands as ephemeral as opposed to the immortal soul and is the untamed "Dionysian" for Nietzsche and the "wild" in Rousseau in continental philosophy. It is the "wild" as opposed to the "civilized" form of thinking in Lévi-Strauss's binary structural division

(1973/1989) and signifies effeminacy as opposed to the privileged role of masculinity in Christian cultural accord. As Shapiro (1996) and Elisha (2011) demonstrate, it is but a short step from these binary cultural presuppositions, to formulations of primary-instinctual processes as inferior, bodily symptomatology as contingent and the direct presentation of the body at large as primitive and undeveloped. These are also the predominant views in 19th-century anthropological discourse on which Freud drew (Chaney, 2007).

From a 'cultural studies' perspective, Leder (1990) highlights the paradoxical experience of "bodily absence" as *promoting* Cartesian dualism in Western culture. A similar claim is reiterated from within psychoanalytic critique: from an inter-subjective (Relational) perspective, Reis (2006) criticizes Bion for "placing the testimony of the senses in abeyance" (p. 187), suggesting that Bion's approach reinforces Cartesian dualism. For Bion, following Klein, it is the *absence of the breast* that accounts for the activation of thinking phenomena. From both cultural and psychoanalytic perspectives, the revision of dualistic formulations requires the incorporation of the existence of sensual and physical realms as both constituents and manifestations of consciousness.

Despite Freud's original inculcation under the founder of phenomenology. Franz Brentano, the phenomenological and psychoanalytical traditions parted ways before the First World War: Jaspers's (1913/1963) descriptive phenomenology and Husserl's (1913/1931) disparagement of "psychologism" marked the rift between the phenomenological outlook and Freud's objective-scientific analysis of the psyche. Whereas in Cartesian intellectual traditions, one could not surmise the existence of another human subject from the presence of a body, phenomenology makes clear the associative 'pairing' of my own body with the perceived body ... as ... someone else. Hence the sensual-sensitive body itself – *presented and present, rather than imaged, imagined, symbolized or represented* – forms the tie that exposes and binds two human subjectivities. In this primary, non-subservient role, the body is key to the constitution of both individual subjectivity, social reality and empathic bonds.

Husserl's (1913/1931) phenomenological account of the body as the axis and vantage point of subjectivity resonates in Merleau-Ponty's *Phenomenology of Perception* (1945/1962). Where Husserl distinguishes a corporal mode of consciousness and empathy. Merleau-Ponty goes a step further: his image of a "blind man with a cane" is a reaction to the notion of the primacy of mental *representation* of reality: for Merleau-Ponty, consciousness is not derived from sensual-tactile input and auditory signals (picture the blind man with the cane) conveyed to the mind and processed by the 'mind'. Rather, he depicts the blind man's cane as a psychical-mental apparatus, an extension of awareness forming a direct continuum of subjectivity with the mental apparatus. It thus reflects a departure from both the Kantian notion of subjectivity and from Cartesian dualism.

## Body as subject in psychoanalysis

Historically, Merleau-Ponty's outlook was consonant with psychoanalysis's growing emphasis on pre-verbal developmental stages. A major contribution to substantiating the soma's essential role in psychoanalysis was the study of developmental stages pre-dating symbolical representation. Bowlby's (1969/1997) Attachment theory lends ethological support to the hypothesis of enduring physical, somatic and behavioural – as opposed to verbal-symbolical – manifestations of affectivity. Historically and conceptually allied to Bowlby's research, Spitz's (1965) findings substantiate the role of concrete aspects (rather than unconscious-repressed aspects) of affectivity – such as touch – in the genesis and aetiology of developmental arrest and emotional distress: in the orphan population he researched, children who were not touched simply failed to thrive. Esther Bick's (1968) Tavistock project of infant-observation lent further support to the growing body of evidence pointing to the continuous role of concrete somatic *presentations* as a major factor of emotional reality in pre-verbal life, and their persistence into childhood (Briggs, 2002).

Alongside Object Relations theories, these findings suggest that somatic aspects of the heretofore supposedly metaphysical 'psyche' are forceful in determining psychic thriving: the enigmas of a mysterious "leap" or of "leaps" had begun to re-form as a study of reciprocal continuous cross-dependent emergences of somatic, affective and mental attributes. Revoking Cartesian dualism or Kantian subjectivity, these findings realign hierarchical and evaluative positions: the two-way compound body-mind matrices between corporality and affectivity substantiate the developing paradigms directed towards unitary outlooks.

This entails charting

> a path ... for a ... new hierarchy between the sensuous and the non-sensuous. ... *not simply ... revers[ing] matters with the old structural order, now reverencing the sensuous and scorning the non-sensuous ... [it is] the ordering structure [itself, that] must be changed.*
> (Heidegger, quoted in Proimos, 2001, p. 155, my italics)

## A new "ordering structure"

In seeking a meta-theoretical stance supporting a new ordering structure of psyche-soma relations in psychoanalysis, four relevant axes of investigation are pertinent:

1. *Phenomenology*: stressing the paramount role of the body in the psychoanalytic experience.
2. *Ontology*: the soma as a foundational "real" standing outside the symbolical order.
3. *Epistemology*: the recognition of primary bodily subjectivity.
4. *Structure and deconstruction*: a new ordering of 'psyche' and 'soma'.

## Phenomenology: the body in the psychoanalytic experience

Nufar is a middle-aged doctor who has sought therapy with me after attending a workshop I gave on 'embodiment'. At the time she approached me, I had a dual therapeutic practice: of Eastern medicine, meditation and body-work and of psychoanalytically informed clinical psychology. To dispel doubts – so I had imagined – the two practices were held in two different rooms in the same clinic. Seeking clarity, I would then suggest – at each given session – that they select which room to go into. Some patients, however, aware of this arrangement, would stop in the corridor and request that we integrate the two. They would hope to incorporate the body-work with materials that were becoming available through verbal work, or integrate bodily manifestations by working through them verbally.

Nufar was one of these patients. Reluctant to comply with my arrangement, she often challenged me: "You are pretending to integrate, but in reality you are perpetuating a split; this is not what I came to you – specifically – for."

I indicated that we could enter the 'psychotherapy' clinic and continue our discussion there.

Still in the corridor, she hesitated. "If I go in there, we'll only talk," she said. "Yet it is my body that doesn't understand."

"I can do my best to seek an explanation with you, for you," I replied. Registering my own feelings, I realized that I was feeling drained and impotent.

She grew grave.

> No, you don't understand. When we *talk* about the body, I know the explanation, but it doesn't help. The words are irrelevant. It's as if my body, my face, my belly, my teeth – especially my teeth which are in a terrible shape – are psychotic.

She then uttered a sentence which has since stayed with me: "My body doesn't need an explanation, it requires understanding. It needs to be met in its own, real, terms."

What were the terms Nufar was pleading with me to offer? Were they to do with my own feelings? With a bodily-bound empathy? With self-disclosure? Phenomenology countered empiricist psychologism and Kantian subjectivism from its outset (Husserl, 1965), contending that "Kant's account of perception leaves no room for the body ..." (Battersby, 1998, p. 70). The celebrated Davos debate between Ernst Cassirer and Martin Heidegger sketched the contours of this intellectual duel: opposing Cassirer's (1945) Neo-Kantian proposition that man constructs a world of symbols which he then confronts, Heidegger made clear a view which unravels the sensual-perceptual construal and contextuality of human experience and communication: prior to symbolical construction, he postulated that

> Dasein ... [is] ... essentially codetermined ... [by] ... the relatedness of a human being, which to a certain extent has been fettered in a body and which, in the fetteredness in the body, stands in a particular condition of being bound up with beings.
>
> (Gordon, 2010, p. 196)

Consequently, within the phenomenological variant of psychoanalysis termed "Dasein Analysis" (Boss, 1963), participatory involvement –

tantamount to the body's *presence* in the therapeutic scheme – came to be seen as paramount. Merleau-Ponty (1968) has termed this an "interweaving" of the "flesh". Based on this, Reis (2007) described the emergent clinical situation as "a prereflective 'interweaving,' a fitting together of 'sensibilities' rather than ... a meeting of minds" (p. 378).

Contemporary psychoanalyst and philosopher Donna Orange (2010) evokes Gadamer's hermeneutics – lodged in the 'human sciences' – to establish an allied line of reasoning. As if responding to Nufar's plea, Orange claims that involved 'understanding' – rather than detached 'explanation' – furthers particular aspects of insight. Following Gadamer, she shows mental life and its understanding to initially arise independently of logical-explanatory-scientific language. Rather, it arises within the 'Erlebnis' – experience, and 'Ergebnis': 'Ergebnis' implies the empirically established "givenness" of reality; 'Erlebnis' denotes "the immediacy with which *something real is grasped ... which precedes all interpretation, reworking and communication*" (Gadamer, 1991, p. 61, my italics).

## *Ontology? The body, words and 'reality'*

Ellman and Moskowitz (1980) suggest that a major confabulation, lying at the root of psychoanalytic theorizing, is the confusion between the ontological reality of participative experience and its verbal representation: since "in psychoanalytic propositions ... it is often unclear whether a psychoanalytic statement is presenting primary phenomenon or whether it is meant to be an explanatory statement" (p. 656). Consequently, concepts such as 'the unconscious', the 'id', 'primary processes', and so forth are alternatively regarded as 'phenomena' and as 'concepts', as participatory experience or as symbolical representation.

Rorty's philosophy of language takes this idea to task on conceptual grounds: Rorty (1970) refutes the possibility of a representational fit between reality and the way it is represented, rejecting the notion that seemingly axiomatic verbal referential-definitions constitute a correspondence to an external truth. The rupture between explanation and an embodied sense of understanding is inevitable since "language changes ... [and] ... what people call now 'sensations' might be discovered to be brain processes" (ibid., p. 211). In Rorty's view, it is this practicality, and not the essential differential qualia of the 'psyche' and 'soma' that lead to "the distinction of mind and matter as two fields of inquiry..." (Rorty, 1979, p. 80). Rorty's views in this respect are in sync with Wittgenstein's (1953) proposition that verbal expression inevitably precludes – rather than expresses – the original somatic experience. This is consonant with contemporary psychoanalytic propositions: global aspects of "lived" experience are foregone in their transformation through the use of language (Stern, 1985, pp. 67, 174–175).

Within the above conceptual trajectories – generally known as "the linguistic turn" in philosophy – words attain substantiality through public accord: rather than presupposing intrinsic attributes of 'psyche' and 'soma', their respective roles are derived from the common usage of the words referring to their consensual actions. Philosophically, the sense of the world "lie[s] outside the world" (Wittgenstein, 1922/1999, Section 6.41) of cognitive mindedness; psychoanalytically, the private-personal experience of 'body' stands outside the precincts of the symbolic sphere, consistent with the notion of a Lacanian "Real". It is the body's subversive-sensual-unaccountable qualities that exclude it from public accord: its immanent materiality sustains an elusiveness whereby it continuously evades 'representability'. It thus remains outside the conventional psychoanalytical ken of symbolical or imaginal psychical material. Reminiscent of the notion of the body as the subversive (grotesque), the 'body qua body' and its sensations evade and defy both 'public accord' and 'language'.

## The body as knowing-subject: present or represented?

If the body itself eludes interpretation, if it no longer serves as a sign or a metaphor, what then comprises the revised relationship between body and psyche/mind in psychoanalysis?

I sit in a Zen-shiatsu group designed to help parents get in touch with their adopted children. I watch one of my students demonstrate a sequence of massage movements, his hands fleeting over the child's body, sensing – rather than touching – it. At one point, he stops and empathically asks the child: "It hurts here, doesn't it?" The boy turns his head towards the student in surprise; the father reacts as if he has unexpectedly encountered a successful conjurer and is trying to decipher the trick. "How did you know?" he asks, incredulous.

I sit in the clinic and an old-time patient of mine arrives. She has lately given birth. She tells me that her mother is watching over the baby in the waiting room. Suddenly, in mid-sentence, she stops, embarrassed, and I perceive a damp spot on her shirt. Milk. At that very minute her mother knocks on the door asking to be let in with the baby. "He was totally calm up till now," she says, "but now he has started crying and casting about ... I think he's just hungry."

How was this connection established? How did they "know"?

I exit, for the umpteenth time, from my own therapy. My therapist is an analyst who was supervised by Winnicott for many years. At the end of the session, she hugs me strongly, briefly. From time to time, as the therapy progresses she notes, in these partings: "You are much more here; you are more present within your body."

Aware of the truth of her observations, I ask myself: what does she know? And how does she know it?

I sit in the clinic with Rotem, who has recently suffered severe trauma. Ordinarily a healthy young woman, she now comports herself as if her body and legs are disconnected. In the clinic she stands up, trembling in sheer weakness, her muscles taut with exhaustion, afraid to let go, wary of sitting or of lying down.

I respond to her body language and her sparse words with my own words, hoping that – taking note of each and every aspect of her presence – my resonance with her is giving rise to helpful remarks.

I suggest that – if and when she considers sitting down – she turn to the right where I have placed an armchair.

"Which side is right?" she asks.

I touch her right hand and indicate: "This side is right."

What has she forgotten? I wonder.

Epistemology – the conditions of and for acquisition of knowledge – is conventionally associated with the study of subjectivity – hence of the cogitating mind, "having to do with opinions and their justifications" (*Oxford English Dictionary*, 2014). The absence of a corporeal component – other than brain tissue – from these constructs of 'mind' is striking. However, both developmental and neuro-psychoanalytic research regarding the interface between experience, consciousness and semiotics in an intersubjective context offer an alternative (Stern, 1985, 2004, 2010; Varela, Thompson & Rosch, 1993). Anthropology teaches us a similar lesson: the body binds semiotics – signs conveying meaning –

with embodiment as a means of articulating the phenomenological experience of "being in the world" (Csordas, 1994); it is thus indispensably relevant to the psychoanalytic investigation of the relationship between symptomatology and meaning formation. Within these conceptual trajectories, *consciousness arises as an emergent feature of the development of the body in its interaction with environmental provision and constraints.*

"Embodied consciousness" thus construed is reflected in the capacities of self-cohesion and self-agency, and manifests in proprioceptive awareness, introception and kinaesthetic motility. This implies that – through early interactions – *the body of the "object"* is internalized, forming the foundations of a subjective self; hence subjectivity is inter-subjectively established through physical interaction (Detrick & Detrick, 1989). Psychoanalyst Sheets-Johnstone (2002) equates bodily subjectivity with Husserl's concept of self-agency – "I cans" – maintaining that bodily agency subtends and gives rise to "nonlinguistic concepts that develop on the basis of bodily life" (p. 41). Accordingly she succinctly surmises that *"nonlinguistic corporeal concepts are in no sense inferior to their linguistic relatives"* (ibid., my italics).

Jung, in his cultural comparative studies, describes a Pueblo Indian chief who thinks white men insane because they claim to "think with their heads", whereas his folk thought with their hearts (Redfearn, 1966): Jung's somewhat sarcastic observations underscore the convention of a 'mind-consciousness-head' trio, delineating a seemingly indisputable correlation between brain function, mental function or consciousness and physical topology. Within this convention, the 'mind' is popularly located in the head, owing to three intertwined and pervasive attributions:

1 Physiologically the bodily aspect of the psyche-soma is equated with the brain: "The body self, assuming brain as a core component of body, is seen as synonymous with the self..." (Meissner, 2003a, p. 279).
2 The brain's neurological functions are equated with consciousness (Crayne & Patterson, 2000).[1]
3 The brain is situated in the head, which is the highest part of the physical body, thereby perpetuating the metaphor of 'higher is better', as in "higher" faculties, for example.

Over the past four decades, Johnson (1987, 1993) and Lakoff and Johnson (1980, 1999) have pioneered an inter-disciplinary study of the relations between the philosophy of language and the body. Challenging the above postulations on philosophical and scientific grounds alike, they have reformed philosophical paradigm relating to body epistemology and subjectivity. Based on early Greek philosophy, they suggest an alternative paradigm within which the psyche "cannot be conceived of spatially ... to be localized ... in any particular site" (Van Peursen, 1966, p. 4), since "in every part of the body the entire soul is present" (ibid., p. 5); it follows that the inquiry into the localization of consciousness is also an inquiry into the body as a constituent-participator in the formation of subjectivity, as opposed to being an 'object' of 'subjective awareness': in the past, the body was clearly implicated in the co-creation of subjectivity when participating in physical activity such as dancing (Meissner, 2003b; Kolod, 2012) but was excluded from this privileged role in the construal of 'subjectivity' per se; Lakoff and Johnson's prolific innovative research into the philosophy of language fundamentally challenges this ingrained paradigm, maintaining that the body forms the basic – rather than the contingent – strata for an alternative "philosophy in the flesh" (1999) contesting the conventional "metaphors we live by" (1980).[2]

Contemporary psychoanalytic formulations reflect a similar diffuse and de-constructivist model of consciousness: Winnicott (1954) hypothesizes that the attribution of the particular allocation of 'consciousness' to the head may be a contingency derived from tissue-trauma due to the head's position during birth. As a consequence, cultural and psychoanalytical accord are "caught up in the ... false localization of the mind in the head, with its sequel, the equating of mind and brain" (ibid., p. 252). Following a similar train of thought, Ferrari (cited in Lombardi, 2002) gives the following outline as to the topology of consciousness: the vertical axis, connecting the belly and the head forms a *temporal-spatial present-time presentation* of the body-psyche, while the horizontal axis reflects historicity and expressions of interpersonal relationship: horizontality confers *representability* on the vertical dimension, which it could not otherwise have.

## The psyche-soma dynamic: towards a new ordering structure

The relative ascension of the body as an essential and particular part of subjectivity has radically affected psychoanalytic efforts at establishing a meta-theoretical paradigm; notably, it has led to an ipso facto recognition of the concrete body as "the repressed" par excellence, that is, the repressed of psychoanalysis itself (Anzieu, 1990; Elisha, 2011). Seeking to redeem psychoanalysis of this embarrassment, Anzieu (1990) states that, unless it integrates "everything to which ... bodily therapies draw attention, ... it will be shelved in the storehouse of obsolete accessories, that are no longer talked about" (p. 69). Accordingly, in *The Skin Ego* (1989), he introduces a model of embryonic development which diffuses conventional distinctions between 'psyche' and 'soma' and between perceptual-sensual faculties and mental-cognitive ones.

For Anzieu, the fact that skin and the central nervous system (i.e. the brain) both emerge from a common embryonic cellular layer engenders a novel ordering of consciousness, blurring distinctions between internal and external, higher and lower faculties. Anzieu thus engages with the following possibility: *"what if thought ... were as much an affair of the skin as of the brain?"* (ibid., p. 9, my italics). In this equation, Anzieu postulates a dual reversibility-complementarity of functions within which "the 'Ego' – now defined as the 'skin-Ego' – has the structure of an envelope" (ibid.), rather than of a nucleus. Anzieu contends that these equations, i.e. the composite structures of "lining-nucleus", "brain-skin" and "skin-ego" function as a particular form of "sign-signified" grid, creating both a metonymical and a metaphorical relationship between the 'I' and the skin. The inherent paradoxes of these terminologies punctuate the inapplicability of separate-specific words to the task assigned them; the diffusion is conducive to a reordering of both categorical delineations and evaluative registers.

Post-structuralist and de-constructivist theorists have gone even further in the obliteration of the boundaries between "Things and Words" (the original title of Foucault's (1970) book, entitled "The Order Of Things" in its English version); whereas the dualistic paradigm was culturally set within the religious dogma of "the Word was made flesh", Derrida (2005) endorses an intrinsic inseparability of 'words' from 'flesh'. Through his manipulation of phrases such as "tactics of tact" (ibid., pp. 266–276), he creates a mesh wherein the body reflects its tactile faculties and touches upon its own reflexivity through being "a thinking body of thought" (ibid.). Parading a host of words simultaneously serving as indicators and indicated, as bodily references and referents – such as "tact", "regle", "index", and "right" – he suggests that corporeity and language are inextricably intertwined.

## The soma's role in clinical theory and technique: the clinical body and the reflexive mind

An inevitable outcome of the body's ascension in a revised ordering of the 'psyche-soma' is the recognition of breaches with orthodox methodology and technique. Winnicott's quintessential approach to interpretation follows these breaches through:

> A patient dug her nails into my hand at a moment of intense feeling. My interpretation was "ow". This *scarcely involved my intellectual equipment* at all, and it was quite useful because it came immediately (*not after a pause for reflection*), and because it meant to the patient that my *hand was alive...*
> (Winnicott, 1968, p. 95, my italics)

Approached thus, interpretation is perceived of as a means of *conveying the environment-analyst's bodily aliveness*, rather than as a means of uncovering the unconscious significance of verbal utterances. Significance and meaning, supposedly metaphysical concepts, are seen to be derivatives of somatic experience whereas verbal communications, in certain instances "are not experienced by the patients as interpretations" (Balint, 1968/1979, p. 18) and are perceived as meaningless. In these instances, *the phenomenology of unmediated experience – rather than thinking – becomes the predominant category of existence, and nonverbal communication – rather than interpretation – the mode of its explication:* Lombardi (2002) asserts that "the assumption that the body has no 'language', as some theoreticians claim, is … dangerously biasing for a psychoanalyst. *Perhaps body-language is the* only *language that cannot lie!*" (p. 366, my italics). I shall return to this issue in Chapter 9.

In recognition of a discontinuity between analytic theory and the lived experience as regards the body's place in psychical life, Wrye (1996,

p. 28) pertinently inquires: in the "inchoate, ungendered, nonverbal sensorium of the body ... how does one find ... ways to reinscribe consciousness?" (ibid., p. 284). In a clinical setting this may read: if and where "body" is an essential phenomenon, appearing both as a primary presentation and via its mental representations, how may the relations between 'psyche' and 'soma' be redefined so as to accommodate theoretical complexities arising from its concurrent presentation, representation and communication in therapeutic interaction?

In the 1980s, Atwood and Stolorow (1984) pioneered the harnessing of phenomenological terminology to the explication of the body's role in the clinical situation and hypothesized a conceptual basis for relational modes of psychoanalytic interaction. Within these modes, the former shift from a "one-person" (classical) to a "two-person" (Object Relations) psychology was extended to include a "two body psychology" (Aron, 1998, p. xv). What had begun as an epistemological project by Husserl (1913/1931) – who recognized the body as a formative locus for the structuring of subjectivity – transformed to include the ontological situation of the psychoanalytic therapeutic encounter. This ongoing shift connotes the inclusion of two distinct parameters:

1 The body's role as regards consciousness, substituting conventional, mental aspects of consciousness – such as "memory" – with attributes ascribed to and embedded in the body, such as "body memory".
2 The body's role in communication, with the physical body presenting as an illocutionary act, a "text" which may be "read": the body carries forth "prosodic elements of communication, such as rhythm, force and tonality ... acknowledged as better carriers of the affective messages than linguistic elements of language" (Schore, 2002, p. 24). In this formulation implicit-procedural memories are carried by the body and semiotically transmitted to the recipient; enactments manifest as particular patterns of unconscious conduct, bearing symbolical significance (see Atwood & Stolorow, 1984, pp. 91–97).[3]

## Conclusion and dialogue

In this chapter I suggested that the ascension of the body to an equivalent status in the formation and communication of psychosomatic life involves revisions of psychoanalytic dogma. Loosening its Cartesian footing –

maintain Lakoff and Johnson (1999) – 'the embodied mind' constitutes a challenge to the Western philosophical tradition. Delineating variegated aspects of this challenge I suggested that it manifests in psychoanalysis as a "reordering" of convention regarding the relations between the psyche and the body; this reordering is dependent upon experience prior to, or different from, symbolic formulation and representation. Since it manifests in present-time therapeutic encounters – in resonance, in movement, in enactments – concomitant therapeutic technique is adapting to accommodate these findings.

In 'Psychical or mental treatment', variously dated 1890 or 1905, Freud suggests that what appears to be the somatic contingently concomitant phenomenon is, in fact what is truly psychical (ibid.). In Chapter 1, I explained that this line of thought was curtailed by the failure of "The Project", leading to Freud's compromise in comporting himself "as if only the psychological lies before me…" (Ammon, 1979, p. 6, quoting Freud's letter to Fliess). However, divergent (and subversive) theories have persistently formed an undercurrent of psychoanalytic theorizing: bodily manifestations came to be viewed as primary, inseparable and valuable components of the psyche-soma, largely through Wilhelm Reich's (1933/1972) polemic extrapolation of Freud's original ideas.[4] These include intertwining psyche with body on three different planes: body as a concrete object, as metaphor, and as a potential substrate of underlying subjectivity and communication; in contemporary theory, these amalgamations re-emerge to form a site of convergence wherein semiotics and hermeneutics, metaphor and concrete presentation align so as to enhance, refine and confer meaning.

In her book, *The Conscious Body*, psychoanalyst and body-therapist Elisha (2011) has shown the aspiration that the body should partake in subjectivity to be true "across" psychoanalytical schools; following her, I propose that the body's direct presentations are non-contingent, non-symbolical, discrete and non-pathological aspects of the psyche. It is this depiction of the body's essential non-contingency in psychical life that renders the formulation of "a unitary picture of the human being in which all functions are complementary" (Mancia, 1994, p. 1284, my italics) a theoretical plausibility.

Incorporating the body in the psychoanalytical scheme requires paying attention to the inchoate, to sensations, to experiences not mediated by language or text; alternatively, it necessitates ingeniously making up a new language and rewriting the psychotherapeutic textual canon (as in Anzieu's 1989, 1990 case). Laying stress on 'experience' as a core component of analytic content-matter has paved the way for a theory based on 'structures of subjectivity' that are not limited to the 'res cogitans': in loosening the link between knowledge and the cogitating mind, psychoanalysis turned to phenomenology as a theoretical framework: Merleau-Ponty's phenomenology – in particular – lent psychoanalysis an "embodiment of understanding and cognition" (Frie, 2007, p. 64) which had hitherto remained outside the purview of psychoanalytic theory and practice. In *Phenomenology of Perception*, Merleau-Ponty (1945/1962) develops a thesis of body-based subjectivity that provides a conceptual scaffolding onto which psychoanalytic theory can cling: he retains the concrete while stepping outside it in the formation of symbolic forms that are irreducible to strictly cognitive interpretations.

Transposed onto the clinical arena, these reformulations engender a revised insight as to the question of a "mysterious leap" and of interpersonal "leaps". Where bodily presentation prevails, patients' silences often render standard analytical procedure impotent: in this sphere the talking cure's mainstay – interpretations – is deemed *meaningless* for some patients. The semiotic significance of bodily presentations and enactments – on the other hand – is crucial to the psychoanalytic reconstructive procedure. Accordingly, "psychoanalysis as a technical procedure must … use semiotic tools … [in] … retrieving procedural memories [that] may not involve cerebral cortex … [and] may be recovered only through … repeating certain postures, or gestures…" (Levin, 2011, p. xvi).

Lombardi (2002, 2009) reassesses "the mysterious leap/leaps" in similar terms. In a revision of the entrenched "head-brain-higher faculties" credo Lombardi integrates the vertical (intra-psychic and psychesomatic) and horizontal (bodily resonant and interpersonal) spheres. The vertical plane lays a heightened emphasis on the phenomenology of psyche-soma participation and aliveness. The horizontal plane stresses *somatic resonance* between patient and analyst and *the role of concrete bodily presentations within the interpretational mode of interaction*. Thus, the ascension of the body as a core existential-phenomenological constituent and determinant of experience has definitely given rise to the 'psyche-soma' experience as a co-joint phenomenon; in the clinical context, it is seen as communicated reciprocally on a non-verbal as well as on a representational-symbolic level: my therapist "knew that I was more present"; the mother "knew" when the baby was hungry. Eitan's psyche-soma could make better sense of Eastern common-sense based on psyche-somatic epistemology than on psychosomatically informed interpretations; and I definitely relied on my somatic counter-transference in order to decipher Nufar's assaults on my psychotherapeutic procedure.

While the present chapter extrapolates on the 'psyche-soma's sensations and experiences, it also punctuates the inconclusiveness of this resolution: is this 'psyche-soma' a "primary phenomenon or ... meant to be an explanatory statement"? (Ellman & Moskowitz, 1980, p. 656). Put differently, can 'experience' substitute for the biological body, or verbal-textual communication as the foundational substrate of theoretical formulation? Can the flux of – by definition – ever-changing experience provide a substantial philosophical foundation for a revised meta-theory? For an alternative ontology? These incertitudes have made the dynamic tension between poles of objective-subjective, representation-presentation, concrete-symbolic statements regarding the somatic aspects of the psyche-soma the crux of contemporary theorizing: for lack of a matching meta-theory, however, it is not clear whether the psyche-soma duo constitutes a concept explaining certain experiences or an entity in its own right. This tension tends to stabilize around one or the other default polarities – positivistic-biologistic or hermeneutic-linguistic:

- *positivistic-biologistic*: the body is construed as the concrete aspect of the 'psyche-soma' and equated with the brain; thus "the body self, assuming brain as a core component of body, is seen as synonymous with the self..." (Meissner, 2003a, p. 279).
- *hermeneutic-linguistic*: the body is depicted as the "Real", standing outside the symbolical order altogether. It is recognized through verbal explication or subordinated to a hermeneutic deconstruction (as in Derrida, 2005).

The two default positions, however, prove disappointing when one seeks 'understanding' of the body in its own terms (as did my patient, Nufar) "rooted in our carnal, sensorial experience in the world and of each other..." (Reis, 1999, p. 412). A mode of explication that phenomenologically welds the incompatible poles of "Sense and Nonsense" (Merleau-Ponty, 1964) in an integrated mesh intertwining sense and sensibility, "tactics and tact" (Derrida, 2005), "skin and ego" is still an elusive project. Prompted by interdisciplinary discourse "psycheanalysis" is seeking such a *'new ordering'*, a way to methodologically and conceptually integrate the psyche and life-vitality.

It is consequently not surprising that – informed by Zen-Buddhism – analysts' aspirations to a state of "being with all one's faculties..." (Horney, 1952/1998, p. 36), and to conceptualize selfhood as "a combination of physical and mental aggregates" (Moncayo, 1998, p. 66) represent a dual pathway: the first pertains to epistemology and methodology, the latter to 'psyche-soma' ontology. These are matched by psychoanalysis's search for a corresponding vocabulary of innovative nomenclature: remembering Anzieu's formulations of "lining-nucleus", "brain-skin" and "skin-ego", we are reminded that psyche ($\Psi v \chi \acute{\eta}$) in its original meaning means "life-breath". In order to preserve it, we must take care in our use of verbal explication lest it smothers and kills (as Lacan warns) rather than nurtures and creates.

Seeking to break through the convention of dualistic constraints, psychoanalysis endeavours to integrate 'sense' and 'sensibility'. With this in mind, one can relate to the arborescent conceptual dialogue phenomenological philosophy has had with Eastern 'body-mind' philosophies (Yuasa, 1993; Park & Kopf, 2009). Broadly speaking, the Zen-Daoist critique is this: for all its advantages, Western phenomenological theory still retains its intellectual substrate, inevitably thematizing and separating objects of consciousness. In Daoist and Zen-Buddhist conceptualizations, the welding of sense and sensibility is axiomatic, manifest in the image and concept of the "body *flowing* perceptually, personally, interpersonally and pervasively ... also flow[ing] thinkingly..." (Kuang-Ming, 1997, p. 17, italics in the original). Adopting both philosophy and religion as disciplinary partners (see Chapter 1), three strands of psychoanalytical theorizing, in particular, have gone a long way in contending with this compound challenge: I have proposed that they distinguish 'unitive experiences' and delineate a 'unitary turn'. I shall review and develop their hypotheses pertaining to a new ordering of unitive experiences and unitary formulations in Chapters 4 and 5.

## Notes

1   1 and 2 also connote two modes of body-mind differentiation: a topological division wherein the head stands in opposition to the trunk and periphery of

the body, and a substantial division wherein autonomous neural functioning is contrasted to the materiality of body-tissue.
2 Both titles of books written by them.
3 Merleau-Ponty terms this "the unconscious as manifest" – "the act aspect of consciousness" (see Dillon, 1971). In a similar vein, neuro-psychological research converges with a semiotic approach to suggest that somatic empathy, defined as the act of paying attention to non-verbal, somatic cues, such as posture and gesture, enables an understanding of what is going on in the thoughts, feelings or actions of others, by mentally mimicking them. This capacity may be developed through a "postural mirroring" and "mental mimicry of the patient" (Gallesse & Goldman, 1998, p. 493).
4 Reich viewed the body as reflecting a direct communication of the unconscious, largely due to the fact that, developmentally, physical, affective and mental constructs all appear to intertwine and compound to create stable characterological formations.

# Chapter 4

# Unitive experience and a unitary turn

Is 'experience' an acceptable ontological terminology? Does the 'psyche-soma' constitute a distinct entity – a mode of subjective experience – in its own right? Can we formulate the joint perspectives of 'sense' and 'sensibility' within psychoanalytic nomenclature? Can categorical, evaluative and developmental distinctions between body and mind be substantially rethought, re-felt, reformulated? The previous chapter confronted these issues: drawing attention to the gradual ascension of the body as a focal point in psychoanalysis, I delineated a re-evaluation of conservative attitudes as to 'mind over body' supremacy. I stressed that the body's growing role emerged concurrently with a growing emphasis on performative aspects of interaction, action and enactments as constituents of meaning formation. Accordingly, I postulated that within the therapeutic matrix a focus on reality as 'present-presented' rather than as unconsciously 'represented' leads to a radical conceptual shift: instead of relying solely on symbolical elucidations and linguistic elaborations, therapy has come to incorporate present-time *experience* as a form of "phenomenological ontology".

Concurrently, the search for an accompanying epistemology climaxed in new orderings of orthodox sign-signified, reference-referent matrices: a unified field, straddling meaning-seeking hermeneutic investigation, and concrete, perceptual, physical presentations was hesitantly introduced. I pointed out psychoanalysis's attempts at psyche-soma metonymies (for example, Anzieu's "skin-ego") as the linguistic counterpart of these innovations; these attempts were, in turn, supported by kindred paradigm shifts in the philosophy of language.

In this chapter I propose to demonstrate how – in regard to psyche-soma relations – distinct strands of contemporary psychoanalysis implicitly embrace 'unitive experiences' and attempt 'unitary' formulations:

conceptually, these innovations converge in a 'new ordering'; in terms of psychoanalytic practice, they pertain to and affect both clinical theory and methodology. While not – as yet – constituting a clear, unified theoretical statement, they share significant tendencies, propensities and episteme. While not declaring innovation, they demonstrate innovative methodologies and theoretical elaborations that revolutionize psychoanalysis in essaying categorizations and formulations implicitly embracing non-duality. Together they verge on a paradigmatic turn regarding unitive experiences and unitary conceptualizations.

## Unitive experience and unitary epistemology

A relatively unitary conceptualization of 'psyche-soma' unity was a common feature of both Eastern and Occidental medical disciplines in the pre-Socratic era, as apparent in a cross-cultural survey of medical texts at the time (Gundert, 2000). In what became a clear East–West philosophical divide, this approach was later eclipsed by adopting 'logos' and Christian evaluative stances as guiding principles in Western therapeutic disciplines: equating consciousness with psyche, psyche with logos and logos with divine transcendence marked a trajectory that eventually led to Cartesian "bifurcative" psychology. Within this ideational framework, both 'theology' and "logy" marked the estrangement between man and the natural world. It was only with the advent of Heidegger's phenomenological outlook – that brought together pre-Socratic, Daoist and Zen-Buddhist perspectives – that unitive experiences and unitary formulations were again ushered into the Western mainstream investigation of the human psyche and psyche-soma.[1]

### Unitive experiences

The definition of unitive experiences is elusive. Their acceptance and assimilation into psychoanalysis's mainstream terminology have been gradual and tenacious. Freud (1927) first mentioned unitive experience as a defensive strategy. Responding to Romaine Rolland's plea for an explication of an "oceanic feeling", which is experienced as an unconstrained experience with no perceptible limits, Freud (1930) reductively portrayed it as replete with oral-regressive characteristics: Freud's response attributes the feeling of absolute union to a regressive wish fulfilment of utter merger.

In contradistinction, prominent strains within contemporary psychoanalysis uphold unitive experiences as primary: Christopher Bollas (1989) even goes as far as to suggest that "embodiment ... refers to a certain success in becoming a spirit, moving freely as an incarnated intelligence" (p. 157). Following William James, Merkur (1989) proposes unitive experiences comprise distinct psychological phenomena: he counters argumentation designating them as *exclusively* 'mystical' or 'religious', proposing, rather, that they may be seen as "experience[s] that portray the self as a totality of being" (p. 57). Leavy (1995) stipulates that their particular characteristics may be the outcome of "meditation ... or ... increasing relaxation of the body and control of breathing ... [that is] ... devoid of verbal content and thereby open to unity with the totality of being ... unarticulated by words" (p. 355). Leavy's position emphasizes the body's germane role as the vehicle of unitive experiencing: in its unarticulated presentation, it is characterized by the seemingly paradoxical equation of the metaphysical-mystical with the physiological-physical.

Many clinicians will find the practical implications of the above propositions part and parcel of their everyday practice. Object Relations theory, in particular, presents 'primary processes' as potentially unitive experiences: Eigen (1983), in a tribute to Marion Milner's work, relates to potential areas of "oneness, undifferentiation, merger or fusion ..." (p. 415) as a "valued state"; he holds up Balint's references to a "harmonious interpenetrating mix-up" (ibid.) of self and other, together with an intra-personal experience of "boundless expanse" (ibid.), as demonstrating similar unitive qualities. These qualities, described in "terms such as union, permeability ... interweaving, and the like" (ibid., p. 420) denote a benign state of primary fusion. Together they reflect a revised perspective of subject–object relations in both philosophical and psychoanalytic terms and, accordingly, impact on clinical procedure and the therapeutic encounter. The following vignette may serve to demonstrate some of this.

Nathan is a 50-year-old man whose vocational career involves religious and mystical studies. The father of seven, he experiences his wife and children as distant and feels unable to make himself available to them. Nathan has had a psychotic breakdown in the past and approached me for therapy following a period of mounting depression which – he fears – may impede his ability to financially support his large family. He has always experienced his father as not present in his life. His mother's presence, on the other hand, has been and still is most pronounced: he describes it as "a wall", a solid entity, with no sutures, with sealed-off orifices. Pointedly, he notes that he has never experienced softness or a sense of nourishment from her.

A few months into therapy, Nathan began to perceive his own presence as disembodied. "My presence", he described, "inhabits only the top part of my body, mainly somewhat to the right of my face; the face itself feels like a rigid mask. Everywhere I go I am not fully there; I'm never wholly comfortable." Over months of work – as these sensations recurred – Nathan gradually recognized the affinity between these sensations and his father's "unpresence", on the one hand, his mother's "impermeability", on the other. 'Space' and 'distance' became extremely relevant to our interaction as, allowing himself to physically move about in the clinic, he gradually learnt – to his great relief – to attain self-agency regarding our respective distance from each other.

As time passes, he is – and experiences himself as – less constrained; however, when I note the marked decrease of tension from his face, he is worried.

"Why are you telling me this?" he asks, intently, as rigidity immediately re-establishes itself, an almost visible visor over his facial features.

I feel as if I am under interrogation and tell Nathan that – before responding directly – I would like to point out that I found the tone of his question unusual for him.

He sniggers: "I am like a wall. I am like mother when she asks me questions."

"But walls don't move about so intently and passionately investigating their ability to be in the presence of others", I find myself thinking, feeling silly when I think of voicing this. Instead, beckoned by his sincerity and self-denigration to reveal something of myself, I notice my own presence and facial features softening. My words come forth as an extension of this soft feeling: "I am touched by what you just said", I share with him. As the words are uttered, I am surprised to feel warm tears gathering in the corners of my eyes. Apparently this is perceptible: Nathan looks at me in surprise: "This is a mystical feeling for me", he says, "*and I should know*. In your eyes, now, I perceive my own expression. So I have an impression that you sincerely feel me." To our joint surprise, tears form *in his eyes* and *he* begins to cry, then to sob, finally heaving and puffing, breathing in deeply.

Gradually breathing more freely, he notes: "I have never felt the air go in like this. It's sweet; it's expansive. I can feel it permeating my whole body."

"There was softness and warmth", I mention. Then, as an afterthought: "And freedom."

As if in reply he mumbles: "I'm here."

Eigen (1983) acknowledges this dual-track revision of a joint transposition of 'subject–object' and 'body–mind' into a new non-dualistic matrix: he terms this "a revolt against Cartesianism" (p. 420), stipulating that Independent School and Object Relations innovations reflect "a dual, union structure (*of self-other, mental ego-body ego*), wherein ... the law of contradiction is suspended in both" (p. 426, my italics). Eigen's contributions highlight the fact that the specification of 'psyche-soma' unitive experiences in psychoanalysis arises coincidentally with a reappraisal of categories relating to subject–object relations in general: within these innovative formulations, the body ceases to be the object of the psyche's subjective investigation.[2]

Gellman (2005) aspires to provide philosophical categories and terminologies that encompass non-dual unitive experiences and unitary ontology. In a paper, "Mysticism and religious experience", he suggests that mystical experiences stem from either a 'sub-perceptual' or a 'supra-perceptual' position, both circumventing intellectual reflective capacities. Rather than searching for a cognitive way of linking or binding two distinct entities – "the mysterious leap from the mind to the body" – these formulations presuppose a *sub*-stratum or a *supra*-ordinate stratum of unified ontology and experience. In line with Eigen's and Gellman's formulations, the quest for the conceptualization of unitive body-mind experience is recast so as to define and describe unitary formulations: these are, typically, *common denominators which may be attributed to both 'body' and 'mind'*.

## The unitary turn: a hypothesized paradigm shift

To date, no major school of psychoanalysis has declared itself as espousing non-duality. However, in order to accommodate clinical innovation, to linguistically conceptualize 'psyche-soma' unitive experience, and to integrate both within existing paradigms, psychoanalysis has indeed stretched its conceptual boundaries. In what follows I shall delineate three divergent attempts within psychoanalytic theorizing to address the conceptual lacunae regarding unitive experiences. I propose, however, that due to the persistent lack in overarching categories and metapsychological formulations these attempts reflect theoretical and methodological efforts *within these strains* rather than generalized meta-theoretical unitary propositions.

## Intersubjective and relational formulations

Adopting conceptualizations originally espoused by humanistic and existential branches of psychotherapy and psychoanalysis, intersubjectivity has adopted hermeneutics, phenomenology and modern structuralism as its theoretical axis (Atwood & Stolorow, 1984). Eschewing intra-psychic positivist one-person theorization, intersubjectivity introduced the "two person psychology" formulation, incorporating a "two body psychology" (Aron, 1998).

Relying on the subjective and intersubjective formulation of psychological experience, Atwood and Stolorow, forefathers of the intersubjectively-based psychoanalytic schools, profoundly altered the view as to the stratification and contents of the unconscious: notably, the equation of unconscious with untamed primary-process bodily forces is rejected. Instead, 'psyche-somatic' organizational patterns lodged in 'the unconscious' are seen to form the basis for unitive experiential schemas as the substrate of consciousness; humanhood is accordingly re-conceptualized to reflect the fact that "personality structure [is] the structure of a person's experiencing" (Atwood & Stolorow, 1984, p. 33). Accordingly, the conservative 'dynamic unconscious', in the form of psychological structures that – having entered the sphere of awareness and reflection – are repressed or denied, is recast to include *experiential, pre-reflective* building-blocks. These constitute compounds of complex "pre-reflectively unconscious" psychic reality (ibid., p. 36), comprising conglomerated physio-psychic schema-units, manifest in thought and action, emotions and behaviour.

It is now easy to see what has led psychoanalytic intersubjective approaches to embrace Merleau-Ponty's phenomenology. Merleau-Ponty's exposition of 'perceptual experience', culminating in pronouncing "flesh" as that which "precedes the division of subject and object..."

creating "instead a prereflective 'interweaving', a fitting together of 'sensibilities'" (Merleau-Ponty, quoted in Reis, 2007, p. 379) defines a *pre-symbolical, pre-verbal consciousness*. Upholding the plausibility of a pre-reflective ego, Merleau-Ponty proposes that the construction of meaning is derived from "a level of the 'expressive' relationship of body and the world" (Besmer, 2007, p. 32), *and that subject–object relations are already established when reflection begins*. Moreover – according to Merleau-Ponty – affect surfaces in this constellation as an emergent property of gestural conjuncture, dependent on perception, its meaning "internal to the gesture itself" (ibid., p. 35).

For Merleau-Ponty the appearance of language is inextricably interwoven with the living flesh, with the compound and indivisible experience of the subject, and thus with the "bodyhood" bearing the spoken word. *In its relation to the material realm in general and to corporality in particular, language is an involvement*, rather than a detachment, maintaining a signifier-signified joint unit, rather than an arbitrary 'sign-signified' or symbolic relationship. Concurrently, knowledge assumes a corporal dimension, as other human beings are known "through their glances, their gestures, their speech" (Merleau-Ponty, 2002, p. 82). The subject who knows is thus inseparable from the subject as known, as reflected upon, as "languaged"; both are inseparably intertwined with the corporality of other perceiving-perceived, touching-touched subjects.[3] The perception and theoretical construal of psychoanalytic terms such as dyadic infant-mother "proto conversations" (Trevarthen, quoted in Lyons-Ruth, 1999), and the "analytic third" (as constructed and construed via the analyst's reverie in Ogden's formulations) implicitly lean on these conceptualizations.

## Involved subjectivity

The phenomenological propositions of an intertwining of mind and body in actional-involved corporeity carry in their wake significant implications for psychoanalytic meta-theory. It is seminal to the phenomenological outlook that active involvement confers meaning: it is an extension of Heidegger's revolutionary proposition that one comprehends the function of objects through their manipulation and not through reflecting on them; only active involvement and manipulation of real objects construe psychic reality. Thus, involved participation – acts, actions and enactments disclose – rather than disguise – meaning.

In harnessing Merleau-Ponty's phenomenology of perception to its needs, psychoanalysis distances itself both from its positivist routes and from a reductively hermeneutic reconstructive meta-theory. In their stead, it postulates a new outlook on hermeneutics and interpretational procedure and on the interweaving of subjectivities. 'Knowledge' is accordingly redefined so as to include embodied, relationally constructed, moment-by-moment joint efforts of two experiencing and perceiving individuals (Reis, 2007). This is far removed from the orthodox ideal of an interpreting subject (analyst) uncovering a temporally-distant-predetermined-psychic-reality, and a non-perceiving – non-perceived, "interpreted" object (the patient on the couch). Rather, it is applicable to key contemporary theoretical innovations such as Stern's "core" and "emergent" selfhoods or Ogden's unitive (1989) "autistic-contiguous position".

Let me give an example: When I was an intern, the heart-rending – or infamous – instance in which Melanie Klein had offered a cup of tea to an analysand whose close relative was killed by the Nazis was presented as a mark of transcendence – or transgression – of the 'symbolical' transference relationship. Ogden's formulations – on the other hand – "make sense" of this: Setting the world of objects – *in their literal meaning* – as a basic stratum of psychological experience, he implicitly suggests a continuity of experience from the intra-personal to a wider 'interconnected' sphere of experience,[4] broadening the scope of potentially analysable material to include relations with the inanimate world. In the spirit of Heidegger's and Merleau-Ponty's phenomenology, physical acts – handling and interacting with the concrete world – *confer meaning*: comfort and safety are conveyed via smooth, yielding surfaces; separateness by unyielding, sharp objects, etc.: the continuity between presentation and representation and between the world of materiality and subjectivity is established. Reclining on the couch, the patient experiences 'softness' – not just a smooth surface; being offered a cup of tea he experiences – and responds to – 'warmth', not 'politeness' – or a breach of professional etiquette. Klein's touching-infamous gesture is thus *meta-theoretically* reframed as an unsolicited example of a unitive striving, a presentation of warmth and tactile contact.

Involved participation thus stands in radical contradistinction to the hermeneutical plea to a psychoanalytic meta-theory: hermeneutic theory of narrated communication claims that one "cannot grasp the act of existing except in signs scattered in the world" and that, consequently, "reflection must become interpretation" (Ricoeur, 1970, p. 46). Conversely, redefining consciousness as preceding speech and symbolization compromises the hegemony of language, including that of analytic interpretation as psychoanalysis's one unchanging stable mainstay. As Leavy (1995) suggests, "language is intrinsically divisive of experience" (p. 355): in embracing unitive experience incorporating bodily awareness, reflective consciousness ceases to provide a watermark of "correspondence to truth", and the plausibility of reflective "knowability" represented by language becomes, in its turn, the object of a questioning scrutiny, rather than the watermark of the objective "real".

In another ideational outcrop stemming from a phenomenological stance, Kohut (1977) suggests substituting positivist outlooks altogether: Kohut proposes that quantum physics – rather than Newtonian physics – is prerequisite for a realistic reflection of the interpenetration and co-dependence of subject–object predication in contemporary psychoanalytic paradigms. 'New physics' undermines positivism in suggesting that complementarity, connoting the mutual and equivalent symmetrical co-existence of a *two-fold truth – rather than a substantial and a contingent one –* is not a metaphysical postulate: rather, it is indivisibly inherent in the physical world. Kohut's proposition is reiterated by Scharff and Birtles (1997) who maintain that the "new ... physics conceptualize[s] physical bodies as composite entities that contain an inherent potential that is actualized by means of active interactions with the external environment" (p. 1092).

*Critical appraisal*

Having gone a long way towards acknowledging unitary formulations, the terminology of the intersubjective schools rests largely on the phenomenology of a 'pre-reflective' unitive experience. Their subjectivist and inter-subjectivist formulations consequently contain two immanent shortcomings in terms of meta-theorization of unitary categorization:

1   In terms of ontology: by the very addition of the prefix 'pre', experience defined as 'pre-reflective' doubly favours the reflective capacity over the bodily one: In terms of developmental progress (a temporal 'pre') and in terms of evaluation, the 'pre' suggesting a more basic, primitive mode of experience.

2   In terms of epistemology, 'pre-reflective' is a binary unit: in structuralist terms, it comprises two signification units ('pre' and 'reflective') rather than a specific-precise terminology, exclusively designating unitive experience.

## Religious-mystical psychoanalysis

While traditionally held to be contingent upon "primary process" and "regressive tendencies", "psychological needs" or "pathology" (Freud, 1927, 1930; Salzman 1953; Ross, 1975, respectively), spirituality has attained a primary status within specific psychoanalytic theorizations: a "watershed mark" distinguishes psychoanalysts who see mystical-religious experience as primary from conventional psychoanalysts. Embracing unitive experience as a primary human attribute and motivational impetus and acknowledging its unique role within subjectivity radically alters perspectives regarding psyche-soma relations. Works entitled "Opening psychoanalytic space to the spiritual", *Spiritually Oriented Psychotherapy* and *Psychoanalysis and Religion in the 21st Century* (Stone, 2005; Sperry & Shafranske, 2005; Black, 2006b, respectively), go as far as suggesting that – in embracing the substantiality of religio-mystical experience – a paradigm shift in the scope and aims of psychoanalysis is implicated. Within this theoretical shift, compound 'psyche-soma' processes, interaction, complementarity and unitary formulations play a major role.

From a Lacanian vantage point, Moncayo (1998) comments that "only paradox comes near to expressing the nondual basis of life. Nonambiguity and noncontradiction are one sided and therefore unsuited to express nonduality" (p. 403). Moncayo sees Lacan's, Winnicott's and Bollas's views on the mystical 'psyche-soma' unity as converging to form a cohesive paradigm, regarding a pre-conceptual *and supra-ordinate* reality. Contrasting conventional conceptions of ego functions and of subjective self with Lacanian and Jungian perspectives of the self, he stipulates that "the key point is that access to the larger unknown subject requires an ego death" (ibid., p. 402).[5] Along similar lines, from within the Winnicottian tradition, Marion Milner's work outlines a "divine ground" in which the cathexis of the whole body "if properly understood, is not a rejection of the outer world, but ... a renewed and revitalised cathexis of it" (1987, pp. 237–238). Milner describes this experience as dependent upon a form of reverie, that is substantially different from "discursive, logical verbal thought" (ibid., p. 236).

Bion is often designated "the psychoanalytic mystic". Pelled (2005) comments that this may well be a reductive view of Bion's contribution and its radical challenge to conventional psychoanalysis since "the alternative suggested by Bion to the pleasure/reality principle is not 'mystical' in the conventional usage of this concept" (p. 56). Rather, she claims, it is mystical in its inclusion of *a particular facet of reality*, the element of the primary unknowable element. In a similar vein to Milner's and Lacan's postulations, Bion's consciousness includes a preconceptual mode of being in the form of a "proto-mind, originally not discriminated from the body, [that] remains in the born personality ... allowing embryonic intuitions to persist throughout life" (de Bianchedi et al., 2002, p. 106). Note that this is a 'proto-formation', inclusive of a primordial state anteceding and pre-dating the distinction of psyche-soma components, and a supra-ordinate organizing function at one and the same time: it is this pre-conceptual mode of consciousness that is aligned with "true knowledge", Bion's "O", wherein the analyst-patient interaction resides within "a realm of mental experiences that seems to make assaults on the sense of time, space and other conditions of limitation" (Van Buren, 2002, p. 150). Within these recurrent 'proto' states of being, "mysterious leaps" between "psyche-somas" may give rise to the capacity of "at onement" (Bion, 1970) with the patient.

Finally, Heinz Kohut's self-psychology has inspired research and clinical work with mystical underpinnings. Kohut's (1966) references to a quasi-religious "supra-ordinate" order with transformative potential, defined by an "expanded, transformed narcissism: a cosmic narcissism which has transcended the bounds of the individual" (p. 266) have paved the way for what constitutes a new trajectory within self-psychology and psychoanalysis. Kulka (2012) proposes that this dimension of the human condition suggests a "permanent oscillation between emergence states of the individual self and the state of dissolving into transcendental selfhood..." (p. 267), "emergence" denoting a dualistic constitution of reality and "dissolution" a non-dualistic 'psyche-somatic' reality. Kulka's proposal is the basis for a profound integration of Buddhism and psychoanalytical inquiry, elaborated upon and made manifest in his visionary "Buddhist Psychoanalytical Training Foundation" (Gabrieli-Rehavi, Green, & Kulka, 2014).

Mystical-religious positions within psychoanalysis go a long way towards dissipating Freudian orthodoxy's qualms as to the primary place mystical experiences hold in psychic reality. In proposing 'proto', 'pre', and 'supra' positions, the mystical perspectives circumvent traditional positions within psychoanalysis: they propound psychic states that either transcend or form pre-conscious holistic infra-structures of consciousness. Moreover, mystical perspectives perceived as 'primary' define a novel conceptual arena, facilitating the introduction of novel epistemology such as "proto-mental phenomenon" and "at one-ment" (Bion, 1952 and 1970, respectively), the "unthought known" (Bollas, 1999) or "cosmic narcissism" (Kohut, 1966). This new epistemological infrastructure is indispensable for the conceptualization of unitive experiences and the formation of unitary conceptualizations.

## Critical appraisal

Despite going a considerable way towards a delineation of a unitary 'psyche-somatic' entity, mystical-religious conceptualizations display some significant shortcomings. A growing distance from the objective, 'biological' object, present in the therapy room, often involves a hypostasis of meta-physical aspects: the mystical-religious position often seems to cement dualism in inhabiting the 'mystical' end of the mystical-scientific continuum: Bion's "thoughts without a thinker", suggesting psychic-mental contents as an existent separate from a physical human thinker, is a pertinent example – pointed out and criticized by relational analysts for this very reason (Reis, 2006). As Reis points out, "Such theories have paradoxically elevated the contents of the mind to a privileged status over perception, making what is in the mind even more 'real' than the world as experienced..." (ibid., p. 177).

Relational criticism of the mystical-religious position brings another of its shortcomings to the surface: orthodox theory strove to fulfil a 'correspondence to the truth' theory of validation, and inter-subjectivity denotes an espousing of post-modern subjectivity as its theory of truth; the mystical-religious position regarding 'reality' and 'truth' is less clearly defined. Its lack of consistency, its movement away from accepted meta-theories (both hermeneutic and biological) and its partial upholding of a transcendental-noumenal truth as primary components of the human 'being', has created a substantial breach with much of mainstream psychoanalytical theory.

## Neuro-psychoanalytic and developmental perspectives

Representing the other end of the idealistic-materialistic spectrum, neuro-psychoanalytic and developmental research has, in the past three decades, promoted unitary conceptualizations of the body-mind question. Whereas in the past, mind-brain 'identity theories' were criticized as being reductionist forms of materialism, it is currently accepted that the "scientific project is grounded axiomatically in a unitary ontology of mind and matter, and in the mandate that this unity be explicated" (Opatow, 1999, p. 97). Consequently, research-based neuro-psychoanalytical heuristic terminology now includes terms such as 'chaos', 'complexity', 'connectionism' and 'systemic' rather than 'binary', 'discrete', 'specific' and 'definitive' – all reductive propositions; instead of particular features of 'body' or 'mind' 'emergent properties' which are procedural outcomes of their constant-infinite interplay feature as unitary formulations.

Over time, orthodox and neuro-psychoanalytical findings have notably converged. Accordingly, non-dualistic contributions of neuro-psychologists such as Allan Schore and Antonio Damasio – as well as neuro-psychologically informed psychoanalysts such as Mark Solms – have contributed to a mounting body of what has come to be termed neuro-psychoanalysis. This discipline readily proposes that "brain and body, self and other, nervous system and environment ... riff ... off each other as jazz musicians do" (Carrol, 2014, p. 12).

Antonio Damasio's now canonical thesis *Descartes' Error* (1994), demonstrates these affinities, openly confronting Cartesian dualism as to the relations between the 'res cogitans' and the 'res extensa'. In his model, affect and cognition are inseparable from spatiality and temporality within a "proto self" which precedes the conscious self. This substrate-self supports a primitive order of representation of current, emergent sensual-affective-somatic states, providing the substrate for "the something to which knowing is-attributed" (Damasio, 1999, pp. 158–159). Perceiving of the self as a potentiality of consciousness thus complements Bollas's (1987) notion of a pre-conceptual content of 'unthought-known' and Bion's (1962) pre-conceptualization capacity.

Earlier I showed that Freud (1930) contested the possibility that oceanic feelings were primary, suggesting that unitive experience constituted "something rather in the nature of an intellectual perception..."

(p. 12). Now the primacy of unmediated and unmodulated subjectivity has turned the tables, attributing *primacy to preconscious representations, sensations and feelings* – including those accompanying unitive experiences. Neuro-psychoanalytic research has provided the theoretical substrate for this profound re-appraisal: emotions and feelings have replaced the 'mental' (ideas) binding with 'drive' (bodily, energetic) as the strata available for – and amenable to – analysis. Concurrently they have substituted Freud's (1900) idea of "mental energy" with the postulation that mental structure and content are joined by "*an affective charge*" (Scharff & Birtles, 1997).

Damasio's (1999) second book, *The **Feeling** of What Happens*, Allan Schore's (1994) book, ***Affect** Regulation and the Origin of the Self* (my bold), and Daniel Stern's (1985, 2004, 2010) exhaustive research have cut across conventional divisions in the definition and description of human experience, creating totally new *cognitive-affective-action-focused* categories of experience – such as 'temporal patterns', 'vitality affects' and 'intensities' (Stern, 1985, p. 67). Stern's innovations effectively span mental-affective-physiological conceptualizations, as he himself stipulates: "The elements that make up these ... organizations are simply different subjective units from ... thoughts, perceptions, actions and so on" (ibid.). In creating new categorical delineations, he also formulates new positions of pre-verbal, pre-symbol-formation selfhoods: "core" and "emergent" "selves".

Neuro-psychoanalytic formulations serve as sound foundations for a reappraisal of conventional psychoanalytic conceptualizations regarding 'psyche' and 'soma' relations, inasmuch as they highlight four striking departures from it:

1   Damasio's (1999) conceptualization of feeling presupposes the integration of introceptive, proprioceptive and spatial cues as crucial for the formation of internal images and conceptions of one's relationships with one's human and natural surroundings: both affect and cognition are seen as contingent on the experiential and relational integration of temporal and spatial cues. This viewpoint is supported by research displaying the cross-modal synthetic-connectionist – as opposed to the analytic – aspects of experience as paramount to acquisition of realistic knowledge of the world (see Stern, 1985; Beebe & Lachmann, 2002): in the *intra-psychic sphere*, transcending

"the boundaries of the [linear] sequential, paradigm of the mind, [this] connectionism has developed a theoretical model based on the concept of work in parallel" (Bucci, 1997, p. 13). In the *interpersonal sphere* Trevarthen (1980) distinguishes global features of non-verbal interactions – "proto-dialogues" – comparable to jazz music improvisation. Not surprisingly, this is reiterated in markedly similar terminology in relational psychoanalyst's Steven Knoblauch's (2005) paper entitled "Body rhythms and the unconscious: Toward an expanding of clinical attention", thus attesting to the affinity between these diverse contributions to the unitary *Zeitgeist*.

2   Time itself is construed differently, with a distinct emphasis on the experience of 'now' as paramount. In his book, *The Present Moment in Psychotherapy and in Everyday Life*, Daniel Stern (2004) stresses the "idea of presentness as key" (p. xiii), recasting consciousness as an intricate, ongoing 'psyche-somatic' emergent process, rather than as an entity given to reflective or introspective scrutiny. Phenomenological consciousness resides in the present and includes a non-differentiating (i.e. unitive) experiential dimension, implying a bi-hemispheric interaction of the brain (Gazzaniga, 1985), providing the basis for an "expanded dyadic consciousness" (Stern et al., 1998, p. 125). These notions are in line with what Merleau-Ponty has – paraphrasing Freudian depth psychology – termed "breadth psychology". Technically this implies a "language of continuous process" (Knoblauch, 1999, p. 36), challenging analytic conceptualizations of linearity, traditionally leading to a deterministic, re-constructivist explanatory framework.

3   Through referring to 'aliveness', 'vitality' and 'rhythm' as basic cornerstones of consciousness – the idea of energy has re-entered mainstream psychology and psychoanalytic formulations. This is apparent in Stern's (2010) book, *Forms of Vitality*, in which "five theoretically different events – movement, time, force, space and intention..." (p. 4) consolidate to form a pre-reflective unified gestalt.

4   Mutual non-verbal regulation of affect defines the relaxation of subject–object distinctions and is utilized, almost off-handedly, to explain metaphysical unity inasmuch as a common, shared affect, involving mutual regulation is an emergent property within this conceptualization (Lachmann & Beebe, 1992). Both ideas – Stern's 'vital' experience and Lachmann and Beebe's implicit relational

knowing, imply a potential unified "unthought known". Both are reminiscent of a neuro-psychoanalytical proposition of the "mind ... [as] an emergent property of ... interaction in relation to sensory and motor processes connecting brain and environment" (Sperry, quoted in Meissner, 2003a, p. 293). To scholars familiar with Eastern traditions of consciousness, the affinity of these conceptualizations with Zen-Buddhist ones is self-evident: relational psychoanalyst and Zen instructor Magid (2002) notes: "The capacity of the self to engage with any and all moment to moment experience ... [rather than] ... the lapse into some mystical oceanic state ... is the hallmark of a life of oneness" (p. 46).

## Implications

Neuro-psychoanalysis and rigorous developmental research transpose unitive experiences and unitary formulations from the realms of subjectivity and mysticism to the purview of "objective" science. They have done much to establish a totally new nomenclature of the mind-psyche, in researching and defining new categorical delineations, eliding conservative ones. Moreover, they have been viewed as supportive and definitive of distinct domains of unitary formulations in fields as disparate as integrative body-psychotherapy, self-psychology and relational psychoanalysis. Relational psychoanalysts, in particular, tend to quote neuropsychological research, in substantiating their claim to pre-verbal and non-verbal relational paradigms (see Knoblauch, 1999, 2005, 2011, 2014). Furthermore, the unitary potential of their hypotheses has been gratuitously adopted and melded with mystical-religious propositions, and particularly with Buddhist propositions of intra-personal, inter-personal and unitive inter-connected reality (see Suler, 1993; Varela, Thompson & Rosch, 1993; Molino, 1998; Magid, 2002; Epstein, 2005; and Alfano, 2005, for examples).

## Critical overview

As opposed to intersubjectivity, on the one hand, and mystical-religious off-shoots of mainstream psychoanalysis, on the other, neuro-psychological research does not have its roots in the psychoanalytic consulting room. Its revolutionary implications are tempered by its restricted claims: It purports to investigate consciousness as a discrete extant, rather than as a derivative of biographical historicity, and, qua discipline, lays no claim to clinical implementation. Recognition of its potential contributions has, however, increased its aspirations and, concomitantly, its scope of influence, especially in the interface between developmental research and psychoanalysis. Backed up by neuro-psychological research, Daniel Stern (1985) has written profusely on "the clinical baby", and Allan Schore has supplemented his initial epigraph of *Affect Regulation and the Origin of the Self* (1994), with the clinical slant of *Affect Regulation and the **Repair of the Self*** (2003, my bold). Meanwhile Trevarthen's (1980), Beebe and Lachmann's (1994, 1998, 2002), and Damasio's (1994, 1999, 2003) contributions to contemporary psychoanalytic theorizing – as demonstrated in professional literature and scientific presentations – are invaluable. Consequently, the neuro-psychological base for neuro-psychoanalytic theories appear as necessary addenda to the hypothesized unitary turn, in promoting its scientific credibility, in much the same way as Freud had hoped his "Scientific Project" would.

## Conclusion and dialogue

Bollas, of course, was being slightly provocative: how seriously may we take the stipulation – quoted in the present chapter – that "embodiment ... refers to a ... success in becoming a spirit, moving freely as an incarnated intelligence"? Nevertheless – in his prolific style – he touched a sore point as regards the theoretical status of unitive experience and unitary conceptualizations. Let me give an example.

When introducing the concept of unitive experiences in a psychopathology post-graduate course, one of my students confronted me:

> Are you suggesting that when my patient describes having an expansive feeling, standing on the road and feeling like a free spirit, I should regard it as normal? What if I were disregarding the preliminary signs of the onset of a psychotic episode?

After dismissingly replying that that would depend on whether he was standing in the middle of the road or on the pavement, I responded on a more serious note: I urged my student to feel what her initial impulse was in response to her patient's statement.

Her immediate response – I noticed – was physical: she made a movement with her palms, as if to draw them nearer each other, holding something between them.

"What is this interpretation?" I asked.

"I would like her to remain within bounds, to shrink as it were", she replied, embarrassed.

Unwittingly my student and I were overstepping the bounds of Cartesian paradigm: we were attributing an 'extended' quality to the patient's mental state. This was not metaphor but a sensed reality, as my student's palm movement indicated. However, it could not be conceptualized otherwise than 'metaphor' since there is no theoretical accord as to the properties of "size" or "movement" of mental states (see Rorty's and Wittgenstein's argumentation in Chapter 3). How can psychoanalysis affirm and incorporate unitive experiences within these confines?

In this chapter I traced the history of unitive experiences – originally termed "oceanic experiences" – and showed the transition in their status, rising from a contingent and marginalized status to one acknowledged as primary. I charted out a dual track of non-duality in contemporary psychoanalysis: the ascent in embracing theory regarding the phenomenology of unitive experience and the persistent efforts at unitary conceptualizations. More particularly, I postulated that seemingly discrete strands of psychoanalytic thought interweave to display a hitherto unnoticed affinity as regards non-dualistic propositions: representing opposing camps within their original psychoanalytic milieus, the trinity of intersubjectivity, mystical-religious and neuro-psychoanalytic theorizing brings together such unlikely partners as Wilfred Bion and Heinz Kohut, Michael Eigen and Daniel Stern.

Non-discriminative unitary conceptualizations – including (body) consciousness and (body) memory – were seen in the past, as connoting a "category mistake" of attributing subjectivity to somatic experience. However, as the rift with orthodox epistemology widens and growing inconsistencies arise, it is becoming clear that the categories themselves are deconstructed. Accordingly, theoretical re-evaluation arises in regard to both meta-theory – as biologically or hermeneutically derived – and to psychoanalytic technique and methodological theory.

What are these methodological implications? Within the intersubjective field, the analyst's and analysand's subjectivities interact in ways that incorporate the psyche-soma's constitutive role in meaning attribution, affect regulation and the attribution and creation of significance. This has far-ranging implications. Leaning on Heidegger's – and more particularly, Merleau-Ponty's – phenomenology, it suggests a diminution in the role of verbal explication's exclusive contribution to therapeutic interaction and success. The therapist's role ceases to be that of an impartial expert surgeon (Freud, 1912) or even a skilful sculptor uncovering the unknown (Freud, 1933a); it is recast as an active, physically involved caretaker, instantiating new psycho-somatic patterns. The analyst has become a creator, seeking a way to compound text and body, narrated history and its bodily marks, hermeneutics and biology: only a profound level of "merger", "interpenetration" and "un-differentiation" – a mark of the divergence from the Cartesian dual 'subject–object' and 'psyche-soma' bifurcation – can explain the concurrent appearance of warm tears in Nathan's eyes and in mine; only the creation of overarching categories – such as warmth – can serve to override the notion of "a category mistake" when attributing a physical quality to a mental event, such as Melanie Klein's empathetic involved interpretation in the form of a cup of tea. Only an 'extended' psyche; and the 'cogitating body' can overturn Cartesianism and show the two – body and mind – to be essentially indistinguishable.

While the present chapter has established the affinity between otherwise divergent schools of psychoanalysis, and has pointed to the proliferation of non-dualistic psychoanalytic references in contemporary professional literature, it has also delineated some of the inherent shortcomings of current theories. All attempts to create a meta-theoretical framework – with a 'pre' symbolical substratum, a 'supra' ordinate one, or a 'proto' type psyche-soma – fall short: none of them has, to date, enabled psychoanalysis to formulate a satisfactory grid bringing together the phenomenology of mystical-religious propositions, the epistemology of intersubjectivity and developmental research and the ontological aspirations pervading neuro-psychoanalytic research. Thus, unitive analyses, observations and hypotheses tend to stand out as idiosyncratic: subordinate to existing categorizations and adhering to the hermeneutic-biologistic oppositions, they are labelled as 'mystical' at one pole, 'reductive' at the other extreme; being incongruous and incommensurable with the mainstream of existing theory they do not, as yet, contribute sufficiently to a paradigmatic meta-theoretical transition.

From within a neuro-psychoanalytic perspective, Opatow (1999) urges us to temporarily suspend our hopes of attaining a unified meta-theoretical statement. Instead he proposes that, due to "the limited capacity of our present conceptual resources ... we willingly take on this [meta-theoretical] deficiency in order to preserve a belief in the unity of Being and sustain the hope of a progressive unification of scientific knowledge" (ibid., p. 97). In Chapter 5, I intend to take this statement to task: elaborating on the conceptual data-base provided in the present chapter, I shall elucidate the main features of non-dualistic overarching conceptual efforts made to date. Then, bearing the propositions of the present chapter and the following one in mind, I shall provide the rationale for the book's transition from Part I – focused on the emergence of unitary formulations within psychoanalysis – to Part II: the latter will show to what extent these propositions may be substantiated by unique epistemological, ontological, hermeneutic and linguistic conceptualizations borrowed from the Zen-Buddhist tradition.

## Notes

1 This stipulation relates to dominant trends within the scientific study of the psyche-soma, thus disregarding Spinoza's theorems, for example. Currently Spinoza's contributions have been integrated into mainstream psychological research due to prominent neuro-psychologist Antonio Damasio's *Looking for Spinoza* (2003).
2 Winnicott (1954) sees this as a contingency to begin with, and attributes the erroneous location of subjectivity in the "mind-head" to the fact that organs of perception are located in the head. The ensuing illusion is that it is the "mind-head" that views the body from outside, looming above it.
3 For Merleau-Ponty, this is an obvious extension of Husserl's principle of tactile 'reversibility', the person being touched inevitably touching, the hand actively touching inevitably being touched (see Reis, 1999, 2007, for a psychoanalytic elaboration on this issue).
4 Interconnectedness is a Buddhist term defining the indivisible nature of reality as a whole.
5 Moncayo (1998) claims that the only valid unitary formulation of the true subject is derived from Buddhist conceptualizations. Therein the subject comprises "a combination of physical and mental aggregates" comprising "a series of clusters or groups of self-functions and processes that conform to the empirical, functional self ... body ... perceptions, feelings, impulses or mental formations-representations, and consciousness" (ibid., p. 391).

# Chapter 5

# The unitary turn
## Overarching conceptual structures

In Chapter 4, I sketched out the outlines of the phenomenology of unitive experiences. I suggested that intersubjective, mystical-religious and neuro-psychoanalytic theoretical strands incorporate clinical observations pointing to psyche-somatic confluence; these, in turn, support the plausibility of 'body-mind' unitary paradigms, represented in the preponderance of prefixes such as 'pre', 'supra' and 'proto' to designate 'unitive' configurations. The emergent nomenclature of co-joint psyche-somatic convergence creates a scaffolding for pioneering unitary formulations. However, I also stipulated that – despite these theoretical innovations – well-structured heuristic argumentation of unitary configurations remains sparse: to date, no coherent and parsimonious *meta-theoretical* standpoint exists that enables psychoanalytic experience, clinical observations and theory to converge around the theme of composite 'psyche-soma' relations.

Despite the fact that, for decades, "most contemporary philosophers have been in revolt against the Cartesian framework" (Bernstein, 1971, p. 5), psychoanalysis is still rethinking its dualistic heritage in a way that incorporates "new kinds of facts" (see Kuhn, 2012, in Chapter 1); similarly, it is still contending with acknowledging unitary formulations and rethinking paradigm so as to create a "new ordering" (see Heidegger, 1962, in Chapter 3). Acknowledging the shortcomings of extant propositions I shall delineate some of the theoretical resolutions that Ernest Hutten, author of *The Origins of Science: An Inquiry into the Foundation of Western Thought*, has thought conducive to "fit[ting] [psychoanalytic] theories to the facts of life" (Hutten, 1961, p. 277): these comprise attempts to incorporate both clinical observations and theoretical considerations in regard to 'psyche-soma' *overarching*, parsimonious, unitary formulations. Building on the propositions adumbrated in previous chapters, I shall compile nomenclature introduced thus far under the following specific conceptual headings: "paradox", "complementarity", "mysterious undercurrents", "connectionism, systems and chaos models". Finally, I shall introduce the elusive category of a 'something more', that denotes elements that consistently avoid categorical and symbolical reduction.

Finally, towards the end of the chapter, I shall chart out the conceptual outlines of the terrain leading to Part II of the book in which I suggest that Zen-Buddhist formulations and terminology may prove invaluable for conceptually substantiating the 'unitary turn' in psychoanalysis.

## Concepts

### Paradox

Try to consider the predicament of Nathan – the patient I described in Chapter 4 – within the constraints of Cartesian dualism: the idea of an expansive 'feeling' or 'thought' (i.e. extended in space) would be heretical; the certainty of a shared warm-teary feeling theoretically unsustainable. Think of the patients described in Chapters 3 and 4 and consider: how can a 'body' evince 'knowledge', 'consciousness' or 'memory'? For Cartesians, a unitive experience is an absurdity. For Kantians, no unitary formulation exists, due to the hiatus between bodily perception and mental categorization, "between the psychological 'inner' and the 'outer' of the empirical self". For "Kant ... introspection has no spatial co-ordinates: nothing 'inner' is spatializable..." (Battersby, 1998, p. 70). Based on these conceptual foundations, Freud's modernist, Renaissance-style attempt to reconcile empiricism and the humanities seems heroic but futile.

In stark contrast to these pioneers of modernity, 'paradox' – juxtaposing two propositions with 'truth values' as regards a certain phenomenon – is immanent to *post-modern formulations* in more ways than one. *Paradoxical positioning and juxtaposing conduce 'seeing through' supposedly veridical truths* embedded in particular cultural milieus: from this vantage point, what has traditionally been accepted as irrefutably axiomatic is not absolute: rather, it is seen to be transient, relative and context-dependent, a "presumptive principle that we hold normatively until and unless [it] cease[s] to serve our enquiries over the long run" (Johnson, 1993, p. 109).

Johnson's cognitive-linguistic research demonstrates that the distinction of 'body' from 'mind' stands as such a "presumptive principle": 'body' and 'mind' constitute essentially different-separate entities within a given Occidental philosophical-cultural context. From the linguistic standpoint, Occidental languages lack an overarching category that is "neither disembodied spirit, nor pure matter" (Leder, 1999, p. 206): adherence to orthodoxy in Occidental philosophy generates the paradox of an impossible "empirico-transcendental" entity (Foucault's *ad absurdum* portrayal; 1970, p. 335): since traditional philosophy fails to acknowledge the feasibility of a definitive empirical-transcendental or psyche-somatic heuristic – Eastern categorizations of such an "overarching" nature are often designated 'paradoxical'.

## Paradox in psychoanalysis

Paradoxical paradigms have, accordingly, arisen in psychoanalytic theorizing as a perceived resolution to the simultaneous existence of contradictory propositions, markedly inherent in Winnicottian conceptualization and clinical procedure. Eigen (1981) highlights the Winnicottian position pointing to "an inexhaustible paradox built into the very structure of self-feeling" (p. 426), while equating paradox with a "mystery or faith expressed through dialectical thinking" (p. 429). From within a philosophical appraisal of the psychoanalytic theory of intersubjectivity, Orange (2000) extrapolates on this, maintaining that, in confronting seemingly inherent chasms within psychoanalytic conceptualizations, "for many 'postmodern' critics of Descartes and his tradition, the answer is to accept paradox and dialectical oppositions" (p. 424).

In addressing Winnicottian paradox, Jones (1992) enriches these stipulations by adopting the notion of an 'embodied subjectivity'. This implies a merger of phenomenological and epistemological viewpoints, inasmuch as the subjective nature of experience reflects the way the world appears – differently – to the embodied-engaged subject. By adopting this standpoint, he suggests that a particular transitional mode of being allows for disengagement from "the usual distinctions of inner and outer, subjective and objective … promoting a 'deeper level of mentation'…" (ibid., p. 236). Adopting Winnicott's terminology, he maintains that "the transitional experience collapses the dichotomy of objectivity and subjectivity for it is 'an intermediate area of experiencing'" (Winnicott, quoted in Jones, ibid., p. 224).

Is paradox then a valid meta-theoretical unitary proposition for psychoanalysis? Moncayo (1998) reminds us that Jung already replied in the negative, "point[ing] out that all spiritual statements contain logical contradictions that are impossible in principle" (p. 403) since they are tautological: either the two are one (unison), or they are complementary; in both cases paradox is refuted. In Jones's argumentation, we encounter a similar philosophical slippage when the unitary nature of the paradoxical position is described as "characterized by the metaphorical nature of experience" (Jones, 1992, p. 236): since 'metaphor' implies conceptually juxtaposing entities from *two distinct* domains,[1] paradox arises only if and when oneness is denied a priori; Jones's argumentation is thus tautological.

In sync with this line of thought, Orange (2009) – a philosopher of psychoanalysis – points to the fact that what psychoanalysts often mean by paradox circumvents the inherent clash between two veridical ontological truths: rather than admitting true paradox or an inevitable tautology, psychoanalysts refer to the epistemology of "dialectics", "interdependence" or "ambiguity". Clinically-minded rather than philosophically-minded, they are concerned with transcending "Cartesian mind-body duality..." in order to explore "the paradoxes inherent in a mind–body continuum as transitional phenomena" (Wrye, 1996, p. 285). In this context, paradoxical thinking amounts to an expediency of furthering a wider sphere of tolerance; it describes an experiential reality under the guise of philosophical argumentation.

## *Complementarity*

In another attempt at avoiding intellectual entrapment in dualistic vocabulary, Orange presents Kohut's mode of intellectual investigation as circumventing paradox:

> [a] post-Cartesian aspect of Kohut's thinking is his resolute refusal of either-or choices...; for a Cartesian, everything is true or false, subject or object, mind or extended matter...; Kohut ... was always looking for a deeper layer of meaning, or a larger context of meaning, or the hidden assumptions giving rise to the dichotomy or bifurcation under discussion.
> 
> (2000, p. 424)

In accordance with Orange's contention, Kohutian and "post-Kohutian" self-psychology has engendered its own distinct resolutions to the issue of dualism, such as a dual-process complementarity of a conglomerated self, with the "body self" as one constituent thereof (see Krueger, 2002).

A more radical post-Kohutian exegesis is presented by psychoanalyst and Buddhist scholar, Raanan Kulka: rather than a dualistic transition between corporeity and mind, Kulka (2003) suggests that oscillations between "diffusive" and "emergent" states converge to form transitory yet complementary states of consciousness. Complementarity thus defined is "not a derivative of the conventional dualistic fissure between body and mind; rather, it is defined by states of existence of consciousness, comprising two facets of the absolute reality" (ibid.). The proposition here is of a new categorization and a 'new ordering structure' – which is complementary: both "diffusive" and "emergent" states of consciousness may include somatic and mental components; both are transient; both are features of selfhood and, what is even more striking: both are complementary features of the 'absolute'. Since 'body' and 'mind' do not stand as exclusive a priori categories, this configuration of complementarity defies paradox.

## Mysterious undercurrents

Patients tell us that they "know in their bodies", that they feel "harmony-with-life-itself", that they experience "spaciousness", that they feel "at one with all" (or "at odds with all", which implies that they have an intuition of an opposite sentiment). "Why?" We tend to ask. Or: "how do you know?" In a candid discussion of the challenge that unitive experience poses for psychoanalysis, Leavy (1995) demonstrates the superfluous nature of our queries, portraying unitive experience as a "connection with the world around ... through an *immediate feeling which is from the outset directed to that purpose...*" (p. 349, my italics); their very 'immediacy' nullifies unitive experiences' rational justifications. Leavy's depiction communicates the mystical underpinnings and the teleological yearning of immanent-transcendental, psyche-somatic unity. Couched within this portrayal is another popular attempt at resolution of unitary formulations: the ascription of foundational substantiality to unitive experiences.

Bollas (1989) portrays his non-dualistic vision of the 'psyche-soma' in its substantialist configuration as an inborn destiny made manifest through 'idioms', which are resident in the body, in its capacity of the 'true self'. True embodiment, he proposes "reflects ... a certain success in becoming a spirit..." which he defines as being "an expressive movement of an individual's idiom through the course of his ... life" (ibid., p. 151). To this, Lawner (2001) adds: "it is as though *immaterial, spiritual currents run beneath literal, sensory surfaces*" (p. 545, my italics). The teleological proposition of a composite genetic (i.e. biological) and environmental selfhood, striving to fulfil its completion is reiterated by Kohut whose postulation of a supra-ordinate self is "beyond the laws of psychic determinism and outside the limits of traditional psychoanalysis" (Chessick, 1980, pp. 471–472).

## Connectionism and systems models

In previous chapters I have already sketched out the dilemma involved in the inveterate breach between explanatory theory and meaning-seeking theory: the former tends to be cast in substantialist terminology and the latter in a process of hermeneutic reconstruction. One is biology, membranes, synapses, drives and instincts; the other is psyche, mental attributes, thoughts, a search for significance and the formulation of meaning. Acknowledging the need for a common ground between explanatory science and meaning-seeking disciplines, Scalzone provides an alternative vision in describing material structures as "the warp of our psychism" and psychic processes as the weft:

> *structures* are stable processes at a low speed of change, whereas *processes* are structures in rapid movement and consequently labile. In this way, ... [it is] ... demonstrated how they are in some way very similar things that belong to a *continuum*: two faces of the same coin. ... they belong 'contemporaneously' to the *res cogitans* and to the *res extensa* and ... they can be both symbolic and sub-symbolic.
> (2005, p. 1411, italics in the original)

How can this continuum be conceptualized? What are the categories that enable us to "reinscribe consciousness" (Wrye, 1996), and embrace a psyche-soma conglomerate that psychoanalyst Sommers Anderson terms an "unspoken dimension", the "cognitive, emotional, imagistic and visceral elements difficult to convey precisely in words" (2008, p. 7)? In my twenties, through repeated experiences during my first visit to Japan, I had begun to develop an intuition as to the feasibility of this endeavour. I attended Zen-Shiatsu classes in a temple which welcomed *gaijin*, i.e. non-Japanese students. The teacher demonstrated, we imitated. Using me as a "body" for a demonstration I could hear my teacher muttering something in his broken English.

I asked one of the older students to translate.

"Tense, very tense", he said. "The teacher says you are a very tense person," he offered.

I was at that time undergoing a period of intense emotional turmoil following a painful separation. I wondered what and how he knew.

"He said some heart trouble was affecting your shoulders", was the diagnosis.

"Heart?" I asked.

"Heart, kokoro, shin, spirit ... affecting your emotional energy, in your chest and shoulders" was the prompt reply.

Establishing new warps and wefts, neuro-psychological and relational perspectives create "connectionist" and "systems" meshes and webs in response to conventional bifurcative terminology. Within these formulations, no single component predominates and no existent is solipsistic, self-contained or exclusive. Rather, seemingly discrete components are intermeshed and connected in myriad ways, pro-creating organic units and producing emergent features, not inherent in any distinct part of the "system": this is true of and inclusive of the seemingly discrete categories of 'psyche' and 'soma'.

From a relational perspective embedded in psychoanalytic research, Bucci (1997) succinctly summarizes that, in order to transcend the conventional "paradigm of the mind, connectionism has developed a theoretical model ... in which the elements are not discrete, organization is not categorical, ... and explicit processing rules cannot be identified" (p. 13). Systems and connectionist networks address the challenge of definitive unitary formulation by suggesting that spontaneous emanation and emergence represent a continuum and a continuity: the dynamic continuity between structures and processes and between the psychic and the somatic domains presents as an alternative to accepted nomenclature and conservative conceptualizations.

Waiting for Cathy in my clinic often brought on a feeling of irritation. It was not the sort of tension that might accompany the arrival of a "difficult" patient. Cathy had been coming to therapy for a long time and was punctual, soft-spoken and eloquent. The only thing I could point to as the cause for irritation was that she never – ever – displayed emotion, and that there was always the slightest – slightest! – moment of hesitation before she would respond to questions or suggestions. A successful business woman in the making, her depiction of lovable and affectionate parents – a perfect and loving, academically-oriented family – was marred only by her brother's provocative life-style.

For me, every person has a specific "entry point" into therapy, an almost palpable moment in which one senses that it is not only a matter of two individuals communicating in the office, but, rather, there exists some ulterior connection, a benign, interactive symbiosis. With Cathy, it was her account of a dream: having achieved a breakthrough at work, her mother is on her doorstep waiting to congratulate her. She opens the door and – on seeing her unexpected visitor – vomits all over her mother, elegant dress and all.

I suggested Cathy's minute hesitations before commencing speech were not only an inevitable delay – as we had formerly imagined – in order to formulate a well-phrased reply. Rather – we now noticed – it was a moment in which she could sense a blend of bitter gall, irritation and ultimately, a gloating feeling. She could not confront her well-meaning, dominant and constrictive mother. Instead she – ever so slightly – hesitated before producing the expected reply; when accompanying her mother to her shopping sprees she would – almost imperceptibly and definitely unconsciously – slow down, inevitably getting – literally – entangled in her feet, making both of them stumble.

Cathy had found a fool-proof mode of communication, solely comprising misattuned tempos, unfitting rhythms, consistent contagious irritation resonance. It was a compilation of near-perfect strategies, allowing her irritated body-mind state to be known through unconscious body-mind interactions, without consciously acknowledging any bad will, anger or action taken.

In the clinic, the matrix of ongoing dialogues modelled on connectionist systems-oriented theorizing, preclude, precede or accompany discrete-linguistic parameters of dialogue. Consequently, new dialogical and communicative non-verbal components of interaction come to the fore. These are designated "affect contagion" (Stern, 1985), "resonance" (Demos, 1984), "attunement" or "mutual regulation of affect" (Beebe et al., 2003), and psyche-somatic modes of reciprocal "patterning" (Fast, 2006). None of these display specific-discrete bodily *or* psychic attributes. Rather, both the intra-personal and the inter-personal domains are regarded as composite, mutually and reciprocally affected-affecting systems, creating composite shared psyche-somatic patterns, connections and regulatory affective dialogues.

## *Aliveness: a "something more" nomenclature for unitive/unitary formulations*

In the leading archive inventory for psychoanalytic literature – P.E.P. – the most frequently cited article at the time of writing this book is entitled "Non-interpretive mechanisms in psychoanalytic therapy: *the 'something more'* than interpretation" (Stern et al., 1998, my italics). Strikingly, most articles in the site's current "most cited" list explicitly or implicitly refer to what I have termed 'unitive' experiences, reliant on 'unitary' formulations stemming from Independent School, Intersubjective, Relational or neuro-psychological conceptualizations. While differing in methodology and proposed clinical implementation, these diverse strands concur as to the inherent limitations of the exclusively symbolic sphere in encompassing the full scope of human psychology. Accordingly, all seek conceptualizations that encompass and include a rationale for the elusive "something more" that evades interpretation: terms that redefine psychoanalysis as involving and encouraging mutual co-determination of involvement, engagement and 'aliveness' – such as 'rhythm' (Tustin, 1978; Aisenstein, 2008), 'aliveness' (Biancoli, 1995), 'intensity' (Køppe, Harder & Væver, 2008)[2] and 'patterning' (Fast, 2006) – proliferate.

Their proliferation suggests that new classes and clustering orders are evolving in order to accommodate an internal world comprising global and coenesthetic dimensions of experience: these do not adhere to discretely divisible functions, amenable to verbal distinction such as thoughts, perceptions and actions. Rather – they are defined by new and compound categorizations of experience, such as "temporal patterns", "intensities" and "hedonic tones" (Stern, 1985. p. 67); they are tangential to 'a new ordering' as they comprise 'new kinds of facts'. Stern's (2010) *Forms of Vitality* provides the ground rules for a radical and innovative meta-theorization of human psychology based on the gestalt of vital manifestations as a succinct distillation of the wholeness of human ontology and phenomenal experience.

The word 'aliveness' makes a first hesitant appearance in P.E.P. cited literature in 1939 and is sparsely mentioned in the 1940s to the 1980s. This is followed by a surge: roughly 1,200 out of 1,500 articles of the inventory, in which the word 'aliveness' appears, were published in the last two decades. Similar results may be seen in regard to unitive and unitary terminology in general: as the focus of psychoanalytic endeavour veers towards 'psyche-somatic' unitive experiences, 'affect' and 'soma' – rather than mental contents per se – are depicted as inherently enmeshed with (and definitive of) 'consciousness'. 'Rhythm', 'intensity', 'aliveness' and 'patterning' define attributes of a psyche-somatic nature that hitherto were not formally formulated. None of these terms is appropriated by any particular school within psychoanalysis; all reflect an overarching new psychological landscape, encompassing physio-mental phenomenon.

In the clinic, relational psychoanalyst Lewis Aron embodies this transition, describing it in his evocative language:

> in the course of a psychoanalytic journey, patient and analyst come to share a psychoanalytic skin ego … mutually regulate each other's behaviors, enactments and states of consciousness … each gets under the other's skin … reaches into the other's guts … is breathed in and absorbed by the other.
>
> (1998, pp. 25–26)

Clearly, at a different time in the history of psychoanalysis, his words would have carried a metaphysical undercurrent. Currently they bear token to the fact that the science and art of psycho*analysis* have come to display and boast *a composite, unitary and synthetic world-view, alongside the traditional analytical outlook.*

## Traversing the "leaps": preliminary outlines for unitary formulations

Twice in my lifetime, I have been involved in setting up integrative mental health services. The first, a private one, was directed by myself and a colleague whose integrative training included Buddhist-oriented psychotherapy and Oriental medicine. The second was set up by an integrative team of mental health practitioners as part of a hospital psychiatric unit, headed by Dr Alon Reshef; it evolved to become *the* psychiatric service the hospital offered, integrating psychoanalytical psychotherapy, body-oriented psychotherapy, meditative practices and Oriental medicine. The unusual synergy created an exciting interdisciplinary clinical and theoretical arena, which we – initially hesitatingly and gradually more confidently – presented in a variety of professional settings. One recurrent issue has pervaded our endless case presentations, supervisions, discussions, symposiums and conferences: viewed through an integrative prism, the patient's unitive experience was at odds with medical protocol, psychological divisive terminology and clinical specialization. So much so, that it inspired a member of our team to embark on an anthropological research scheme related to the multi-level disciplinary fissures arising in the hospital in response to the implementation of the evolving, alternative unitary body-mind protocol.

First-time patients are the case in point since they have not had the socialization of hospital units and specialized medical care. Seeking the relief that accompanies a degree of certitude they would often ask: "Is this a mental disorder or a physical one?" In the meantime, we were facing the same dilemmas. Our staff meetings and consultations – in which *we* would seek certitude – reflected mirror images of the patients' predilections: is he/she displaying with psychosomatic symptoms? Somatoform ones? Factitious? Dissociative? "Straight" hysterical conversion? Any mental health professional of integrity will attest to the pervasiveness and inscrutable nature of these recurrent dilemmas. How many of these diagnoses vary or change as we change medical setting? As time passes? As "diagnostic norms" or typologies change? As new D.S.M manuals are written?

In a series of articles on the conceptual quest for unitary formulations within the neuro-psychoanalytic domain, Opatow (1993, 1999) questions the plausibility of transcending what he terms psychoanalysis's "recalcitrant dualism" (1999, p. 97). Opatow maintains "that our present methodology employs a provisional conceptual apparatus that ... [is] ... admittedly deficient (i.e., dualistic)..." (ibid., p. 97). In particular, he stresses the fact that, since experience cannot be transcended, "we are forced to create solutions that isomorphically preserve within the process-terms attributes of the experiences they were designed to explain..."

(Opatow, 1993, p. 438). In plain terms, Opatow is pointing to the fact that both the design of empirical research and the formulation of qualitative research cannot transcend the boundaries of dualism due to an inherent tautology: we define experience by a specific language; we construct a vocabulary to match our experience. This tautology implies that in order to generate "out of the box" conceptualizations, the "isomorphism" binding experience and its explanation must be transcended: since "no breakthrough in empirical findings alone will furnish the needed conceptual framework..." (ibid., p. 439), novel categories of experience and their corollary nomenclature are required. Pertinently, Opatow states that such a framework, assuming the inherent and "axiomatic ... unitary ontology of mind and matter..." (ibid.), has, recently "fallen from the precincts of philosophy and theology into the purview of ... science" (ibid.).

Opatow's propositions succinctly summarize some of the deficiencies of current unitary models, and some of the requirements for transcending or amending these deficiencies. Specifically, he determines that ontology and phenomenology, on the one hand, and methodology and epistemology, on the other, inevitably march hand in hand, each using aspects of the other as prerequisite to its own establishment. Consequently *"the [conceptual] framework itself"* (ibid., my italics) becomes the object of research, requiring a reappraisal of theoretical underpinnings and presuppositions, and the instantiation of a new language: in order to accommodate the conceptual modifications involved, a meta-theoretical shift, rather than a strictly theoretical one is implicated.

## *The framework itself*

It is my contention that the converging theoretical propositions outlined in Chapter 4 and earlier in the present chapter provide the preliminary building blocks that support such a non-dualistic theorem of psychoanalysis. Expounding 'a new ordering structure', they respond to the queries raised in the preceding chapters as to a mind to body "leap" and as to the mutuality of reciprocal mind-body "leaps". They acknowledge the accumulation of 'new facts' and their gradual conceptual integration; and, ultimately, they acknowledge their transmutation to the status of 'new sorts of facts', thereby annunciating a full-fledged paradigm shift. They also begin to address the quest for a corresponding vocabulary and nomenclature straddling the 'body-mind' and 'psyche-soma' divide. Brought together, they comprise a set of overarching configurations, conceptually redefining the framework itself.

In order to clarify these statements, I shall briefly redefine my main arguments pertaining to unitive experiences and unitary formulations:

- I use the concepts of 'paradox' and 'complementarity' to designate modes of conceptualizing – and accommodating – the tension of inevitable polar oppositions. I propose that terms such as 'dialectics', 'interdependence' and 'ambiguity' are conducive to a reshuffling of categories and to generating overarching categorizations that do not defer to the psyche-soma divide.
- I propose that the existence of 'idioms' and 'immediate feelings' – i.e. not exclusively determined by the dynamics of personal psycho-history – reflect *'spiritual undercurrents'* that define a *realm of primary, unified material-ideal, psychic-somatic existence*.
- I postulate that in 'systems' or 'connectionist' theorizing, the duality inherent in the 'psyche' to 'soma' ordering is loosened: emergent properties of 'psyche' and 'soma' form the warp and woof of a fabric, testifying to their inextricable, mutual and constant inter-constitution. The mechanisms and conceptual frameworks of these theorizations point to *a unified field* engendering a 'new ordering'.
- I suggest that 'rhythm', 'intensity', 'patterning' and sense of 'aliveness' straddle psyche and soma: within these categories intense mental effort shares a defining quality with intense physical exertion, for example; shared features of conventionally-held-as exclusive attributes of 'structure' or 'process', 'psyche' or 'soma' are implicated; an *interchangeability of substantial features of 'psyche' and 'soma'* is implicitly presupposed.
- In postulating a unified field of 'psyche-soma' experiencing *a linguistic re-formulation of conventional categories is implicated*, within which the "reification of metaphor" (to borrow Orange's (2000) term) is minimalized: rather, the new terminology reflects an alternative vocabulary which straddles two conceptual realms.

These innovations are concomitant with implications regarding clinical methodology and theory adumbrated in Chapter 4 and in the present chapter:

- In positing the therapist's mental disposition as promoting 'psyche-soma' formation and experience, a potentially unitive-evoking mentation is implicated – *the therapist's unitive predisposition aiding the formation of the patient's unitive experience.*
- Monitoring a shared psyche-somatic reality – via perpetual minute-by-minute 'affect contagion', 'affect regulation' and psyche-somatic 'attunement' – seemingly 'psychical' and 'somatic' categories become demonstrably non-isolatable.
- Both of the above – along with 'attunement', 'rhythm', 'intensity', 'patterning' and a sense of 'aliveness' – enhance the propositions of 'undifferentiating' and 'interpenetrating' qualities of 'psyche-soma'.

The accumulation of these observations – coming as they do from disparate theoretical strands – does not adhere to any distinct, conventional conceptual framework. From a bird's-eye perspective, however, they converge: together they represent a new, more unitary approach, to the age-old question of psyche-somatic relations, converging to indicate a paradigmatic shift.

## A motivated dialogue

The need for an alternative paradigm, accommodating and integrating the growing body of "new sorts of facts" but sidestepping the "mistaken cultural assumption that the only alternative to objectivism is radical subjectivity…" (Lakoff & Johnson, 1980, p. 185) is clear: thus, in order to substantiate the emerging paradigm, new ideational terrains are invariably explored. Conversation with the East has offered psychoanalysis the sought-after new terrain.

Initially drawn to a meticulous discipline of scientific research of consciousness, gradually fascinated and eventually acknowledging resemblances (see Molino, 1998), Buddhist and Zen-Buddhist conceptualizations have been introduced to psychoanalysis due to a dual, composite motivation. One is *comparative dialogue* – emerging mainly in the United States in recognition of an affinity between psychoanalysis and Eastern traditions as "ways of liberation" (see Watts, 1975). The other marks an acknowledgement of the distinct and exclusive contributions these disciplines may offer to psychoanalytic theorizing. This applies particularly in areas where dualism is perceived as a hindrance to incorporating and formulating the full scope of experience which, lacking a parsimonious overarching theoretical framework "become[s] highly problematic, [a] 'mysterious' notion, ... which set[s] aside the usual notions..." (Berger, 1996, p. 60): in these areas, theoreticians come to recognize the need to incorporate non-dualistic perceptions as definitive theoretical concepts in an explanatory grid that "includes the tension of ambivalence – polarity..." (Hutten, 1961, p. 277).

In what may be seen as a belated reply to Freud's pejorative views on unitive phenomenon, Barry Magid, a psychoanalyst and Zen instructor, seeks to delineate an alternative:

> To non-dualistically inhabit reality does not involve regression but constitutes true developmental maturity.... Dualism itself constitutes a developmental failure ... [In non-dualism] ... the self engages with any and all moment to moment experience ... *it is this functioning, not the lapse into some mystical oceanic state, that is the hallmark of a life of oneness.*
>
> (2002, pp. 45–46, my italics)

Part II of the book will be directed to clarifying, developing and elaborating this conceptual trajectory.

## Conclusion and dialogue

The present chapter has focused on two levels of organization – paradigmatic and conceptual – that address the issue of body-mind dualism in psychoanalysis:

- Initially I suggested that theories pertaining to unitive experience and unitary formulations came under the somewhat confusing headings of "paradox", "complementarity" "mysterious undercurrents", "connectionism, systems and chaos models".
- I then went on to suggest that psychoanalysis is acknowledging and incorporating an array of conceptualizations – such as 'aliveness', 'rhythm' and 'intensity' – that have arisen in disparate psychoanalytic schools. Not conforming to any of the above theorizations, they amount to a *"something more"*, describing phenomena that evade conservative dualistic divisions.

Following Opatow (1993, 1999), I showed that these two orderings represent a new framework, requiring a revision in theory and generating a methodology requiring *"something more* than interpretation" (Stern et al., 1998, my italics). Straddling the perceived 'psyche-soma' divide, this new framework is shared by the three major psychoanalytic strands delineated in Chapter 4: brought together, they coalesce in redefining a common field of shared theoretical and clinical nomenclature. They thus reform the conceptual mesh of psychoanalysis, implicitly addressing the key issues presented in the Introduction and in Chapter 1, yet – still – seek an explicit, salient terminological corpus on which meta-theoretical statements may be based.

The proposition of an alternative meta-theory – based on an alternative set of presuppositions – has haunted psychoanalytic inquiry since the advent of Jungian analysis. However, brought before the "psychoanalytic court", the line for the defence is clear: unitary propositions are self-defeating inasmuch as they are inevitably construed as resident within the metaphysical-spiritual pole, and are thus inevitably disparaged "as the spawn of conventional religious forms, fundamentalism, or 'New Age' fashions" (Lawner, 2001, p. 526). Consequently terms such as "mysterious" (Berger, 1996; Reis, 2006), or "idiom" and "destiny" (Bollas, 1989) that purportedly reflect the foundational and primary nature of a proposed ontology are difficult to integrate. Their self-evident idiosyncrasy suggests that their conceptual underpinnings are still regarded as "foreign bodies" within the psychoanalytic construal of unitary theorizations. On similar grounds systems and 'connectionist' formulations are often dismissed since they bear an affinity to chaos theory. The presupposition that apparent chaos "implicitly contains a profoundly spontaneous ordering process" (Eigen, 1983, p. 415) is reminiscent of metaphysical rather than scientific argumentation.

Thus, in order to fully investigate and gradually incorporate the findings described in this and in previous chapters, we must look beyond the precincts of psychoanalysis itself. However, in so doing, we may easily re-enter the now familiar vicious circle: within conservative paradigms one must adhere to the conservative 'psychical' or 'somatic' division; adopting novel nomenclature denoting new overarching categories – in the hope of addressing theoretical lacunae – lacks congruence and cohesion within the established theoretical context. As a consequence, the gap between what clinicians perceive and describe and the inherent inadequate conceptualization often ushers in straight metaphysics, philosophical deconstruction, or post-structuralist formulations.

Under the heading "What next?" in an article entitled "Science or hermeneutics? Psychoanalysis in search of self-definition", Irwin (1996) urges psychoanalysis to transcend the constraints of its major meta-theories. He thus concurs with Opatow's (1999) contention that "the conceptual framework itself ... [is] [the] ... ultimate goal of research..." (p. 97). Irwin makes it clear that

> For the field of psychoanalysis to move forward, beyond self-destructive fragmentation and useless bickering, it needs to come to a[n] ... understanding that the truths it seeks to discover ... about the human condition are of such a profound nature, and include so much that seems ... paradoxical and incompatible, that only a theoretical model capable of incorporating comfortably both Naturwissenschaft and Geistewissenschaft could possibly be adequate.
>
> (1996, p. 86)

Irwin's plea thus calls for a 'new ordering': it emphasizes psychoanalysis's need for a meta-theoretical stance that will non-dualistically and parsimoniously accommodate and incorporate objective inevitabilities and the subjective and inter-subjective viewpoints. In this enterprise a stepping outside cultural a prioris, stepping beyond conventional suppositions and challenging inveterate, apparently axiomatic presuppositions is required. This is a concern of all strands and theories within psychoanalysis which see the potential of psychoanalysis as an "art which concerns the life and the aliveness of a person" (Biancoli, 1995, p. 109), as well as achieving more conservative goals.

In the following chapters I shall describe the manner in which Zen-Buddhism and some of its Daoist underpinning provide such a non-dualistic framework. Alluding to – and providing the heuristics for accommodating – issues such as 'interdependence', 'non-duality', 'interpenetration', 'vitality' and 'body-mind', they offer sophisticated argumentation for the inextricable intertwining of body and mind. I shall therefore argue that they potentially provide the psychoanalytic quest for models of 'psyche-soma' unitive experiences and unitary formulations with satisfactory paradigmatic resolutions, with pragmatic intra- and inter-personal models and with adequate linguistic nomenclature.

## Notes

1 This does not imply that Winnicott's propositions are in themselves erroneous: I am suggesting that bringing them together as *explanatory resolutions* is antithetical to Winnicott's philosophy and terminology. This may well be one of the reasons that his contributions are not recognized as a "school" or "discipline" within psychoanalysis.
2 An editorial survey of relevant literature.

Part II

# 'Body-mind-one'

## The psychoanalytic riddle and the Zen response

### Introduction

In Part I of the book I delineated the shortcomings of 'psyche-soma' theories in psychoanalysis. In particular, I noted the contrast between the richness and complexity of clinical intuitions regarding a compound 'body-mind' and the ineptitude and paucity of their theoretical counterparts. I showed that this breach conforms with the long-standing cultural heritage of dualistic presuppositions, conceptualizations and nomenclature in Western philosophy. I argued that, owing to an inbuilt "recalcitrant dualism", their accumulation constitutes a substantial – but inevitable – failure at achieving a valid, parsimonious 'psyche-somatic' meta-theory, congruent with contemporary practice.

Consequently, the basic premises of the exposition in Chapters 1–5 was that a conceptual affinity and continuity exist between the age-old Western-philosophical 'body-mind question' and the psychoanalytical 'psyche-soma' question: both supposedly reflect an inveterate duality between two distinct entities. Since accruing evidence in the consulting room of contemporary psychoanalytic practice is proving incompatible with this axiomatic presupposition, it has inevitably led to an accumulation of aporias such as the fact that:

1  The non-verbal simultaneous presence of two subjects – therapist and patient – has a mutual emotional impact, without demonstrating a reliable mode for such an influence.
2  Unspoken *and* non-enacted contents are communicated and comprehended without postulating a consistent mechanism for such communication.

3   Body and mind of separate individuals prove to be mutually constitutive and interdependent without embracing subject–object non-duality.
4   The body bears aspects of consciousness – such as memory – without redefining consciousness so as to include the soma.
5   Verbal communication of cognitive content affects the soma – and its development and physiology – without embracing metaphysics.

All of the above underscore the fact that conventional theoretical formulations have failed to describe and elucidate the full scope of empirical occurrences in the clinic. Hand in hand with this goes the methodological implication: a consistent failure of verbal interpretations in representing the full scope of mental contents has led to an upsurge in the acknowledgement of, and concomitant research effort to assess, non-verbal components of communications. Symbolical representation has been joined – and to an extent usurped – by the semiotics of direct, concrete, actional and enacted presentation.

Consequently I further suggested that, as "new facts" accumulated, they provided the impetus for an ongoing paradigm shift. However, lacking a sound and parsimonious base in theory, this tacit paradigm shift is incommensurate in impacting meta-theory since it fails to recognize in these "new facts" "new *sorts* of fact", in Kuhn's (2012) terminology. Leaning on the long-standing psychoanalytic-Buddhist conceptual dialogue, I suggested that Zen-Buddhist conceptualizations and their formulations of the mind-body connection may be of assistance in addressing these perceived lacunae. This is my intention in Part II of the book.

## *Structure of Part II*

Chapter 1 surveyed the question of psychosomatic relations in psychoanalysis within the context of a pervasive body-mind dualism in the Occidental-philosophical foundations of psychoanalysis. Veering from 'psychosomatics' to 'psyche-somatics', Chapter 2 explored some proposed resolutions, culminating, however, in an "either/or" position of positivistic *or* hermeneutical meta-theorizing. Chapter 3 provided germinal unitary propositions involving the recognition of somatic aspects of subjectivity and inter-subjectivity and their phenomenological underpinnings. The wedding of a 'psyche-somatic' phenomenology with relational embodied intersubjectivity was shown to alter the perception of both "intra-" and "inter-" psychic leaps.

Finally, in Chapters 4 and 5, I surveyed common denominators of three major strands of contemporary psychoanalysis – intersubjectivity, neuropsychoanalysis and mystical-religious – that proclaim innovation. I suggested that these form the basic strata for disciplinary innovative configurations and propositions regarding unitary 'body-mind' relations and unitive experiences in psychoanalysis at large: taken together, they constitute a state-of-the-art collation of innovative conceptualizations regarding psyche-soma relations. These relate specifically to the subtending dilemmas regarding the three key controvertible positions outlined in Chapter 1:

1 *Categorical position*: the view of the body and mind as substantially different and/or belonging to mutually exclusive categories.
2 *Evaluative position*: the view of the body as inferior and the psyche as the superior counterpart within the 'psyche-soma'.
3 *Developmental position*: the view of the body as the early, primary-primitive aspect within an epigenetic model wherein the contents of the mind gradually supersede the body-based primary processes.

In opposition to these deeply embedded positions, the three aforementioned fields in contemporary psychoanalysis embrace unitive experience and implicitly assume a unitary psyche-somatic ontological predication in proposing:

1 Psyche-somatic cohesive unity as demonstrated in 'systems' and 'connectionist' theories and in overarching terminology – straddling body and mind – such as 'vitality'.
2 An overarching or a priori ordering under which body-mind is subsumed – i.e. a 'supra-ordinate' or 'post-representational' order, or a 'pre-reflective', 'proto' selfhood or predisposition.
3 An elision of traditional equations of "mind = conscious = subject" as opposed to "body = material = object", manifesting in novel unitary terminology such as 'the psyche-soma',[1] 'the skin ego', 'the body-self', etc.

Concurrently, formulations positing the body as an epistemological construct – one has a "conscious body", "body memory", etc. – gradually appear. In conjunction with the above ontological configurations they serve to eradicate the substantial 'body' *and* 'mind' division, illustrating the potential for 'unitive experiences'. Moreover, they reflect the proposition that these experiences are not solipsistic, pathological or mystical-transcendental phenomena: analysand and analyst experience unitive experiences, both separately and co-dependently, as these arise in interactive 'merger' and 'interpenetration' within the psychoanalytic matrix.

I consequently suggested that, once *non-duality* is recognized as an organizing principle, it is clearly apparent 'across theories', in key concepts and configurations pervading contemporary psychoanalytic clinical methodology, such as:

1  Injunctions of radical suspension of the – intellectually – knowing subject, as in Bion's technical dictum urging the analyst to retain no memory or knowledge[2] (Bion, 1970), or the concepts of the "unthought known" (Bollas, 1989) and "unformulated experience" (Stern, 1983), etc.
2  Acknowledgement of "embodied subjectivity" (see Muller & Tillman's 2007 compilation, *The Embodied Subject*).
3  A reformulation of counter-transference so as to include joint and shared therapist-patient contents of consciousness, with both somatic and psychic counterparts (see Schore, 2002; Ogden's 2008 elaborations on the concept of "reverie").

The above innovations thus involve a transition in psychoanalytic sign-signified matrices: this applies particularly to the elevation in the status of the sensible-sensual-perceptual attributes of the body, originally cast contingently, as "signs" of "signified" mental conflict. These innovations, in turn, require linguistic reformulations precluding 'body' 'mind' discreteness and divisive terminology: since the philosophical substrate of psychoanalysis is largely devoid of appropriate non-dual terminology, innovative nomenclature, particularly tailored to these new needs, is required. In implicit recognition of "new sorts of facts" and "a new ordering" – for which extant terminology was lacking – unitary innovations such as 'vitality', 'merger', 'interpenetration', 'aliveness' and 'proto-selves' have emerged, accompanied by putatively a-dualistic terminology such as "at one-ment" (Bion, 1970).

In confronting all of these issues, particular thinkers within psychoanalysis have borrowed, employed, adopted, adapted and frequently implemented aspects and particles of Eastern terminology, epistemological constructs and ontological claims. These, in turn, have influenced theoretical language. These contributions have not, however, been directed to elucidating the potential contributions of Zen-Buddhism's essential a-dualistic world-view to the field of mind-body relations. In acknowledgement of this, I propose to undertake – in Part II of the book – the clarification of extant and potential contributions of Zen-Buddhism (and, to a limited extent, underlying Daoist presuppositions), to the issue of psyche-soma non-dualism in psychoanalysis.

Part II will thus constitute a mirror-image of the picture presented in the preceding chapters: demonstrating the robustness of non-dualistic formulations in Zen-Buddhist philosophy, I shall show their potential theoretical validity in providing a substrate for novel psychoanalytic perspectives pertaining to 'body-mind' theory and meta-theory: Chapter 6 presents the immanence and substantiality of non-duality in Zen-Buddhism; Chapter 7 – the place of the body and 'vitality' within this non-dualistic scheme. Both will refer to 'potentiality' and 'change' as substantial, thus arguing against the substantiality of 'body' and 'mind' as apodictive and definitive predications. In Chapters 8 and 9, I review notions of 'paradox', 'complementarity', 'mystery' and the immanent entanglement of 'representational' language and 'presence'; in light of these notions I shall reconsider 'direct presentation' and 'embodied mindedness' as furthering both unitive experiences and unitary formulations. Brought together, I shall suggest in Chapter 10, this reappraisal of ontological, epistemological, phenomenological and linguistic perspectives constitutes a comprehensive meta-theoretical statement supporting an alternative, overarching framework for theories presented in Part I.

## Buddhism, Zen and psychoanalysis: an introduction

As opposed to the foundational texts of psychoanalytic-Buddhist dialogue (Fromm & Suzuki, 1974; Watts, 1975) and the romantic atmosphere of earlier 'dialogical' studies (Becker, 1961),[3] my emphasis is *not* a comparative one; neither do I seek to substantiate affinities. Rather, my point of departure is that "Western mentality is complementary to that of the East ... but profoundly different" (Humphreys, 1971, p. 15), owing to "*differences in the basic premises* of thought and in the very methods of thinking" (Watts, 1957, p. 24, my italics). Utilizing these differences I develop what Thomas Kasulis (1989; Kasulis et al. 1993) – Zen scholar and former chair of the Department of Comparative Studies at Ohio University – terms the "provocative" function of comparative research: rather than serving the prevalent heuristic the provocative function is used to highlight dissonance, thus "transforming the object of our concern so that we may see it in a new way" (ibid., p. xii). In the context of the present study this entails pondering "why our western tradition ... make[s] the distinction between the mind and the body so absolute" (ibid., p. xiii). In adopting this stance and relinquishing inveterate presuppositions I hope to introduce a conceptual trajectory "that emphasizes the ... continuities between mind and body instead of their ... separation" (ibid., p. xvii). Through highlighting Zen's distinct approach to body-mind' issues, I wish to address its potential contributions to psychoanalytic theory and meta-theory of psyche-soma relations.

Compared to earlier dialogical-interdisciplinary studies, my purpose is thus to attain focus – rather than accord – concentrating on body-mind relations as the specific field of study.

### *Cultural underpinnings*

In his *Sociology of Postmodernism*, Lash (1990) maintains that postmodern counter-culture has forked to form two discrete trajectories: along one route, conventional disciplines are challenged by employing hyper-symbolical postmodern argumentation, based on a reification of the verbal-referential domain: Lacanian and strictly hermeneutic reconstructive theories represent this trajectory in psychoanalysis. Along the other route the bodily-concrete, perceptual and sensual is paramount: in psychoanalysis, Bowlby's Attachment theory and Winnicott's contributions in the 1940s and 1950s precede this new and forceful 1960s counter-culture appearance of concrete, physical reality as constitutive of intra-psychic life (Sella, 2015).

Owing to the pervasive lacuna in psyche-soma meta-theory, the viability of this latter trajectory within psychoanalysis itself has, however, proved tenuous, necessitating the incorporation of supportive theoretical domains. As Sawyier (1973) – a psychoanalytic-philosopher engaged in meta-theory research – aptly puts it, "in the absence of external feedback, the ... language of a discipline grow[s] increasingly arcane...", in which case, a "serious attempt to come to terms with a major new theory ... is appropriate" (p. 216). One such theory – or theoretical domain – was indubitably post-war phenomenology, addressing "Being" (Heidegger, 1962) and proposing body-mind "interweaving" (Merleau-Ponty, 1945/1962), supplemented by existentialism's "existence precedes substance" credo. Both phenomenology and existentialism provided a substrate for reparatory efforts directed towards the integration of 'corporal-consciousness'. It is against this cultural-intellectual-historical backdrop that a reigning classic in comparative Buddhist-psychoanalytic research – Anthony Molino's (1998) *The Couch and the Tree*, an anthology of over 70 years of scholarly and psychoanalytic comparative research – was compiled. Along with phenomenology and existentialism, the "mystical-concrete" vocabulary of Buddhist philosophy and Buddhist-inspired therapeutic disciplines addresses orthodox Occidental philosophy's crises and assuages contemporary psychoanalysis's incompetence in embracing non-duality.

## Contours of the psychoanalytic-Buddhist discourse: a brief history

Carl Jung was the first major theorist within the analytical tradition to consider Eastern contributions to Western psychotherapeutic theorizing, noting that they "lay far beyond anything known to academic psychology ... [and] overstepped the borders of medical ... psychology" (Wilhelm & Jung, 1984, p. xiii). He also recognized that what he termed the conceptual underpinnings of the Orient's "findings" had to do "with an extensive phenomenology, to which hitherto known categories and methods could no longer be applied" (ibid.), and acknowledged his indebtedness to Daoist philosophy for affording the first external source of support for his own findings. Jung recognized that Daoist non-duality opposites "cancel out in non-discrimination" but are still potentially present (ibid., quoting Wilhelm).

In the first major work representing a favourable appraisal of Zen-Buddhism's contributions to psychoanalytic theorizing and technique – that of Fromm, Suzuki and De Martino (1974) – Erich Fromm considers the welling interest in Zen-Buddhism, from a vantage point strikingly similar to that of Jung: Western man's spiritual crisis following the Second World War. Inspired by Zen-Buddhist approaches, Fromm reconsiders man's relationship with nature and the 'natural': described as "instinctual" and "primary", they are not regarded as disruptive qualia to be sublimated, transcended or repressed, but as constructive of the fabric in which human life is embedded. The unconscious thus perceived, says Fromm (loosely quoting Suzuki), does not comprise ideas or mental contents alone. Rather, it "is something to feel. Not in the ordinary sense, but in what I would call the most primary and fundamental sense" (ibid., p. 131). This portrayal of the unconscious, says Fromm, enables us to perceive of "a deeper and not conventionalized area of experience" (ibid., p. 130) that is both basic and primary.

Elaborating on this theme and pursuing a similar theoretical thread, contemporary psychologist and inter-disciplinary scholar, John Suler (1993) proposes that a "close look at the psychoanalytic view of how the mind works, at its deepest level, can parallel the Oriental view" (p. 6). He then goes on to quote Loewald's definition of primary processes:

> insofar as they are unitary ... undifferentiating and non-differentiating, unhampered by laws of contradiction ... and by the differentiation of ... subject and object. ... they do not manifest or establish duality, no this and/or that ... no action as distinguished from its agent or its goal or its object ... the perceiver and the perceived.
>
> (Ibid.)

Leaning on "Eastern" conceptualizations – and in opposition to established psychoanalytic wisdom – *these primary processes are perceived and upheld not as precluding consciousness, but as a form of consciousness*, hitherto unrecognized as such in psychoanalysis.

In his retrospective study, Molino (1998) traces a historical progression to show how Buddhist contributions to psychoanalysis have shifted from supporting unorthodox psychotherapeutic endeavours and formulations, to posthumous dialogue with mainstream theory over the years. Contrasted with the marked scepticism encountered in their initial debut, Molino maintains that their current proliferation within contemporary psychoanalytic texts attests to radical changes in theory and practice. Rather than arousing suspicion and opposition, they currently assist the formulation and incorporation of robust (as opposed to unorthodox, subversive or anecdotal) theoretical innovations. In contemporary psychoanalysis, Buddhism enhances an understanding of a wide existential matrix (Safran, 2003). This serves as the basis for a historical compromise with religious sentiments (Simmonds, 2006) and the establishment of an incumbent ethical standpoint (Kulka, 2003). It also interlaces with the proclivity for embracing phenomenological paradigms of unitive experiences. Even more pertinent to the present discussion is the fact that Buddhist-psychoanalytic discourse furthers and promotes the substantiality of non-duality in general, and specifically as pertains to the question of body-mind relations. This serves to enhance methodology and technique: enriching concepts, such as 'presence' and 'embodiment', it lends weight to the embodied manner in which interpretations are delivered (see Cooper, 2010).

The 'embodied' rather than the intellectual level of discourse reflects a substantial shift pertaining to the methodology of investigation within the psychoanalytic-Buddhist interface: whereas the pioneering era was characterized by intellectual endeavour and fascination coupled with a reticence regarding embodied practice,[4] contemporary dialogue is nourished by psychoanalysts and researchers acquainted with meditative practice. Consequently, they recognize the 'body-mind' both as an object of study and as the actual vehicle of research: the embodied subjectivity inferred from this conceptual trajectory provides the initial inklings of a new mode of categorization, supporting a paradigm shift as regards mind-body relations; the generation of appropriate nomenclature and terminology required to meet the needs of emerging non-dual formulations in psychoanalysis is a direct outcome.

Consistent with this approach is the fact that therapeutic foundations derived from Zen-Buddhist conceptualizations provide the necessary perspective and support for psychoanalysis's hesitant attempts at non-dual *clinical* formulations. Within Eastern Daoist and Buddhist-informed systems of medicine a "*[specific] disease can manifest itself with [either] 'psychological' and 'physical' symptoms* according to western terminology..." (Ng, 1985, p. 450, my italics). Accordingly, Eastern terminology, incompliant with Western medicine's bifurcation "cannot see the necessity of classifying the symptoms into the two groups or saying which group of symptoms are primary or secondary" (ibid.). Rather, Buddhist world-views consider human beings' suffering in terms of "a constantly changing complex system ... for which no linear explanation is appropriate" (Magid, 2002, p. 135). In Part II, I show how this non-linear philosophy, of an embodied/spiritual selfhood and essential interconnectedness, provides a parsimonious scaffolding for a non-dualistic theoretical reformulation in psychoanalysis.

## Notes

1 On one occasion Winnicott (1956) goes as far as to refer to a composite "psychesoma" unit, followed by Marion Milner (1969).
2 Bion (1970) particularly stresses that this predisposition is crucial for structuring a non-dualistic experience of "at-one-ment".
3 For Becker (1961): "Zen ... fit[s] without embarrassment into the most strict definitions of psychotherapy, and even into a loose definition of psychoanalysis..." (p. 13).
4 Cooper (2010) makes note of Alan Watts's reservations and Fromm's compunctions concerning "sitting". Rubin (1996) makes a similar observation concerning Jung.

Chapter 6

# Non-duality in Zen-Buddhism
Implications for the mind-body question in contemporary psychoanalysis

The formative Buddhist text known as "The Awakening of Faith in the Mahāyāna" states that "all things from the beginning are neither matter nor mind, neither wisdom nor consciousness, neither being nor non-being..." (Hakeda, 2006, p. 78). What does this text literally mean, and what spirit does it convey? Is it a tale of genesis? A nihilistic philosophical statement? An inscrutable enunciation of Mystery? And where and what is this singular "beginning"? Does it convey historicity? Psycho-history? Most importantly: what relationship does "neither matter nor mind" bear to the psychoanalytic conundrum of body and mind as substantially distinct and inextricably interactive, as conceptually different and phenomenologically indivisible, as both 'represented' and 'presented' within the individual's psyche-soma compound and in the dyadic interaction?

The present chapter will focus on the above dilemmas from within a Zen-Buddhist outlook. Providing both a continuation and a mirror image of the first two chapters, I propose that Buddhism as a whole sketches a non-dualistic conceptual framework accommodating physical matter and metaphysical form. Zen-Buddhist notions of non-duality in particular provide a parsimonious non-dualistic alternative to seemingly inevitable and indispensable body-mind antinomy and bifurcation. I shall demarcate these notions within their theoretical framework, taking the following steps:

1 Delineate the basic tenets of Buddhist Mahāyāna[1] approaches to non-duality.
2 Chart out the conceptual basis of Zen-Buddhist approaches to non-duality.
3 Introduce the constructs of pre-ontology and potentiality.

4 Reflect upon the contribution of Zen-Buddhist non-duality and kindred conceptualizations to contemporary psychoanalysis.

## Non-duality: Mahāyāna roots

Buddhism as a whole views every feature of reality as totally, inevitably and inescapably dependent on all other features for its formation and existence. No existent and no concept evade this overriding edict: accordingly, both material objects and mental contents co-create each other, arise and subside incessantly (I expand on this theme in greater length in Chapter 7). However, drawing on the work of 2nd-century Indian Buddhist philosopher Nāgārjuna, Mahāyāna schools share a more particular credo of non-duality, based on a configuration of reality as predicated on 'emptiness'[2] (Skt.: *śūnyatā*) of intrinsic essentiality or substantiality (Skt.: *svabhāva*). From Nāgārjuna's radical perspective, even the sine qua non of Buddhist paradigm – the intrinsic all-pervasive interdependence – termed 'dependent co-arising' or 'dependent origination' (Skt.: *Pratītya samutpāda*) – is considered a tenuous proposition, since it implicitly postulates a substantiality of its interdependent causations and outcomes. How so?

For Nāgārjuna, the dependent aspect of 'dependent co-arising' presupposes that "the effect's essence is the conditions" that have given rise to it. However, Nāgārjuna argues, "the conditions [themselves] don't have their own essence. Therefore "How could an effect whose essence is the conditions come from something that is essenceless?" (MMK, 1.13, in Garfield, 1995, p. 5). Consider in this light, for instance, Freud's view of bodily symptoms as contingently dependent upon the psychical apparatus, which is itself dependent upon the body, since ego is "first and foremost a body ego". Can we still consistently claim that 'ego', 'body' or 'psyche' have a distinct essence that definitively and exclusively demarcates their existence? Psychoanalysis uses constructs such as "paradox" or "mystery" in an attempt to make sense of this tautological conundrum: 'emptiness' provides a more robust heuristic in this context. Viewed through it, reality is construed "as an endless web of events issuing forth ... with no duality, with no constancy of division and differentiation, valid relative to their time and place" (Raz, 2007, p. 22).

Let us now proceed a step further with Nāgārjuna. True to this line of reasoning, Nāgārjuna stipulates that even 'emptiness' itself does not constitute an ontological statement relating to "a" reality, since this would connote an ontological-essentialist conceptualization: it is not an ultimate truth-hood, but rather, a process of emptying oneself of one's views, a progression towards a state of empty-hood. He therefore proposes that "emptiness of emptiness" is the prerequisite for an understanding of the Buddhist teachings or overarching order (Skt.: *Dharma*) which is "a truth of worldly convention *and* an ultimate truth" (MMK[3] 24.8, in Garfield, 1995, p. 69, my italics): transposed onto the present work, we might call these – respectively – the 'concrete' as against the 'metaphysical' truth; the 'physical-bodily' as against the 'mental-spiritual'. In sync with this, he cautions against interpreting 'ultimate' as 'ideal' or 'superior', suggesting that the two truths – conventional and ultimate – maintain an equilibria-continuum of mutual subsistence (see ibid., 24.10). 'Emptiness' means an ultimate – rather than either 'particular-personal' or 'absolute-ideal' – understanding of the relationship between binaries.

I am reminded of an episode that may illustrate this point. Some 15 years ago I attended a conference on "The Psychology of Awakening", at which Mark Epstein – a psychiatrist-Buddhist practitioner and an author on the psychotherapy-Buddhist interface – was giving a lecture. Epstein shared his tribulations at the early stages of his own professional integration. He recalled how, during his internship, he attended Gestalt therapeutic sessions. In response to his therapist's exploratory remarks, Epstein (loosely quoted) would iterate:

"Yes, anger arises now."

"Do you mean to say that you are angry?" responded his therapist (Epstein used a somewhat gritty-creaky voice in this imitation, if I remember correctly.)

"I am sharing the experience of this moment" – or something to that effect – Epstein would reply.

"Whose experience is it?" the therapist would inquire – and so they went on and on, the therapist insisting – as we tend to do – that Epstein personally "own" his feeling; Epstein claiming an ulterior, absolute viewpoint, in which anger constitutes a dependent, impersonal entity: failing to reconcile absolute and conventional realities within an integrative, non-dualistic paradigm, both felt frustrated, both felt misunderstood.

One of the concomitant implications of this approach is the negation of a substantial differentiation between 'body' and 'psyche' as "independent, separate, as entities possessing [innate] qualities of their own" (Griffiths, 1986, p. 108): 'body' and 'mind' do not exist separately because they do not possess innateness. They are therefore not 'body' and 'mind' unless they have been defined by their context – such as 'body' contextualized by 'mind' – which is similarly and at one and the same time devoid of innate essentiality – and vice versa. *This argumentation turns the conventional body-mind question head over heels* since it stems from an *opposing set of presuppositions: rather than assuming essentially distinct 'body' and 'mind' – which inevitably remain discrete – Nāgārjuna presupposes contextuality, thus nullifying 'body' and 'mind's' primary essentiality.*

Ergo: no "leap", "paradox", "mystery", etc. are required to explain non-duality.

In a similar vein, the sūtras known as the *Prajñāpāramitā Sūtras* (attributed in Buddhist folklore to Nāgārjuna himself) are exemplary of non-dual conceptualizations. One of the most succinct depictions appears in the Heart Sūtra[4] in which the Bodhisattva[5] Avalokiteshvara instructs his disciple Śāriputra:

> emptiness is not other than form
> form is not other than emptiness...
> ... in that way, all phenomena are empty...
> ... in emptiness there is no ... discrimination.[6]
> 
> (In Lopez, 1988)

In the spirit of Nāgārjuna's philosophical project, the Heart Sūtra refutes the substantiality of each and every aspect of physical, emotional and mental aspect of being, nullifying the essentiality of the formative Buddhist models themselves: since they depict reality as "illusory", they posit it in a dualistic opposition to the "real". In contradistinction, the sūtra's allusion to the total absence of substantiality relates to non-duality in its most stringent sense: all *seeming opposites* are provisional constructs, construed as such in the thinking mind. It thus refutes essentialism in its accepted sense: the implications pertaining to the 'psyche-soma' question are rife.

## Conceptual versus participatory 'emptiness'

Nāgārjuna's radical ideational notion of 'emptiness' seeks to describe a quality of reality that is based on "relinquishing *all* views" (MMK 27.30, Garfield, 1995, p. 352, my italics). Zen rejects the puristic tinge of this argumentation, maintaining that – thus conceptualized – "the deconstructive function of emptiness as ultimate truth lacks a dynamic ... relationship with worldly truth" (Kim, 2007, p. 52): it consequently identifies 'emptiness' with an experiential – as opposed to the solely intellectual – mode of recognizing reality. As pertains to the present thesis: rather than postulating philosophical hypotheses as to the nature and relationship between 'body' and 'mind', Zen stresses the unified 'body-mind' consciousness's contribution to furthering both the unitive process – manifest in praxes – and its conceptualization.

## Non-duality in Zen-Buddhism

Embedded within Zen's critique is the fact that the *philosophical* undertaking of surmounting dualism borders in itself on tautology: Loy (1998) – a Zen teacher and professor of philosophy and religion – suggests that "the problem with philosophy is that its attempt to grasp non-duality conceptually is inherently dualistic and thus self-defeating" (p. 5). "The very impetus to philosophy", he maintains, "may be seen as a reaction to the split between subject and object: philosophy originated in the need of the alienated subject to understand itself *and its relation to the objective world...*" (ibid., my italics).

In the preceding chapters I stipulated that 'unitive' experience stands at odds with this proposition and requires a radical and comprehensive philosophy of 'existence' and 'Being' to counter it. Intuitively many therapists recognize this, but the conceptual underpinnings underlying this intuition are – for the most part – lacking in psychoanalytically oriented trainings. In my early days as a clinical psychologist, I was humbled in learning that – in order to circumvent dualism – an alternative set of assumptions to the one included in my clinical training was required.

I worked with children, some of whom were autistic, others post-psychiatric hospitalization. Noam, a six-year-old child, in particular, comes to mind. He had suffered from hypoxia – insufficient oxygen supply at birth – and, as often happens, his ensuing diagnosis was unclear. He had a sweet sing-song voice in which he would tell me things like "I have a yellow feeling in my lower belly." When I inquired how he thought it had got there, he nonchalantly responded: "Oh, it's always been there, but it comes when it's winter." I would then say something like "It sounds like you are quite familiar with it" and he would chuckle, thump his belly contentedly and roll about on the floor.

I'll never forget the session in which I'd entered the clinic deeply upset after receiving some very bad news.

"You have it yourself today", Noam told me.

"I have what today?" I responded, still somewhat absent-minded, though I already had an inkling of what was coming.

"That thing I told you about in your stomach."

"In my stomach?" I quizzed him.

"In my stomach", he said, pointing to his own belly and laughing, almost hysterically.

In these short interludes – and others during our sessions – Noam taught me much about the three distinct forms of non-duality charted out by Loy (ibid.) that counter the seemingly inveterate inevitability of dualism:

1   the negation of dualistic thinking
2   the non-plurality of the world
3   the non-difference of subject and object.

## *1 The negation of dualistic thinking*

Following Nāgārjuna. Loy (1998) proposes that the very ability to think is dependent upon binary relationships: thinking is by definition a dualistic mode of approaching reality since it inevitably contextualizes objects by consciously or unconsciously conjuring their opposites. From this perspective, conventional philosophy itself, as an intellectual abstraction aspiring to an analysis of an "either-or" nature – including an analysis of consciousness and the contents of consciousness or of object and subject as separate existents – becomes untenable from a non-dualistic perspective. Seeking an alternative, the Diamond Sūtra advises the Zen adept: "Keep your mind alive and free without abiding in anything or anywhere" (in Wu et al., 2003, p. 56).[7] Within this "alive" modus "to abstain from thinking in ... categories is called right thinking" (Hui Hai,[8] quoted in Bloefeld, 1962, pp. 49–50). Where Kantian subjectivity teaches the inevitability of applying categories to experience, the Diamond Sūtra encourages adepts to refrain from applying them, or, once applied, to refrain from considering their predicates as definite, cemented entities.

### 'Not thinking'? 'Without thinking'?

Imagine an artist, or artisan, a performer, a parent – perhaps even yourself – absorbed in some form of external task and in your own internal workings in a manner that is self-absorbed and externally oriented at one and the same time. The now popularized Zen postulates of 'no-mind' (Jap.: *mushin*) or 'freedom from thought' may be equated with such an immediacy of absolute absorption. Repudiating the conventional equation between subjectivity and thinking, Dōgen describes this form of awareness: "As it moves along with beyond [without] thinking, its appearing is immediate. As it is completed ... completeness itself is realization" (Tanahashi, 2010, Zazen Shin fascicle, p. 314).

In the 'Platform Sūtra', Hui Neng – 6th patriarch in the Zen lineage – explains these notions of "beyond" or "without" thinking as "freedom from thought". Within this mode, the mind is aware (conscious) of thought-formations in the same way as the senses are aware of their respective objects; it relates to thoughts in the same way as the eye relates to the objects of sight, the ear to sounds, etc. It is a sixth sense.

> What is freedom from thought? If you see all things without the mind being ... attached, this is freedom from thought ... having the six consciousnesses go out ... [and] the six senses [go] into the six fields of data ... coming and going freely...
> 
> (Cleary, 1998, p. 21)

Dōgen further distils the distinction between 'thinking', 'not thinking' and 'without-thinking' (the latter is roughly equivalent to Hui Neng's "freedom from thought"). For Dōgen, a 'without-thinking' modality (Jap.: *hishiryo*) is an experiential mode that denotes intimate attention, distinct from conceptual, intentional and objectifying thinking. In a key fascicle of the *Shōbōgenzō* – the Genjōkōan – Dōgen states: "To carry the self forward and experience ... things is delusion. That ... things come forward and experience themselves is awakening" (Tanahashi, 1985, p. 69). Within this mode, *hishiryo* connotes a distinct quality of attention that responds to the manner in which things are given to consciousness in "emptiness".[9] When consciousness is not "attached", it doesn't grasp, divide, analyse or pass judgement; things are given to it in an intimacy that neither negates nor affirms.

## 'Without-thinking' and the 'body-mind'

Kasulis (1989) stresses that both 'thinking' and 'not thinking' create distinct categories – the former distinguishes objects as differentiated, the latter distinguishes between states of consciousness. Conversely, 'without thinking' is an intuitive awareness, refuting the equation of 'thought' with consciousness. Kasulis sketches out the following definitions in order to highlight these differences from a phenomenological perspective:

1  'Thinking' denotes a positional (affirming or negating) attitude directed at 'contents' of thought.
2  'Not thinking' denotes a position of negation, in relation to 'thought' itself.
3  'Without thinking' denotes a non-positional attitude enabling an intuitive response to "pure presence of things as they are" (ibid., p. 73).

Kasulis summarizes this position thus: "My self does not *relate to* ... things, my self *is* these things ... directly experienced ... given in pre-reflective experience without the bifurcation between subject and object" (ibid., p. 90, my italics).

## 'Without thinking' and phenomenology

Kasulis uses Dōgen's formulation – repeated throughout his texts almost as a litany – of "body and mind dropped off"[10] (Jap.: *shinjin datsuraku*) to substantiate the position wherein "no separation between body and mind" exists (ibid., p. 91): the body is not an object of perception; one's body-mind does not exist as a represented image, differentiated from one's selfhood at a given moment in time. Drawing on these notions, Shaner (1985a, 1985b) proposes a non-dualistic embodied epistemology of the 'body-mind'. Shaner (1985a) suggests that an 'embodied' consciousness subsists foundationally as a compound in Zen canon. Based on the Heart Sūtra commentaries, he postulates that, since the implicit understanding is that "matter and mind in their essential nature ... [are] ... the same", it follows that "'bodymind' is experienced prior to body-mind distinctions..." (ibid., pp. 122, 120, respectively). Shaner's exegesis emphasizes a 'bodymind' field, within which he identifies five features that define the compound body-mind consciousness as primary:

1 "There is no reflection, analysis, abstraction, wish, hope, fear.... There is only the activity of presencing the horizon in toto as it is given to consciousness."
2 "This mode of experience (total body-mind experience) is ... immediate and spontaneous; there are no mediate intentions which attribute any meaning to the situation."
3 "Bodymind awareness ... serves as a backdrop against which ... changes ... may be understood."
4 This dynamism expresses itself in the awareness of the myriads of possible ways in which one may focus one's ... intentions. At such times one is aware of bodymind as the ever changing dynamic reservoir from which an infinite number of intentional vectors may be posited.

And, finally:

5 "Bodymind is the phenomenological ground for all experience, since all experience is both located and directed" (Shaner, 1985b, pp. 23–24).

## 2 The non-plurality of the world

In dualistic thinking, the world is seen as comprising a plurality of distinctly separate objects; reflecting on Buddhist body-mind paradigms from a psychotherapist's perspective, Watson (2008) maintains that, conversely, in a non-dualistic model "everything is interdependent and interconnected, nothing is absolute and independent ... mind and body, belief and action, object and environment are seen in reciprocal relationship, all constituent parts of a dynamic and mutually causative whole" (p. 71).

We intuitively recognize the non-plurality of the world as we are affected by it. We are affected by it since there are attributes which we share with *all*: we are affected by the seasons, by the moon, by odours, sounds and sights; we know unitive experiences although we cannot "explain them": in her (2014) book *Sensation*, Lobel – former head of the Department of Psychology in Tel-Aviv University – cites numerous articles showing specific interactions between seemingly discrete phenomena. She stresses the fact that seemingly neutral stimuli have the full scale of psychological-behavioural-actional counterparts. Her approach to 'embodied cognition' research teaches that attributes of temperature, texture, weight, light, colour and space – as they appear in our surroundings – deeply affect our body-minds. We share these attributes with the rest of the world. For instance: we have long known that propensity to violence is exacerbated by high temperatures (Anderson, 2001). Lobel shows us that warm room temperature, warm tea and warm surroundings breed good-will and love. In conventional psychology, we are talking about a set of contradictions – between body and mind, physiology and psychology, violence and good-will. In acknowledgement of non-plurality, we are talking about an interconnected mesh: within it, the common denominators of "temperature" and "expansion" – derivatives of the Buddhist "Great Elements" (Skt.: *Mahābhūta*) model – prevail. Within this model the expansive "heated argument", "warm heart", "hot-headedness" and "compassionate glow" share spatial and physical features which determine their non-specific affinity and interaction with the world.

The non-plurality of the world is closely tied to the question of ontological unity. In its seminal formulation this question is confronted through the major Buddhist tenet of 'dependent origination', stated thus: "When this exists that comes to be; with the arising of this, that arises. When this does not exist that does not come to be; on the cessation of this, that ceases" (Bodhi, 1995, p. 655). Refuting any substantiality – since all phenomena are conditioned – the principle of 'dependent origination' claims total non-plurality insofar as no phenomenon is independent of conditions, and all conditioned phenomena are interdependent.

A Mahayanic variation on the topic appears in the sūtra entitled "Indra's Net":

> Far away ... there is a ... net [of jewels] ... that ... stretches out infinitely in all directions.... If we now arbitrarily select one of these

jewels ... we will discover that in its polished surface there are reflected *all* the other jewels in the net.... Not only that, but each of the jewels reflected in this one jewel is also reflecting all the other jewels, so ... an infinite reflecting process occur[s].

(This version is in Cook, 1977, p. 2)

Germane to this point of view is the Mahāyāna doctrine of Hua-yen (Jap.: *Kegon*). Refining the idea of infinite reciprocal reflection of entities, Hua-yen maintains that "the myriad things in the universe freely *interrelate* with each other without losing their own identities. Each and every manifested object ... includes simultaneously all the qualities of the other objects within itself" (Oh, 2000, pp. 283–284). This is called 'mutual identification' and 'interpenetration'. Thus, body and mind both "interpenetrate" as specific entities and dissolve in endless reciprocal interfusion. Kim invokes Dōgen to represent a similar notion from a Zen perspective, suggesting that "in the Buddha-dharma, the teaching of the 'essence of mind' includes the whole reality and does not separate reality from appearance..." (2004, p. 117): For Zen, suggests Kim, there is no separation between the perceptual mechanism, subjectivity and reality; moreover, the overriding non-plurality does not rest apart from reality on a transcendental plane, but requires a perceptual and embodied participation for its instantiation. In Dōgen's words: "the zazen[11] of even one person ... imperceptibly accords with all things and fully resonates through all time..." (Tanahashi, 2010, p. 7): Dōgen's concept of 'oneness' (Jap.: *ichinyo*) or 'as one' (Jap.: *itto*) is predicated upon this line of thinking.

## 3 The non-difference of subject and object

Based on this line of reasoning, the third form of non-duality deduces the non-differentiation of subject and object from the first two forms of non-duality. It supports this deduction by propagating a perceptual form that establishes a substantial dependence – or a tenuous unity[12] – between perceiver and perceived. Rooted in the senses, the Zen-Buddhist claim is to a state of affairs in which apperception is located within the perceptual embodied sphere.[13] Concurrently, the material-world is not experienced as a whole if, in perceiving it, the subject-mind still perceives itself as separate from it. Thus Dōgen says: "What is inseparable from mind ... is not conceived by [discriminating] consciousness. It is walls, tiles, and pebbles. It is mountains, rivers, and the great earth. *Mind is skin, flesh, bones, and marrow*" (Tanahashi, 2010, Sangai Yuishin fascicle, p. 490, my italics).

Aware of the perils of dualistic thinking, Zen seeks to avoid conceptualization as such: after all, binary antimonies inevitably arise from making a direct claim to a concept of 'non-duality', which would imply *duality* as its complementary formulation. Instead, Zen advocates a continuous questioning position; it establishes a non-dualistic frame of reference by default, via didactic dialogue and parable. Examine the following:

> MONK: If self-nature ... belongs to no categories of duality, where does ... seeing take place? (*Is there a distinct subject?*)
> CHI OF YEN-CHU: There is seeing, but nothing seen. (*Alluding to the illusion of truly uncovering the nature of the object through perception.*)
> MONK: If there is nothing seen, how can we say there is any seeing at all?
> CHIH: In fact, there is no trace of seeing. (*If the subject is absolutely receptive, is there truly a subject?*)
> MONK: In such a seeing, whose seeing is it?
> CHIH: There is no seer either.
>
> (Suzuki, 1956, p. 207, my italics)

Suzuki's commentary is that "the seeing is not reflecting upon an object as if the seer had nothing to do with it. ... *seeing ... brings the seer and the object seen together...*" (ibid., p. 160, my italics). Dōgen suggests a similar inherent interpenetration or immersion. The world and the perceiver are experientially one: "A fish swims and no matter how far it swims, there is no end to the water. A bird flies ... [and] there is no end to air" (Tanahashi, 1985, pp. 71–72).

Non-differentiation of subject and object sets the ground for what, in Chapter 3, I termed 'a new ordering' structure, wherein subjectivity defined as constituted solely by the 'solipsistic' mind is a reductive viewpoint. Within this 'ordering', the body and mind are not fundamentally separable; material 'body' is not the object of the perceiving or cogitating subject. Dōgen's concept of the inseparability of the 'body-mind' (Jap.: *shinshin ichinyo*) connotes the interpenetration of body and mind; body and mind thus belong in the same order of being, and may not fully be accounted for separately, or independently of each other. In Dōgen's body-mind project, the seemingly definitively disparate categories, adhering to an "either-or" predication – be it monism, dualism or even pluralism – are recognized to be ultimately interdependent.

## Potentiality and the 'pre' of pre-ontology

In my own analysis I experienced prolonged periods in which I lay silent – thinking, daydreaming, picking my nose, sensing or hallucinating – on the couch. I found my verbal expression limited and limiting. Rather than strain to find words, I came to befriend those – sometimes prolonged – periods of silence. I didn't have a clue when and whence the next verbal utterance would emerge. My analyst – a long-time student of Buddhism – completely respected this. However, at some point during those stretches of reverie he would – for lack of a better word – pre-empt me, gently inquiring:

"What are you experiencing now?"

"Why now?" I would respond – or retaliate. "Why are you intervening at this moment? In what way is it different? How did you know?"

"I honestly don't know", he would candidly, contemplatively, reply.

In previous chapters I quoted psychoanalyst and Buddhist practitioner Wrye (1996) when she inquires: "In the inchoate, ... nonverbal sensorium of the body ... how does one find ... ways to reinscribe consciousness?" (p. 284). Irritated at times by my therapist's innocuous stance, or strangely comforted by his reply at others, I used his interventions as clues to this reinscription or reformulation. I learnt to consider his gesticulations as a cue to my own self-inquiry: did he notice a change in my breathing pattern? Or an impending change? Was there something brewing inside me to which he was responding? Did he sense a potential internal movement that – had he not intervened – would not have manifested?

In Chapter 5, I hinted that a clue to these queries may be found in Scalzone's (2005) puzzling resolution to the body-mind question. Scalzone suggests that the material and psychical planes are not as clearly demarcated as one tends to think, inasmuch as processes and structures are "in some way very similar things that belong to a continuum: two faces of the same coin" (ibid., p. 1411): body and mind differences are a matter of degree rather than a definitive qualitative categorization. Wrye's clinical query and Scalzone's conceptual formulation both approximate an inchoate entity, a primary consciousness that is neither – strictly – an amalgamation of body and mind nor a developmental progression from one to the other.

The philosophical counterpart of these suggestions is found in East–West conceptual dialogue. In a comprehensive text on comparative philosophy, Li (1999) suggests that "roughly speaking, the dominant view in the west has tended to see the world as constituted of basic elements or 'bricks' ... From this perspective ... the world is static at a fundamental level" (p. 12). It follows that, once transfigured, an entity loses its original, underlying characteristics in order to attain an essentially different one: the bricks cease to be bricks once they converge to form a house, for example. This is consistent with substantiality – an either/or status of 'body' and 'mind', of distinct 'somatic' or 'mental' attributes. In contradistinction, Li proposes that Eastern philosophical traditions maintain that *"the fundamental nature of the world is change"* (ibid., my italics): the proposition of *'immanent flux and change' as substantial* refutes western metaphysics of substances with stable and enduring attributes; it consequently challenges the dichotomy of either/or: if transformation is endemic to entities – say, 'body' or 'mind' – we cannot define them in terms of either/or: an underlying 'pre' or 'proto' state may potentially give rise to both.

Confronting similar issues from a Zen-Buddhist perspective, Kasulis (1989) succinctly advances the notion of an underlying and ongoing potential existence, from which differentiated existents emerge. Kasulis relates to the portrayals in Daoist philosophy of the Dao[14] – a radical, definitive influence on Zen – as an endless potentiality, giving rise to the myriad – or "ten thousand" – things:

> From the Tao,[15] one is created,
> From one, two,
> From two, three
> From three, ten thousand things.

And further:

> Ten thousand things ... are created from being.

"Being is created from non-being" (in Chapters 40 and 42 of the D.D.J.,[16] cited in Kasulis, 1989, p. 31).

In Kasulis's view, the Dao connotes a "pre-being" giving rise to "being", a potentiality giving rise to manifestation: yet "pre-being" and "being" do not present as distinct or exclusive categories. Moreover, in contradistinction to linear, developmental progressive models, *they are not temporally distinct.* As opposed to psychoanalytic common wisdom, potentiality is thus not superseded by manifestation. 'Pre' and manifest structures coexist in the same way that 'potentiality' and 'being' constitute two concomitant existents. Coming back to Wrye, my analyst and myself: in the same way 'pre-conceptual' or 'pre-reflective' may be thought of as independent ontological structures, rather than as modes that temporally precede conceptualization or reflection.

## Potentiality and the seeds of consciousness

Kindred argumentations as to the relations between potentiality, change and manifestation are found in key Mahāyāna texts. "The Awakening of Faith in the Mahāyāna" (Hakeda, 2006) argues that the 'totality of being' is designated by 'suchness' (Skt.: *tathatā*), denoting the all-inclusive nature of reality, reconciling potentiality and immanent flux and manifestation. The term '*tathāgata-garbha*' is employed to designate this reconciliation: *tathāgata-garbha* is variously translated as "a womb", bearing a passive, or static, quality or as "embryo," "germ", or "seed", which suggest a changeable, dynamic, active function.

A kindred concept relating to human consciousness – '*alaya-vijñāna*' – is found in the Mahāyāna Lankavatara sūtra. *Alaya-vijñāna* is often perceived as a 'store-consciousness': in this capacity it "contains the seeds of all possible forms ... preceding all discrimination, yet giving rise to all that is discerned ..." (Raz, 2007, p. 26). Pertinent to the present discussion is the fact that the *alaya-vijñāna*'s function is a psyche-somatic one, engendering a joint field that constitutes "a continuous and subtle type of mind that *carries the seeds of both body and mind together...*" (Waldron, 1994, p. 216, my italics). Both concepts thus accrue with the proposition of a 'pre' substrate, suggesting that "all things from the beginning are neither matter nor mind, neither wisdom nor consciousness, neither being nor non-being..." (Hakeda, 2006, p. 78).

## Conclusion and dialogue

In the early stages of the book I outlined a paradox: the persistence of psyche-somatic *dualistic theorizing* – in its intra and inter-personal dimensions – within strains of contemporary psychoanalysis which explicitly or implicitly embrace non-duality. I argued that, consequently, as new 'facts' pointing to non-dualistic aspects of psychoanalytic practice accumulate, they are not acknowledged as a 'new sort of fact', thus failing to contribute to meta-theoretical amendments.

I defined the strains explicitly or implicitly embracing non-dualistic configurations as:

1 The 'mystical-religious' strain that maintains that "we no longer speak of physical, psychical, and spiritual layers, because as long as we do so it appears that the layers could be separated from one another" (Pytell, 2006, p. 491).
2 The neuro-psychoanalytical perspective maintaining that "'awareness' is not ... an exclusive function of the highest level of central-nervous-system functioning, but involves the entire different levels of 'representational awareness'" (Greenspan, 1982, p. 666).
3 The intersubjective relational perspective maintaining that "we are dealing with a constantly changing complex systems (i.e. displaying dependent co-origination)..." (Magid, 2002, p. 135).

In the present chapter I approached this paradox from an external vantage point – that of Zen-Buddhism – presenting a foundationally non-dualistic perspective. I argued that within Zen-Buddhist formulations:

1 Non-duality presents overarching organizational principles embracing mental dispositions (non-dualistic thinking), singularity-inclusiveness (non-plurality of the world) and 'subject–object' relations perspectives.
2 Epistemological attempts at transcending intellectual and discriminatory objectivity via involved, actional, non-intellectual agency give rise to an integrated 'bodymind' compound cognizance.
3 Underlying structures constitute a dynamic potentiality which remains intact as these structures give rise to differentiated manifestations.

The vision of fundamental non-duality is a far-ranging and compelling one: in previous chapters I demonstrated that – in psychoanalytic theory – both biologistic and hermeneutic explanatory models deduce causation in terms of either contiguity or precedence: a linear developmental and evaluative progression leads from the 'somatic' to the 'mental', from manifest to ideational-symbolical. Conversely, configurations introduced in the present chapter repudiate the foundational presuppositions underlying these seemingly inevitable axioms: the notion of a unified, synchronous-simultaneous body-mind nullifies the presupposition of precedence; the concept of 'interpenetration' that of contiguity. More particularly: these notions are in line with complex 'connectionist' and 'systems' organizing principles in psychoanalysis, and readily accommodate the seeming 'paradox', 'complementarity' and 'mysterious undercurrents'. Consequently the inveterate substantial, hierarchical and developmental presuppositions – so characteristic of psychoanalytical formulations – are fundamentally rejected.

If Epstein had only known it during his early years' attempts to reconcile psychoanalysis and Buddhist teachings ... Nāgārjuna's notion of 'emptiness' circumvents the seemingly inevitable meta-theoretical divisions between polar oppositions and sets the foundation for a "two truths" paradigm. This is further developed in the 'Awakening of Faith' sūtra, annotated by Hakeda:

> The Mind is discussed from two view-points: ... one is the aspect of the Mind in terms of the Absolute ... and the other the aspect of the mind in terms of phenomena ... each of these two aspects embraces all states of existence. Why? Because these two aspects are mutually *inclusive*.
>
> (2006, pp. 36–38, my italics)

This proposition undercuts what seems to be an ineluctable axiom – that monism and dualism form a dichotomous, contradictory pairing (see Chapters 1 and 2).

In a similar vein, Li's portrayal of Daoist constant flux and Kasulis's exegesis of the Dao's role in the formulation of a 'pre-ontology' relates directly to the function of 'pre' and 'proto' prefixes discussed in Chapters 4 and 5. It repudiates the conventional notion of 'substantiality' and of inevitable temporal development-progression. As an example, we may review Freud's formulations suggesting that "where id *was* there ego *shall be*" (Freud, 1933a, my italics) and "the body is *first* and foremost a body ego" (Freud, 1923, my italics). Freud's position reflects positivistic conceptualizations – having foregone one status, an entity attains another: that which has developmentally and temporally gone forward and advanced is no longer that which it has supposedly superseded. From these perspectives, id is "egoed" and the body transforms to become "ego" in a temporal developmental progression (and its evaluative corollaries); in the same way the unconscious is revealed to consciousness – and ceases to be unconscious – and the bricks of which a house is built cease to be 'bricks' once they become a 'house': they represent two discrete entities that *appear to be substantial and maintain an either/or position*. But what of the indubitably veridical experience, the compound body-mind potential, the incessant flow of unformulated experience when lying on the couch? Can we dismiss the experiential fact that discrete 'body' and 'mind' are 'moulted' or 'dropped off' to conglomerate in a function of "body and mind cast off", as Dōgen suggests?

Noam, aged six, and suffering from who-knows-what following hypoxia at birth – with his notion of "a yellow feeling in the lower belly" – teaches us much regarding 'non-dualistic thinking', 'non-duality of subject and object' and the 'non-plurality' of the world. Lobel (2014) has shown how these manifest within 'embodied cognition'. Over the past decade attempts have been made at integrating these notions with psychoanalytic theorizing. Jeremy Safran (2006), relational psychoanalyst and Buddhist adept, succinctly notes:

> Nonduality is a mode of experiencing that breaks down the distinction between categories that are conventionally regarded as opposites.… The Buddhist perspective on non-duality is that the natural human tendency to think about things in dualistic terms is … the heart of the problem and that wisdom is the ability to experience things nondualistically.
>
> (Ibid., p. 197)

A conceptually ambitious attempt at integrating epistemological and ontological aspects of the notion of non-duality has been put forward by Kulka. Kulka (in Brodsky, 2007) proposes that "the idea of selfhood must contain the free movement between experience as a nonorganized essence and experience as a formed and structured organization" (p. 170). This formulation supports "the idea of quantum selfhood that moves freely within an interactive network from a state of infinite potential to a state of crystalized existence" (ibid.). Kulka (2003, p. 3) critiques the tendency to equate the finite with the 'somatic' and the infinite with 'mental' attributes. Rather, he proposes a conceptual foray *beyond* the "body-mind question as the derivative of the conventional duality between matter and spirit" (ibid.). Within his conceptualization both corporeal and mental realities manifest in the finite ("crystalized") and infinite domains alike.

Brodsky (2007) maintains that this formulation is shared by Matte Blanco, who, inspired by Bion's theorizing, proposes that selfhood is defined by the ability to oscillate between finite and infinite-potential modes of mentation, reflecting an underlying common denominator to all phenomena. Within the psychoanalytic-Buddhist dialogue this is congruent with Epstein's (2005) portrayal of the affinities between psychoanalytic pre-reflective psycho-mentation and Buddhism. Epstein (2005) refers to Winnicott's concept of 'unintegration' as reflecting this state of non-differentiated, pre-reflective mode of existence subtending 'being'.

Dōgen's contemporary, Mumon Ekai exhorts Zen adepts to "concentrate ... with ... 360 bones and 84,000 pores, making ... whole body into one great inquiry" (Shibayama, 2000, p. 24). Contemporary psychoanalysts have adopted this position: recognizing that non-dualistic awareness requires a distinct embodied enquiry, contemporary psychoanalytic writing encourages unmediated experience, heralding "the embodied subject" (Frie, 2007) as such. The novel perspective of embodied subjectivity prevails in recognizing a rich intra-psychic panoply of "forms of vitality" (Stern, 2010), that gives one "the feeling of what happens" (Damasio, 1999) leading to "understanding experience" (Frie, 2003).[17] The methodological inter-personal implications are presented by Alfano (2005), as she prescribes a potential technical derivative, delineating the form of attention – derived from Zen training – applied in contemporary psychoanalysis:

> I am, thus, proposing a particular method comprising reverie, ... *transcendent attunement* (a fluid state of being in which there occurs a transient suspension of duality between self and other), and a cluster of emergent capacities in both my analysand and myself.
> (Ibid., p. 225, italics in the original)

Alfano's perspective underscores the fact that subject–object–mind-body interactions cannot be thought about independently: they are mutually and continuously constitutive of each other, reflecting a model of reality in which the emphasis is shifted from individual existents to process and relationship. In this model, mind does not – only – perceive the objects of perception; rather mind is perception, and perception of contents of the mind and mind itself are indistinguishable: mind encompasses thought processes within a 'without-thinking' mode; it is not different from (though not synonymous with) tiles and pebbles; it is body, flesh, skin and marrow. Following these notions through in the following chapters, I delineate Zen-Buddhist notions of embodiment, the relationship between discursive-linguistic and embodied awareness, and derivative implications of both issues on the analyst's state of mind within psychotherapeutic interactions.

## Notes

1 Literally meaning 'great vessel' or 'vehicle' in Sanskrit as opposed to the "Hīnayāna" ('small vessel'), a term reserved – sometimes derogatively – for 'early' or 'Theravada' Buddhism. Zen-Buddhism is one of the Mahāyāna schools of thought.
2 The notion of 'emptiness' does not represent a nihilistic outlook, as Freud (1920) might have assumed when pejoratively depicting Nirvana as a mental state bordering on annihilation of response to internal and external stimuli.
3 An abbreviation of *Mūlamadhyamakakārikā*, Nāgārjuna's formative text.
4 The Heart Sūtra is considered to epitomize the Mahayanic perception of 'emptiness'.
5 In the Mahāyāna tradition, a 'bodhisattva' is someone who, having attained 'awakening' turns its fruit to compassionate action for the benefit of all "sentient beings".
6 Some renditions of this text equate "form" with "body" and the sūtra thus reads: "This Body is not other than Emptiness and Emptiness is not other than this Body" (Thich Nhat Hanh, 2009, p. 1).
7 The Diamond Sūtra is considered one of the Mahāyāna *Prajñāpāramitā* canonical texts. Translated as "beyond wisdom", these texts form the basis of the Zen credo of the inherent inseparability of 'practice' (Skt.: *samadhi*) and 'wisdom' (Skt.: *prajñā*) on the one hand, and wisdom and compassion (Skt.: *karuna*) on the other.
8 Hu Hai, an 8th-century Chinese Chan teacher is also known as Linji's (Jap. *Rinzai*) teacher in Zen genealogy.
9 In the ideograph of "without thinking" – *hishiryo* – he uses the ideogram 'ku' suggesting 'emptiness' or potentiality rather than negation.

10 Different commentaries translate this experience in a multitude of ways: Bielefeldt (1988) refers to a "sloughing", Shaner (1985a, 1985b) to "casting off", Kasulis (1989) and Yuasa (1987) term it "moulting" and Leighton and Okumura (2010) "shedding".
11 Zen meditation.
12 The argumentation as to Zen's objections to the outright declaration of 'unity' as a substantiality is beyond the scope of the present thesis.
13 In order to understand the implications of this claim to the psychoanalytic enquiry, we can go back to Winnicott's (1954) exploration of the localization of consciousness in the head, which he attributes to the sensual apparatus' location in the head area: The "head", through perceiving the body, experiences the body as an object observed by it.
14 'Dao', the ideographs of which denote 'The Way', is the basic tenet of Daoism, a philosophy which originated in 6th-century BC China. Daoist terminology is based on inherent change, enabling constant germination of life. Daoism intertwined with Buddhism in China and specific Daoist constructs – such as 'emptiness' – pre-dated and moulded Chan Buddhist paradigms, becoming a constitutive influence on Zen-Buddhism.
15 Wade-Giles transliteration of "Dao" (see "Preface").
16 *Dàodéjīng*, one of the two seminal Daoist texts.
17 All three are titles of books representing strands of non-dual formulations in contemporary psychoanalysis.

Chapter 7

# The body of the Buddhist 'body-mind'

Much water has flowed under the bridges of the Danube, the Thames, the Seine and the Hudson since Freud referred to the body – a constant reminder of pain and limitation, a cumbersome tag-along – by the nickname "Konrad", thus delineating the legacy of psychoanalytic orthodoxy regarding the body and the "bodily". Yet, even today within the evolutionary conceptualizations of corporality in psychoanalysis – the body's status within the 'body-mind' scheme retains an ambiguity. Moving on from the previous chapters' focus on an overarching non-duality, the present chapter utilizes Zen concepts to *focus specifically on the body's role within the co-joint 'body-mind'* accretion. Within the accumulating 'embodied mind' and 'mindful body' conceptualizations, the reciprocal give and take of 'body' and 'mind' make way for an underlying co-joint construct of *'a body-mind' entity* connected and related to the world.

Conceptually, the equal valence of 'mind' and 'body' that converge to form the 'body-mind' requires the "elevation" of the body to be on par with mental and psychical aspects of selfhood. As shown in Chapters 3 and 4 – and demonstrated via the metaphor of "Philosophy in the Flesh" – this "elevation" comprises a compound cultural, conceptual and linguistic philosophical project. With an eye to the ascension in the body's role, we can appreciate the poetic ambience of what Kuang-Ming (1997) – the contemporary philosopher and author of *Chinese Body Thinking* – describes as a "body flowing perceptually, personally, interpersonally, ... pervasively ... thinkingly" (p. 17). This is bodily selfhood of unthought knowledge, of conglomerated 'body-mindfulness', giving rise to intuitive intercorporeal relationality. It also entails neutralizing the seemingly inevitable unconscious coupling of 'bodily' with 'pain' and 'death': the disengagement of 'bodily' from the anxiety-provoking aspects of 'mortality' benefits from Buddhist formulations, up to and including the non-duality of life and death (Sella, 2009).

Complementing Johnson and Lakoff's linguistic project, I previously highlighted Merleau-Ponty's phenomenological one: Merleau-Ponty shows that in order to "walk the talk" – to create an embodied subjectivity – a congruent grasp of the performative-participatory aspect of a cohesive body-mind philosophy is prerequisite. Accordingly, the present chapter delineates a philosophical perspective that inherently includes corporeality in defining subjectivity. Beginning with models in early Buddhism which show body and mind to be inextricably intertwined, I move on to Zen approaches with their fundamentally non-dualistic outlooks. These give rise to the third theme of this chapter – the inveterate non-duality pervading the "Zen-clinic" in the theory of the "clinical body" and the clinical body-mind.

## Early Buddhist models of the 'body-mind'

The Buddhist conception of the 'body-mind' circumvents substantiality, and thus does not adhere to conventional Occidental categorization. Rather, the 'body-mind' as such is conceived of as a continual flux of interrelated occurrences: "It is the basic tenet of Buddhism that what we call an 'individual' ... or 'I' is only a combination of ever changing physical and mental forces or energies, which may be divided into five groups or aggregates" (Rahula, 1974, p. 20). Rahula goes on to say:

> [W]hat we call life ... is the combination of the[se] five aggregates, a combination of physical and mental energies. These are constantly changing; they do not remain the same for two consecutive moments. Every moment they are born and they die.
> 
> (Ibid., p. 39)

Within this configuration, at any given moment the perceived and experienced existence of an individual constitutes a unique psychophysical event. The singularity of the event is defined by the transient nature of its compound mental and physical components (or aggregates).

This is not dissimilar to the concept of compound 'self-states' or of 'multiple coding' (Bucci, 1997) in contemporary Self and Relational paradigms: their conceptualizations acknowledge the invaluable contribution of the body and of somatic-communications to the organization of

150   Body-mind-one

self-states and relational intersubjectivity. In them, however, the underlying psychoanalytic dualistic presupposition is retained: the conceptual infra-structure for deciphering the benign role of sensual-perceptual-somatic aspects of selfhood *as an integral part of self-states* remains obscure. Consequently they are often either pathologized or relegated to the realm of "regressed" or "primitive mental" states.

What are the five aggregates comprising the Buddhist 'body-mind'? The most basic division within this formulation is between the physical aggregate termed '*rūpa*' and four mental aggregates termed '*nāma*'.

The aggregates comprise:

- *Rūpa* (body/form): designates both the body proper and the sensory experience of material objects, inasmuch as they occupy space. Concurrently, it comprises four elements and thus shares the attributes of solidity, fluidity, temperature and motility with the physical world at large.
- *Vedanā* (sensation): based on bodily, sensual and ideational impressions, sensations are divided into three categories – pleasant, unpleasant and neutral.
- *Saṃjñā* (perception): denotes the distinct sensual or conceptual apprehension of an object. It is thus a prerequisite for the capacity to distinguish and allot name-signifiers to material and conceptual objects.
- *Samskara* (disposition): also termed 'will' or 'mental formations', the word designates mental structures and processes which are/have been "conditioned" or "compounded" – by *Vedanā* and *Saṃjñā*, among other things.
- *Vijñāna* (consciousness): this is the faculty that adds awareness to the other aggregates, thus binding together in a reflective mode the material body, sensations, modes of perceptual cognizance and the mental arising of volitions. It also denotes awareness of the arising of thoughts, ideas and emotions.

Since the aggregates do not adhere to conventional dichotomous oppositions, it is futile to attempt a finite distinction of their 'mental' and 'bodily' attributes: *Samskara* (disposition), for example, is seen to include "*bodily reflexes and ... dispositions* such as breathing and walking ... verbal reflexes and dispositions ... *ideational reflexes and dispositions*"

(De Silva, 1979, p. 19, my italics); *Vedanā* (sensation) is a sensational response comprising "five types of possible feelings: *bodily agreeable feelings, bodily painful feelings, mentally agreeable feelings, mentally painful feelings* and feelings of indifference" (ibid., p. 40, my italics).

In Chapter 6, I discussed the principle of interconnectedness or dependent origination as underlying the Buddhist notion of non-duality: When this exists, that comes to be; with the arising of this, that arises. When this does not exist, that does not come to be; on the cessation of this, that ceases. The incessant interplay between the aggregates is an exemplary demonstration of this principle: as conditions arise that bring the aggregates together, the functioning gestalt we call 'a person' appears; as they change, the gestalt changes; if they are removed, the gestalt transforms; their cessation denotes death. In and through their interdependent arising, the aggregates form a chain of continuous 'events', which, at that moment in time, appear to be an "Iness"; none of these, however, deserves the designation of a *definitive* 'I', or 'subject'.

The model of dependent co-arising also annuls any 'self-existence' or 'selfhood' – metaphysical or otherwise – superseding this flux of psychophysical events. The Buddha preaches: "Any kind of ... form whatever ... should be seen as it actually is ...: 'this is not mine, this I am not, this is not myself'" (Bodhi, 1995, p. 123). There is no separate, independent self, psyche or soul that would be left if one removed the constant interplay of bodily form, feelings, perceptions, impulses and consciousness. Rather, the experience of this interplay comprises selfhood. In an early seminal comparative thesis Stcherbatsky writes:

> The Buddhist term for an individual, a term which is intended to suggest the difference between the Buddhist view and other theories, is ... a "stream".... It includes the mental elements and the physical ones as well ... as far as they constitute the experience of a given personality.
>
> (1923, p. 26)

The implications of this approach for psychotherapy are far-reaching since the seeming annihilation of selfhood constitutes a major challenge to the conventional notions of subjectivity and selfhood (see Engler, 2003, for a more detailed exposition).

Nowhere is the perceived need to retain a sense of integration and continuity of our physio-mental experience of self greater than in the face of disintegration, trauma and loss. In 2009, I was asked by the organizing committee of the IARPP[1] annual conference to present my own view as to Buddhist contributions to therapy in areas of trauma and loss. For me, that invitation was a challenge at confronting my own devils, pervasively haunting every aspect of everyday life in my home country, Israel; it also urged me on in my own struggle to attain a personal conceptual consolidation of an ultimate continuity between life and death. This was especially true after having been struck by the stark finality of death of my brother and sister-in-law, both at the age of 23. What follows are two clinical extracts from my presentation:

Ziva is a religious settler living in the occupied territories, whose son was murdered by Palestinian terrorists. Throughout our meetings Ziva evokes her religious upbringing, that encourages an attitude of "it is all for the best", as offering her some condolence. On the other hand she comes to realize that it encourages her to deny and disguise her bitterness and rage and perpetuates frozen aspects of the self.

"I want to be here, alive, and take in his death", she insists.

Paradoxically I, her secular therapist, offer her what she perceives as transcendence, through joint moments of silence with a meditative quality, through contextualizing her grief within natural-seasonal cycles as they present in the therapy room through the Jewish Holiday cycle. I make use of my meditative training to focus on the sphere of sensation and a felt sense of emotional selfhood. Unexpectedly for both of us, very slowly and gradually, moments of unbearable pain and panic fall into patterns, the rhythms of laughter and weeping reframe as cycles; that which we share comes to the foreground and divisions subside.

Avram is a man suffering from numerous long-standing debilitating diseases. I have been seeing him for a number of years, throughout which his medical condition has gradually declined. Our interaction is open and warm, supported by Avram's cryptic sense of humour and his previous Buddhist training. But this time is different – Avram comes into the room obviously shaken and deeply perturbed. He has just received the results of a number of tests and it seems they might not bode well. Only half-jokingly, he looks up and says: "Please assure me that I will not die...."

I find myself letting his words sink with the in-breath and resonate within me as I breathe out. Without any conscious thought I respond: "I can assure you that you will die." I halt for a moment, holding my breath, to take in the shock – my own and his – then continue, almost listening to my own voice as I find myself following, rather than initiating, a litany: "and I will die ... and the doctor who gave you the tests will die ... and that tree" – I nod in the direction of the window – "will die...."

As if struck dumb, Avram looks at me for a few seconds with terror in his eyes – as I sit pinned down to my chair asking myself what a foolish thing I have done. Then he breaks up in laughter – and it is a laughter of sheer relief.

## Six "consciousnesses"

The continuity between supposedly distinct 'psyche-somatic' self-states – up to and including that of death – is complemented by an inclusive perceptual model. Buddhism maintains that the chain of incessant 'events' we term 'I' is concomitant with the world as experienced through the function of the six senses (Skt.: *saiāyatana*). Each of the six sense faculties – eye, ear, touch, taste, body (tactile sense) and mental faculty – has a 'consciousness' that arises at their interaction with the objects of their perception: The meeting of the eye with a 'visual object' confers 'visual consciousness', the ear with an 'auditory object' an 'auditory consciousness', and so forth, up to and including 'mental consciousness'. The Buddha portrays this position of 'bodym-ind' relating to the world as "the all": "the eye and visibles, ear and sound, nose and scent, tongue and savor, body and tangible things, mind and mental-states. That, brethren, is called 'the all'" (Woodward, 1993, p. 8). Implicit within this formulation is the radical claim that the mind faculty – perceiving mental states – does not have a privileged status and is equivalently posited on the same plane as the other sense faculties.

The Buddhist theorem of the relationship between consciousness-awareness and the body-mind thus turns the psychoanalytic model head over heels. The psychoanalytic model considers awareness an attribute of the senses and consciousness an attribute of the mind which is cognizant of awareness; Buddhism takes a strikingly different view: consciousness arises at the meeting of a particular faculty – whether perceptual or cognitive – with its appropriate object. The mental faculty may then add awareness to the consciousness that has arisen. The radical implication is that neither empirical objectivity nor intellectual subjectivity prevail. Since the mental and the physical are set on one plane "we ... have six categories of consciousness, ... beginning with visual sensation ... in connection with some colour ... and ending with [a mental] consciousness accompanying a non-sensuous object" (Stcherbatsky, 1923, p. 9).

## Zen body and non-duality in Dōgen's *Shōbōgenzō*

### The body-mind and the 'study of the way'

Dōgen teaches the body-mind's inseparability as a particular instance within the general principle of non-duality: "You should know that ... the whole reality ... includes the entire phenomenal world ... how can you differentiate this into body and mind?" (Tanahashi, 1985, p. 154). Thinking otherwise may lead to an erroneous privileging of one plane of existence over the other, as Dōgen points out in the same fascicle: "You should know that ... body and mind are non-separate, nature and characteristics are not two. ... you should know that ... body and mind are one..." (ibid.). Thus, although Dōgen's theme of the "Body and Mind Study of the Way" connotes distinguishing the two, it does so non-hierarchically, positing them as necessary conditions for the complementarity of "undivided activity" (Jap.: *Zenki*), of 'body-mind' coalescence and 'body-mind' to 'world' confluence. 'Body' and 'mind' interactions and 'bodymind' and 'reality' relations both adhere to the dictum: "although not one, not different, although not different, not the same, although not the same, not many" (Tanahashi, 1985, pp. 85–86).

A telling example is Dōgen's exegesis of a classical Zen-Buddhist story relating to Bodhidharma's[2] Zen students' initiation. In the original version, students' merits were acknowledged in conformity with a symbolical order: the depth of their understanding was metaphorically equated with the bodily membrane, leading from the exterior (skin) to the interior (marrow) of the teacher's (or ancestor's – Bodhidharma's) body. Dōgen waives this traditional imagery, of gradual penetration from skin, through flesh, to bone and marrow. In his portrayal, the dominant notion is that "the ancestor's body and mind is the ancestor – skin, flesh bones and marrow. It is not that the marrow is close and the skin is far" (Tanahashi, 1985, p. 171). Dōgen thus implies that if we speak of anything but the whole, or if we speak of the whole 'body-mind' as not being "completely penetrated", then that is not the full grasp of the ancestor/teacher's presence. His oft-repeated "the entire body is prajñā (wisdom)" (Tanahashi, 2010, p. 27), or, in Nagatomo's (1992) rendition "the total body is the total mind" (p. 168), captures this sentiment. The same radical trajectory of non-duality underlies and pervades Dōgen's reinterpretation of other early Buddhist texts, bearing far-reaching implications on his configuration of body-mind non-duality (Jap.: *shin-shin ichinyo*).

It is thus not surprising that contemporary psychoanalytic-Buddhist dialogue is replete with allusions to Dōgen's quintessential contributions to non-dual formulations (see Magid, 2002; Cooper, 2010; Kulka, 2012, for some examples). The scope and versatility of his writing lend themselves to psychoanalytic thought in areas as varied as the body's distinct epistemological role, body-mind theory, and the phenomenology of body-mind. His depiction of the interpenetration of phenomena is tangential to what Balint, Milner and Eigen have termed "a harmonious interpenetrating mix-up" (Eigen, 1983, p. 415) between the 'body-mind' of the analyst and that of the analysand. Acknowledging Dōgen's contributions to areas in which the 'body-mind' unit serves as a fulcrum of relational awareness, contemporary psychoanalyst and Zen-teacher Magid (2000) ponders how far this image of non-duality may be followed through: "'Body and mind dropping off,' in Dōgen's … phrase, denotes the dropping off of all separate experience of body and mind. How should we as psychoanalysts understand the 'self' that drops off?" (p. 523).

## Dōgen's actional body-mind: 'just sitting' (Jap.: shikan taza)?

In the Rohitassa Sūtra, the Buddha declares: "I declare that in this very fathom-long carcass [i.e. body – Y. S.], … lies the world, … the cause of the world, … the cessation of the world and course of action that leads to the cessation of the world" (Rhys, 1993, p. 86). Thus – despite the denigration of the body in early Buddhism as unclean and allied with the 'defilements' of 'attachment' and 'craving' – the philosophical underpinnings of

Buddhism's 'psyche-somatic' scheme pave the way for an alternative model of 'body-mind'. Antedating Western phenomenology, the 'body qua body' in this model is a 'conscious body', serving as a conduit of a sensible (dual meaning intended) apperception of the world; it is *the* major vehicle for attaining knowledge, a priori it is on a par with the mind.

Consistent with these earlier teachings, Zen scholar Dumoulin (1989) claims that Buddhism "admits of no meditation or state of higher spiritual consciousness apart from the cross-legged posture" (p. 16). In a similar vein Bielefeldt (1988) suggests that Dōgen's philosophical project is predicated on the meditative state through its embodied injunctions. Dōgen states: "If you let go the mind and cast aside knowledge and intellectual understanding, you will gain the way ... the attainment of the way is truly accomplished with the body" (Masunaga, 1971, p. 47). Bielefeldt (1988) consequently asserts that "in Dōgen's formulation ... [cultivation] ... seems to have to do with more the body than the mind....". He further suggests that in this respect *"The ancient 'mind seal' ... transmitted by the Buddhas ... [has] become a seal (mudra) of a distinctly corporeal sort"* (ibid., p. 170, my italics).

Shaner (1985a) suggests that Dōgen's instructions for seated mediation symbolically and concretely delineate the conditions conducive to an "internal dynamism ... [enabling the] ... experience of presencing things as they are ... [and] ... the infinitude of spiritual awareness..." (ibid., p. 224): focusing on the centre of the body, two and a half finger breadths below the navel, the actional intentionality of 'just sitting' enables a transposition of awareness from the perceptual ascension-aloofness of the head to the somatic core: in "reversing the intellectual practice of investigating words and chasing after talk..." (in Bielefeldt, 1988, p. 176), a welding of physical-emotional-cognitive being-presence occurs. Consequently, "somatic responses of ... (tension, shape, color, form) can be presenced as a reflection of mind-aspect intentions" (Shaner, 1985a, p. 181). In phenomenological terms the body thus portrayed constitutes an experiential-instrumental tool for a non-cognitive cognizing experience and a fulcrum of de-tensionalized intentionality.

## A 'body' study of the 'way'?

The seeming predominance of 'body qua body' in the 'body-mind' relationship and the paramount function of actional aspects of 'body-mind' give rise to a suspicion that Dōgen is proposing a reversal of hegemony, privileging the body over the mind: or is he, at least, charting the outlines of what I have termed – following the phenomenology of Heidegger – a "new ordering", the body on a par with the mind? What, ultimately, is the status of an actional-performative-somatic discipline within Dōgen's theorem of the equivalence of a "Body and Mind Study of the Way"? (Jap.: *Shinjin Gakudō*).

Two divergent interpretations arise, each supported by a distinct exegesis.

1   In the "Samādhi of Samādhis" (Jap.: *Zanmai o Zanmai*) fascicle, Dōgen preaches:

> It is easy to regulate the mind when the body is upright. If the body is straight, the mind is not dull. Instead, the mind is forthright ... and mindfulness is present. If the mind scatters ... gather together your body-mind and resume the upright posture ... gather together all distracted thought ... within this posture.
> (Tanahashi, 2010, p. 669)

In this respect, Dōgen's body-mind paradigm comprises a form of physical 'self-cultivation' (Jap.: *shugyō*) leading to its own superseding. In sync with this proposal, Nagatomo (1992) suggests that a reading of Dōgen that rests on "the physical" determines the state of mind via the corporeal modus. This rendering emphasizes the concrete and actional 'gate' as *the* royal road for the study of the other two 'gates' to Buddhist knowledge: the moral 'precepts' and the attainment of 'wisdom'.

2   While this rendition pays tribute to Dōgen's radical reverence of bodily and actional aspects of Buddhist practice, it is, in other respects, a reductive one. This relates to a subtle but significant difference between Dōgen's perspective and that presented in the early Buddhist sūtras: for Dōgen, the state of the *bodymind's engaged participation* is, in and of itself, an 'awakening', rather than a means of attaining 'awakening'. Rather than suggesting that Zen practice is a mode of 'self-cultivation' designed to attain an ulterior goal, Dōgen maintains the 'oneness of practice and awakening/realization' (Jap.: *Shushō ittō*); within it there is no temporal or conceptual breach

between the actional and material 'form' or 'practice', and the supposedly metaphysical attainment of 'awakening'.

In suggesting no inherent temporal breach between practice and realization, Dōgen very succinctly – and – poetically – preaches:

> You should not have ... expectation for realization outside of practice, since this is the immediate original realization. Because this is the realization of practice, there is no boundary to realization. Because this is the practice of realization, there is no beginning in practice.
>
> (Tanahashi, 1985, pp. 151–152)

In this respect the 'body-mind' for Dōgen *is one compound system of both conventional living and soteriological enquiry tantamount to awakening*: physical uprightness, attuned bodily acumen and wisdom-realization are all tantamount to '*shinshin-ichinyo*' – 'body-mind-as-one'. This, in turn, is tantamount to 'realization' and 'wisdom'.

## The clinical body

In Chapters 4 and 5, I described psychoanalysis's attempts to reconcile the seemingly incompatible categories of 'body' and 'mind' in terms of 'structural-material' and 'procedural-psychic' aspects of the self. At this stage of the manuscript I feel that the time is ripe for reiterating Scalzone's (2005) bold suggestion, already presented in Chapters 2 and 5: imagine for a moment that "they are in some way very similar things that belong to a continuum: two faces of the same coin ... belonging 'contemporaneously' to the res cogitans and to the res extensa ... both symbolic and sub-symbolic" (p. 1411). Imagine an agent exists which – rather than uniting two distinct entities – is the warp and weft of the 'body-mind' entity as such: in this model 'structures' and 'processes', 'organic' and 'functional' are not essentially different. Imagine this is not only a theory – as the psychiatrist I discussed in Chapter 1 magnanimously offered to accept – but a true-to-life depiction of reality, or, at least a comprehensive, parsimonious *Weltanschauung* – a world-view.

The unitary confluence between 'body' and 'mind' and between the 'mind-body' and world is closely allied with the theory underlying the medical viewpoint in Eastern medical practice. Diagnostics, therapy and outcome are all contextualized within, and determined by, a non-differentiated 'psyche-somatic' system: the ontology of health and disease is defined by a fundamentally 'psyche-somatic' indivisible categorization. Body-mind epistemology determines diagnosis: this means that the 'body-mind' of the patient is examined, diagnosed and attended to by a – by definition and vocation – "mindfully-embodied" therapist.

Historically, the medical models adopted in Zen-Buddhist communities largely reflected the Sinicization of Buddhism, manifesting medical paradigms that reflect a confluence of Daoist and Buddhist doctrines (Goble, 2011). Within these paradigms, clinical syndromes present as existential-phenomenological realities. Consequently, the aim of the practitioner is "to establish, maintain and promote integration of all the various aspects" of one's being and their integral connection to the "universal structure" (Sasaki, 1996, p. ix).

Sitting together on a hillock in Hampstead Heath Park in London, my Eastern Medicine teacher prompted me on in my first hesitant attempts at cultivating this perspective. He and I used our breaks from the clinic to snatch a quick bite, practise, meditate and observe passers-by. As one of them caught our eye, my teacher would ask: "What do you think is his diagnosis?" Or, sometimes he might propose his take and say, whimsically: "His liver looks tight", or "His kidneys seem empty." What he was actually conveying to me was not, of course, a medical diagnosis of organ membrane or functional pathology. Rather, he was training me to observe – through my 'six consciousnesses' – a sense of the psyche-somatic-mental-spiritual *functional* compound that relates to particular energetic conduits, named after bodily organs, in their relation to the world. This relationship is dependent on and represented by, the flow of 'qi'.

## *The concept of 'qi'*

Within its confluence of Buddhist and Daoist doctrines Buddhist-oriented medicine wholeheartedly embraced the major concept of Chinese medicine – the concept of 'qi' (Jap.: *ki*), variously translated as vitality, breath, movement or energy. The theory of 'qi' maintains that the major viscera of the body are functional systems rather than solely organic units. Each of these functional units provides (and requires) 'qi' for both mental and physical functions which are unique to a particular conduit or 'unit-organ' system. For example, the functions of the liver system include "storing blood", "governing the tendons" and "housing the ethereal soul" (Macioica, 1989, pp. 77–80); consequently, when my teacher pointed out a man with a "tight liver", he expected me to relate this observation to all these intertwined functions. In a similar vein, the heart "governs blood", "manifests in the complexion" and "houses the mind" (ibid., pp. 71–74). Within these composite physio-mental-spiritual conduits, an imbalance of 'qi' is the underlying cause of all dis-ease.

Various philosophical interpretations of the term 'qi' point to its conceptual richness since it denotes the 'material-mental', the 'concrete-process' function, the missing link sought after by Western philosophers and by psychoanalysts. From a comparative philosophy perspective, Leder (1999) translates 'qi' as "vital force" or "matter-energy", thus loosening the perceived allegiance to either a material or metaphysical definition. She further notes the affinity of the concept of 'qi' to Merleau-Ponty's concepts, stipulating that one might say of Ch'i,[3] as Merleau-Ponty does of flesh, that "there is no name in traditional philosophy to designate it..." (ibid., p. 208). Similarly, one of the main proponents of Zen-Buddhism in the West, D. T. Suzuki, has noted that the "impalpable" nature of 'qi' makes it compatible with the notion of "infinite potentiality", thus "transcend[ing] the centripetence of the ego-consciousness" (Suzuki 1970, p. 149). In this respect, 'qi' is tantamount to a multi-layered unobstructed flow, a physio-mental-spiritual experience on all levels.

We often meet patients who describe themselves as "stuck", who experience a lack of congruence between thought and action, who experience the flow of their life as "obstructed" and "disturbed". Somatic equivalents often appear to be a "tightness" in the belly, back, or back of the neck: this may be what my teacher encouraged me to intuit when he referred to "tightness" in one area, "emptiness" in another. I am particularly reminded of one patient – a psychology graduate – who discovered that his habitual physio-mental pattern of tightness in the belly and back of the neck was replaced by "a warm feeling which begins in my abdomen and extends to the extremities, my hands and feet", following an appropriate clinical intervention. At such times he would feel as if his typical verbal fluidity failed to describe the richness of this experience of "flow". Similarly, a 15-year-old teenager was relieved once he was able to reframe what appeared to be symptoms of anhedonia and mild OCD as – in his own words – "a lack of flow in everything".

Ziva – the bereaved woman patient whom I mentioned earlier on in this chapter – struggled to attain similar sensations. Highly dissociative, longing for her dead son, she would ruminate: "Where is he now?" immediately replying: "I think he has gone on a trip – a long trip, to Thailand. He'll be back," she would smile; "I know he'll be back," she would say, laughing.

As this was happening, I became aware of the fact that I was holding my own breath as she spoke, halting my own internal flow, experiencing a strange split within me. Struggling to keep in touch with the awareness of death, the attendant emotion of sorrow became unavailable to me. Almost concurrently I became aware of the fact that I, too, was, inadvertently, smiling, almost light-heartedly.

I glanced at her almost immobile chest. I imagined her heart, within, solid, unmoving, without a tremor.

"What is happening here?" I asked, pointing at both our chests.

"Here?" She returned my question, smiling. "Nothing", she responded, almost in reprimand.

I waited, still for a moment, searching within me for that which I could not find; that which may – and may not – come forth.

As I finally breathed out, I was aware of a release of control and the words trickled forth: "How does it feel – this nothing – for you?" I almost heaved now.

Gravity was now written on her face. "Nothing" – she repeated – "Nothing – it is like an iceberg that I feel nothing."

"An iceberg?" I enquired.

"An iceberg" – she smiled again. "It is frozen."

"What if there were to be some warmth?" I asked.

She shuddered. "Mummy", she uttered, like a little girl, frightened when hearing a scary tale.

We worked with the narrative. We discovered why she was smiling. We made up a new story that included warmth and fire in the hearth – a warmth that was lacking from her family home where she had learnt to use her smiles to disguise her anguish. We used the concepts of 'warmth', 'thawing', 'flow' and 'energy' to substantiate the newly-found 'psychesomatic' sense of non-obstruction and authenticity, aiding her in her first steps at working through the unutterable, inconceivable truth of finite loss.

Contemporary Japanese philosopher of the body-mind Nagatomo, with his colleague Leisman (1996) – reflecting on similar issues regarding an arrest in psyche-somatic flow – suggest that 'qi' provides the sought-after conceptual suture for the perceived body-mind fissure and experience of discontinuity: "When there is a gap between the movement of the mind and that of the body ... it creates an 'interval' in the otherwise smooth, continuous flow of action" (Nagatomo & Leisman, 1996, p. 444). Nagatomo and Leisman indicate that this "interval" is created because of discursive thinking. Accordingly, they indicate that a loosening of the hold of discriminatory thought leads to a 'psyche-soma' suffused with 'qi'-awareness:

> If you don't put your mind anywhere, it will permeate throughout your body, and in proportion to the degree to which it extends unobstructed to the entirety of your body, it fulfills the use of your hand, when the hand calls for it, it fulfills the use of foot when the foot calls for it, and it fulfills the use of the eye, when the eye calls for it.
> (Ibid., p. 447)

They consequently equate 'qi' with the psyche-somatic phenomenology of non-obstruction and with the internal action-movement described as a "permeation" of the body.

Keeping this conceptualization in mind has aided me substantially in my psychotherapeutic practice. In particular, the issue of patients presenting with obsessive-compulsive symptomatology comes to mind, as reflecting both mental and actional rigidity and "obstructions of flow". One such patient, Or, would vacillate in sessions between sharing sensations of hunger, stretching his calf muscles "so as not to waste time", gnawing-obsessive thinking and a wounding sense of loneliness. Within the purview of conventional psychoanalytic psychotherapy, it was not easy to distinguish a pattern, a personality trait or a dynamic theme underlying these diverse manifestations: I might easily have dismissed feelings of hunger as regressive or interpreted them as representing emotional hunger, his muscle stretches as compulsive gestures or as representing a need to sense his bodily boundaries, etc. Yet, while all of the above are relevant, it gradually struck me that the consistent feature was the intolerability of a sense of diffusion on all levels: counteracting it, a sense of sharp clasping-bounding 'qi' was the common attribute of supposedly divergent physiological, actional, conceptual and emotional manifestations. To use his own words, he could not "let go of the lifeline" and remain "clueless". Tellingly, as symptoms were gradually alleviated, a sense of "unintegration", "merging", "daydreaming" and "almost dissolving" became more familiar.

'Qi' thus provides an indispensable concept, bridging the seemingly insurmountable breach between body and mind. It unites categories that Occidental philosophy generally differentiates, or regards as mutually exclusive – such as psyche, soul, spirit and corporal vitality. Rebutting the notion of "a category mistake" in unitary body and mind categorizations, it provides a non-discriminatory conceptualization, reflecting subjectivity and intrinsic relationality to the "all" in its purest-experiential state. Espousing a bodily-bound hermeneutic outlook, Kuang-Ming (1997) terms this "body thinking", a "situational call to the bodily subject ... the spontaneous life response" (p. 174).

My patients, Avram, Ziva, Or and others, seem to have been responsive to this call.

## Conclusion and dialogue

Why has the ascendance of the body in contemporary psychoanalysis failed – to date – in providing an acceptable account of a non-differentiated unitive subjectivity? How – "dropping off of all separate experience of body and mind – ... should we as psychoanalysts understand the 'self' ...?" (Magid, 2000, p. 523). In this chapter, Zen conceptualizations resound with these psychoanalytic challenges, conceptually seeking "a satisfactory account of how entities of one kind can have ... to do with entities of another kind" (Irwin, 1996, p. 68). The response is: an overarching framework need be provided; within it, 'body' and 'mind' are not of "another kind"; positing them on the same plane does not constitute a "category mistake". Tracing a number of complementary perspectives I have shown how bodily postures and mental states interact, how the non-plurality of the world is grounded in the "six consciousnesses" and how the supposedly deconstructive challenge of "empirico-transcendental" selfhood (see Chapter 5) is met via the empirical-transcendental notion of 'qi'.

The view of the body within the body-mind scheme presented in the present chapter is that:

1 The body maintains incessant interaction with other facets of the self, and the emergent self-hood is perceived as a series of fluctuating interactive 'events' between bodily and mental attributes.
2 The body is inherently immersed in the reality of the world via the properties of the 'elements': 'solidity', fluidity', 'temperature' and 'motility'; the same holds for the 'body-mind'.
3 Consequently, the body does not determine mind, the mind does not determine body and body-mind self-states do not determine subjectivity. Rather, body-mind states are subjectivity.
4 Self, consciousness, pathology and psychopathology are defined by the non-divisible unitive experiences determined by 'qi': 'qi' provides a necessary "missing link", a conceptual configuration for concepts such as 'vitality', 'aliveness', 'intensity' and 'rhythm' of psyche-somatic life.

Independent School and self-psychology authors often conceptualize primitive object usage or self-object relationships in terms of the elements: Balint (1968/1979) writes: "Without water it is impossible to swim, without earth it is impossible to move" (p. 145); Kohut (1959) describes an empathic stance that is "closer to the movement of the water as it interacts with rocks and gravity". In the Buddhist scheme, this is not metaphor. Rather, it is a depiction of a particular type of object-relationship participation by the analyst in a shared "spiritus mundi": 'solidity' (earth), 'fludity' (water), 'temperature' (fire) and 'motility' (air-wind) reflect *qualities and tendencies*, typifying both human-hood and phenomena in general; thus, the body-mind is inextricably immersed and intermeshed with the world: mind, body and world interpenetrate each other profoundly, orchestrating an experience that is concurrently mental, sensual, emotional and perceptual. In this way, "the enclosed body, a concrete particular, expands thinkingly in to generality" (Kuang-Ming, 1997, p. 149); in this way supposedly discrete somatic resonance moulds inter-corporality, so that it manifests as a profound relational state, as a psyche-somatic position of mutuality.

Citing extensive developmental research, Daniel Stern (1985) introduced the concepts of 'core' and 'emergent' selves, postulating that, within them, action, emotion and cognition interweave, inter-modally presenting as "intensities" or "temporal patterns" (p. 73). The body-mind scheme emergent from Buddhist perspectives matches this notion, similarly deconstructing conventional 'body-mind' predication. In an inversion of the dualistic tradition Griffith (1986) writes that *if* 'psyche' and 'soma' were to denote individuated existents, it would violate the fundamental Buddhist principle of 'dependent origination'. Within this scheme, bodily and mental manifestations converge, both presenting under shared overarching categories.

The gist of these lines of thought is that the concept of an "objective" body and "subjective" mind is radically refuted: body and mind are mutually co-creative; they interpenetrate and – through their interpenetration – conduce non-dual subjectivity; in fact, in Dōgen's terms they *are* subjectivity. In 'Genjōkōan' – a key fascicle – Dōgen teaches: "to study the Buddha way is to study the self. To study the self is to forget the self ... your body-mind as well as the bodies and minds of others drop away" (Tanahashi, 1985, p. 70).[4] This is attained within the meditative practice performed in the physical-mental posture of 'just sitting', 'practice-realization'. In Dōgen's scheme, these designations of mindful awareness in order to "presence" the non-duality of self-hood epitomize *a new ordering*.

Major schools within psychoanalysis currently recognize the emergence of 'unthought' and 'unformulated' "knowns". Organizing principles that preclude the ordinary body vs. mind divide include "tactile, kinesthetic, and acoustic dimensions of experience..." while "*discrete state dimensions* ... [are seen to] ... stand opposed to continuous processes..." (Knoblauch, 1999, p. 43, my italics). As a consequence, conceptualizations pertaining to "non-discrete", non-dualistic formulations emerge: relational intersubjectivity embraces "self-states", comprising an agglomeration of sensual, emotional and cognitive attributes. Mystico-religious writers portray a unitive experience that connotes a measure of constant flux and "becoming", that disavows substantiality. Neuro-psychoanalysis demonstrates the manner in which consciousness is an emergent property of the complexity of inextricable body-mind systems.

This connectionist complexity is consonant with the "Zen clinical body" and its underlying concept of 'qi': an "empirico-transcendental" entity – to borrow Foucault's de-structurally provocative terminology. 'Qi' is structure and process, warp and weft, symbolical and pre-symbolical; it is a unique configuration of a *'psyche-somatic' agent*, and an *overarching theoretical concept straddling body, mind and spirit* at one and the same time. From this perspective, Eastern medical theory –

including symptomatology, diagnosis, therapy and prognosis based on these philosophical models – is distinctly and profoundly 'psyche-somatic'. Within it, health, including mental health, is tantamount to a particular body-mind state of "body-mind-as-one" which defines "unobstruction". As I demonstrated through Avram's, Or's and Ziva's histories, Zen's particular convergence of realization-practice is not considered to be simply conducive to health, it – in and of itself – defines health. Accordingly, Existential psychotherapist and Buddhist scholar, Engler (2003) equates this notion of unself-conscious non-obstruction with Kohut's formulation of the outcome of successful therapy.

In a similar vein, contemporary psychoanalysis is gradually rebutting hierarchical, developmental and categorical 'body' to 'mind' distinctions. Espousing 'unitive experiences' and 'unitary' formulations, it has much to gain by accommodating Zen's perception of the 'body-mind' within its integrative theoretical framework. As regards substantiality of body and mind – Dōgen consistently postulates a 'body-mind', or – as Shaner (1985a, 1985b) would have it – a 'bodymind'. The joint phrase denotes a joint entity – missing from psychoanalytic discourse – and a linguistic term which is congruent with unitive and unitary formulations. As regards the 'body' to 'mind' hierarchy, Dōgen tends to – provocatively – privilege the body over the mind, a manoeuvre seemingly designed to rattle the conventional "mind over body" Buddhist convention; in other instances he insists on the concept of 'body-mind(-as-)-one' (*shinshin ichinyo*). As for the developmental aspect, well, if one were to draw a developmental pathway, it would be a soteriological one, culminating in the development of an attuned body-mind's "*feeling* judgment, without forming an intellectual judgment" (Nagatomo, 1992, p. 256, my italics).

Last but not least: repudiating notions as to the mind's supremacy or immortality, Dōgen describes the body as both the intentional-epistemological vehicle for engaging with reality, and an embodiment of the mindfully-saturated reality it thus exposes. How so? Dōgen explains: "Actually ... you hear dharma with ... complete mind, complete body, and complete way ... You can hear dharma with body first and mind last" (Tanahashi, 2010, p. 553). In Nagatomo's (1992) rendition, the same passage is even more explicit: "Studying the way with the body.... The body comes from studying the way ... [and] becomes the true human body" (p. 166). In these propositions non-dual selfhood functions both as a vehicle for perceptually and sensually "knowing" the world and as a derivative of its own actional intentionality. Thus, Dōgen's unique contribution is in recognizing that the "intimacy" with the 'psyche-soma' – and of 'psyche-soma' with reality – is performed via an embodied contextual responsiveness and actional intentionality. Consequently, studied via the 'body-mind', one attains a realization of the unitary core-nature of reality – including the unitary 'body-mind' and the unitive experience of a 'body-mind'. Acknowledging this, Kim (2004) maintains that, for Dōgen, "the activity of the body-mind serves not only as the vehicle of understanding, but also as the embodiment of truth" (p. 100).

In the following chapters I shall trace these themes through, elucidating them within dyadic interactions in order to further establish their specific relevance to psychoanalytic practice.

## Notes

1 The International Association for Relational Psychoanalysis and Psychotherapy.
2 Founder of the Chan/Zen-Buddhist lineage of Dharma teachers or "patriarchs".
3 Leder (1999) uses the older transliteration based on the Wade-Giles system, as opposed to the now standard Pinyin transliteration.
4 This evocative and intellectually enigmatic passage is quoted in numerous psychoanalytic texts, in the context of non-duality.

# Chapter 8

# Embodiment and interpretation – not two

To begin this chapter at the beginning I shall reiterate one of the vantage points of this book: the presupposition that 'psyche' and 'soma' represent discrete phenomena configures verbal categories and terminologies. It thus appears axiomatic that "reality can be described in two languages, physical or mental" (Meissner, 2003a, p. 288): Since language both defines and delineates reality, the limits of psychoanalytic language construe the limits of perceived reality. Language thus replicates the dichotomy of substantialist or parallelistic paradigms since "interaction is ruled out because we have no language to express it – there is only a physical language on the one hand and a mental language on the other" (ibid., p. 288). This being the case, it is fitting for the analyst to strive beyond the dichotomy of habitual mindsets, dispositions and conventional metaphor in order to represent, affect and possibly implement a non-divisive psyche-somatic reality: an alternative scheme of unitive experience and unitary postulations requires an alternative terminological vocabulary. *This alternative will provide a linguistic sign to the 'psychesoma' signified as a co-joint entity in its own right.* Within this overarching signification "bones" and "scriptures" (sūtras) are not separate entities; they are – in Zen words – "not two".

Fifteen years ago I was engaged with two colleagues in the Tavistock Clinic in an intriguing quest. We all had had psychoanalytic psychotherapy training, had all been involved in some form of "body-work" and had all delved to some depth into meditative practices. Through case presentations and peer-supervision we sought to investigate the elements within those disciplines which – consciously or unconsciously – guided us in our current therapeutic interventions.

I started out by presenting a patient whose main complaints were of feeling "alone", "cut off", "behind a glass barrier", not heard and hardly seen. These manifested in everyday life in a lack of intimate relationships, in social anxiety and in a host of physical complaints.

Over time my patient began feeling – quite often – that she was "not feeling", by which she meant that physical pains, intense anxiety and suffering were often diminished. Gradually she began to recognize different gradients within this "not feeling" state: one was "relaxation"; another was "contact" or "connection"– initially to herself and, very gradually, to me.

Concomitantly I discovered that I too gradually allowed myself to relax. My own breathing pattern changed perceptibly, letting myself go into a more 'embodied' state, by which I mean that I could physically sense my own body at the same time as cognitively and feelingly weighing my patient's words. The newly acquired sense of aliveness and presence seemingly enabled us – conjointly – to be more alive and spontaneous in interaction. In response to a comment I made to that effect, she said: "Yes, now when this kind of work is done, it feels as if I suddenly am; I appear rather than disappear."

As I "presented" her to my colleagues, I explained that at that point in time I was often moved to literally touch this patient – pat her back, support her lower back as we were parting, hug her when it seemed as if she was vulnerably exposed. This raised a host of questions: "Why? Why then? What made you feel that? Would you actually touch her? Given your previous training – why not?" Although our joint project was launched in order to confront these very questions I felt very much at a loss for precise, theoretically coherent justifications for what seemed to be methodological breaches, or outright ethical misconduct.

Striving for a unified body-mind field – a 'unitary turn' – my colleagues and I confronted an inevitable breach with psychoanalytical orthodoxy; philosophy's 'linguistic turn' – in support of this orthodoxy – proposes a reality determined and communicated solely via verbal communication (see Rorty, 1967). When contemporary psychoanalysis suggests that "enactments" or "projective identification" are modes of communication, they challenge this proposition, adhering, instead to the bodily basis of communication, to a "philosophy in the flesh" (Lakoff & Johnson, 1999). In a similar vein, relational psychoanalyst Anderson (2008) refers to "bodies in treatment" as "the unspoken dimension". In fact, Anderson refers to a very particular state, an "open state" of "letting go" comprising "cognitive, emotional, imagistic and visceral elements difficult to convey precisely in words" (ibid., p. 7). Anderson follows this rich textural portrayal by presenting the reader with a challenge: "What do you feel in ... your body when you have let go? Can you express it in words?" (ibid.).

In previous chapters I introduced the concept of non-duality, proposing that it made possible the straddling of the 'mind-body' within a unified conceptual mode. The present chapter specifically examines the potential of non-duality to reconcile the polarities of "discursive" versus "embodied" subjectivity, establishing a common ground between presentation and representation, the bodily and the symbolical. Pointedly, this relates to an attempt at straddling the seemingly inevitable rift between the patient's experience and the analyst's explication, between the interpretation and phenomena lending itself to interpretation. This is an undertaking which contemporary psychoanalysis is continually contending with: Stern (1985) long lamented the loss of meaning inherent in the use of language; Lacan (1975/1988) designated the body "The Real" truly because it seemed to evade symbolical meaning-making.

Contemporary psychoanalysis – with its phenomenological emphasis – reminds us that experience is not easily divisible into bodily and mental components. Yet – where words fail – how can we psychotherapeutically understand and relate to non-verbal, pre-verbal or 'unitive' experiences? Does knowledge have a corporeal aspect, a welding of the literal and metaphorical meanings of 'conception', connoting both 'ideation' and 'life-potentiality'? Can we – metaphorically – attempt to go to a beginning before the discursive and the embodied were sundered and parted ways? And by conjecture: can we interpret and confer meaning using "silent interpretations" (Spotnitz, 1969), and derive meaning from "procedural interpretations" (Herzog, 2011), which may include concrete, physical actions and interventions?

In 1966, Winnicott wrote: "The word psycho-somatic is needed because no simple word exists which is appropriate in the description of certain clinical states", and goes on to say that "The hyphen both joins and separates the two aspects..." (p. 510). Winnicott thus describes an inevitable tension, akin to the one described by Kohut when he chose to obliterate the hyphenated 'self-object'. The new (non-hyphenated) term "is designed to denote a newly conceptualized view of the relationship ... where there is either a total or a partial lack of differentiation..." (Gerzi, 2005, p. 1035). Proposing non-differentiation was far from trivial for

Winnicott – having only once, in writing used a non-hyphenated "psychesoma" – nor was it a trivial thing for Kohut to forego his previous formulations and embrace one that included supra-ordinate structures.

Words create concepts, concepts generate the choice of words. "Our ordinary language ... which pervades all our life, holds our mind rigidly in one position" (Wittgenstein, quoted in Blomfield, 1982, p. 296). A unitary formulation of mind and body is – a priori – ruled out, since mind-body dualism is "deeply embedded in ... our shared conceptual systems and in our language" (Johnson, 1993, p. 2); consequently – as the "linguistic turn" rightly claims – we have no language to express unitary 'bodymind' formulations, thus no way of verbally affecting 'it': philosophically we stipulate that body and language belong to two distinctly different orders; linguistically, attributing common attributes to corporeity and psychical aspects of being has long been considered a "category mistake". Basch (1976) contends that, as a result, a semantic resolution to the mind-body fissure is untenable since "'mind' and 'body' are not comparable words, and meaningful conjunctive propositions cannot be established between them" (p. 398).

Accordingly, if we seek to employ concepts springing from unitive experiences and representing embodied subjectivity, it is incumbent upon us to draw upon external resources. Linguistically this requires an effort to "objectivize ... [our] own particular language ... in the light of another language..." (Voloshinov, 1986, p. 69). Within this "other language" a phenomenological 'psyche-soma' outlook may generate a nomenclature which allows the positing of body and mind on the same semantic and lexical plane.

In fact, psychoanalysis is called upon to produce *two* new languages: one is *a conceptual language* relating to psychical events and phenomena now acknowledged as inseparably intertwined with corporality: this engenders concepts such as "psychesoma" (Winnicott, 1956), "skin-ego" (Anzieu, 1989) and "somato-psychic" (Alfano, 2005). The second is *a therapeutic language* acknowledging the intertwining of psyche-somatic subjectivities of patient and analyst in which "patient and analyst come to share a psychoanalytic skin ego ... [as] ... each ... reaches into the other's guts ... is breathed in and absorbed by the other" (Aron, 1998, pp. 25–26). From these perspectives the present chapter re-examines and re-contextualizes the "talking cure" designed to address the "mysterious leap" from the mind to the body. Employing Zen-Buddhist conceptualizations as

Voloshinov's "other language", I examine the relationship between discursive thought and embodiment, and its methodological implications as regards "interpretation" in psychodynamic psychotherapy.

This is done taking the following steps:

1   Examining the *Zeitgeist* giving rise to prevalent configurations of the relations between language and body in psychoanalysis.
2   Presenting non-dualistic propositions in Zen-Buddhism's conceptualization of discursive and embodied knowledge.
3   Reflecting on "Zen language's" potential contributions to psychoanalytic theorizing, as regards the validity of a "fit" between psychic reality and verbal utterances.

## Discursive thinking, language and body in psychoanalysis

### Cultural underpinnings and Zeitgeist

The fissure between reality as perceived and reality as verbally represented played a prominent role within the cultural tradition whence psychoanalysis arose. In 19th-century Europe, it emerged as one of the points of contention between the Romantic ethos and the ethos of the Enlightenment. Representative of the Romantic spirit, Herder (2002) distinguishes between the human act of "naming" and a divine language – beyond the constraints of human verbalization – pertaining to an ineffable transcendental truth. Conversely, modern hermeneutics espoused a humanistic-language-bound view of the fit between consciousness and reality. Within this contending formulation, it is "the linguistic constitution of the world ... that creates the prototypical schemata for our conditions of recognition and knowledge" (Gadamer, 1976, p. 13). This articulation aspires to incorporate and subjugate the corporeal into the linguistic sphere: Only "when we have found the right expression (it need not always be one word) ... then it 'stands', then something has come to a 'stand'"[1] (ibid., p. 15).

Freud's world-view developed within this latter tradition, maintaining that bodily symptomatology constituted a failure in the capacity of verbal symbolization. However, following Freud's death, in post-war Europe, the dual opposition of 'language and body', and of 'thinking versus direct presentation' surfaced as a thematic focus of strife within cultural discourse. The 1960s counter-culture deepened the rift, weaving together disparate philosophical traditions that toppled conventions as to relations of language, body and mind. Innovations presented in incremental works such as *The Order of Things* (Foucault, 1970) (originally entitled *The Words and the Things*, in 1966), *Language and Mind* (Chomsky, 1968), and *Perception and Mind* (Merleau-Ponty, 1964), revolutionized body-mind-language relationships. In his book, *Sociology of Postmodernism*, Lash (1990) underscores this, suggesting that these trends signified "an end to the primacy of ... the text, the word, the signifier ... a bursting out of the 'prison-house of language' ..." (p. 81). From a psychoanalytic perspective, this shift enunciated theories of pre-verbal states, anticipating their counterparts in terms of silent, enacted and procedural interpretations.

Roszack (1969) points out that Zen-Buddhism was incorporated into the 1960s counter-culture as one of the "forces of the 'non-intellective deep' and 'antinomianism', alongside ... 'anarchism' and ... 'body mysticism'" (p. 64). However, "en route", essential aspects of Buddhist non-dualistic philosophy were distorted so as to serve counter-culture credos. Jeffrey Kripal (2007) – a contemporary philosopher of religious thought – writes: "Within this cultural milieu Nagarjuna's profound statement: 'There is not the slightest difference between the world and Nirvana', was paraphrased to appear as: 'there is not the slightest difference between the erotic and the mystical'" (p. 19). These non-dualistic, supposedly-Buddhist creeds, embellished and helped promote a cultural milieu supportive of "a gentle and gay rejection of the positivistic and the compulsively cerebral" (ibid.).

It was these cultural strains that engendered more profound psychoanalytic-Buddhist dialogue. The Jung–Hisamatsu and Fromm, De Martino and Suzuki encounters radically affected attitudes regarding the relationship between experience and verbal interpretations. They induced existential psychotherapists and thinkers – such as Ronald Laing – to stipulate that, divorced from corporal experience, verbalization creates a painful, malignant and pathogenic 'double-bind' communication. In contradistinction, Zen and Daoist-based practices have come to stand for an "Eastern mind ... [that] ... favours pre-verbal and non-verbal forms of being, thinking, and relating..." (Bollas, 2013, p. 3). Together these external contributions have conduced incorporating the 'bodily' into psychoanalytic theory and praxis, thus contributing to the demystification of unitive experiences.

How so?

## Language and body

Deferring to an ideal developmental progression – from body to cognitive mind-ego – psychoanalytic orthodoxy is defined by the body's susceptibility to verbal communication. The talking cure's inherent *raison d'être* is that an appropriate therapeutic 'analysis', verbally clarifying symbolical meaning, would resolve unconscious conflicts. With the underlying conflicts resolved, the body would relent and symptoms diminish.

In an issue of the journal, *Gender and Psychoanalysis*, dedicated to elucidating embodiment's contributions to psychoanalysis, Shapiro (1996) seeks to revise this position, suggesting that "multidimensional, multifaceted somatosensory experience is, by definition, difficult to define and speak about – it is nonverbal" (p. 300). In a post in a contemporary international IARPP internet colloquium (6–19 May 2013), Wachtel carries this notion forward. Wachtel headed his post "The Non-Talking Cure", contending that communication consistently comprises a "focal message" and a "metamessage". The former is the 'content' – what the analyst often thinks he or she is saying. The latter are the many emotional resonances and meanings conveyed in ways that fall under the umbrella category of "nonverbal": tone of voice, body posture, rhythm and timing, etc. *Much of the semantic pathway is thus designated 'embodied', in line with contemporary psychoanalytic unitary conceptualizations such as 'being' and 'presence'.* This is all the more pronounced as applies to distinctively non-dual formulations such as "at one-ment" (Bion, 1970) or "dissolving" (Kulka, 2012), which represent a conceptual foray leading beyond the conventional duality between matter and spirit. Within this matrix, body and mind constitute "existential modes of consciousness, *comprising two differentiated and equivalent facets ... of reality*" (Kulka, 2003, p. 4, my italics).

These sentiments are shared by:

1 Intersubjective thinkers, who recognize meaning to be both embodied and co-construed.

2  Developmental psychoanalysts, who maintain that embodied, orchestrated interactions create 'proto-conversations'.
3  Neuro-psychologists, extrapolating on communication non-verbally transmitted, received, encoded and decoded by specific neural pathways.
4  Mystical-religious thinkers, who propound a unitive experience, indivisible and – by definition – inexhaustible by verbal articulation.

Kulka (ibid.) demonstrates:

> A young woman whom I have been seeing for a few years ... one day ... gets off the chair and stands as if in military 'attention' looking out of the room window. She does not respond to my question, leaving her posture a standing riddle for me.... Every now and again she repeats the ceremony of standing by the window, until one day I feel that I have fathomed the meaning of this stance: Is it the ambulance? I ask, and she inclines her head, indicating that this is so. The parents of this woman were killed in a car accident.
> ...
> My words, oscillating between genetic and dynamic interpretations do not reveal anything of value to my patient about her life and the influence of her parents' death on them. And as I surrender to her ceremonial act ... we are silent together ...; she stands and I sit on my chair, eyes closed, entering into a few moments of meditation, until I hear her reclining in her seat again.
> One day, in the midst of contemplating the ambulance and its passengers I feel a great deepening of empathy and compassionate feelings and something in me is moved in an unfamiliar way. I rise and come to stand beside my patient in silence. [Some time later], ... as the sound that raises us to our feet is heard, she tells me, in a hushed voice, "I no longer need to get up and stand."
> It is verily in the physical act of standing up that – it would seem – we marked the annulment of the difference between ourselves and an-other person. Verily in the physical expression, ... in-corporality emerged in dissolution. In ... returning to our ordinary position of verbal communication ... return to the fissure occurred, return to the duality of individual, solipsistic corporality....

## Dialogical considerations

Part and parcel of the original fascination with 'Eastern' mysticism' in its early phases of the psychoanalytic-Buddhist interface was its 'embodiment'. For Durckheim (1962) – inspired by Jung – the lower abdomen (Jap.: *hara*) represented an alternative order of being: as a "root" of the body, it is portrayed as the physical equivalent and psyche-somatic substrate of un-differentiation and unity of the psyche-soma. In a similar vein, Fromm (2000) intuitively referred to the 'centre-belly' as a seat of consciousness and communion, representing "being", as a polar opposite of orthodox, cerebral, detached, peripheral interaction.

Recent psychological theorizations have followed these lines of reasoning through, affirming Buddhist contributions. In a volume called *Buddhist Thought and Applied Psychological Research*, Pickering (2006) demonstrates how – in the constant flux of feedback loops integrating and incorporating perceptual and conceptual inputs – *"Instead of a Cartesian substance, selfhood is seen as dynamic, interconnected ... and essentially without essence"* (p. 120, my italics). Strikingly, Pickering (ibid.) sees this as pertaining to both the "selfhood" observed and the observing, analytical self: the "experiencing" body-mind and the "inquiring" body-mind are inseparably co-dependent. Contemporary psychoanalyst and Zen practitioner, Alfano (2005) outlines the contributions of this 'co-dependence' to psychotherapeutic methodology and practice: a "somato-psychic" disposition leads to the suspension of duality between experience and analysis; the ensuing "somato-psychic" bidirectional relationship between the analyst and the analysand culminates in a "transcendent attunement".

## Zen non-duality and an embodied language

What particular conceptual strata does Zen provide for understanding and deciphering such "somato-psychic" self-states? According to Zen tradition, Zen itself rests on "a special transmission outside the scriptures", "not founded upon words and letters" yet pointing directly to one's mind. It connotes "reversing the intellectual practice of investigating words and chasing after talk..." (Bielefeldt, 1988, p. 176) embracing the notion of 'direct transmission' from one 'mind-consciousness' to another.

However, even this radical formulation is taken to task by Dōgen: Dōgen's Zen is revolutionary in that it seeks to create a suture, to bridge the gap between the concrete and the transcendental. His "mystical-realism" (a term coined by Kim, 2004) seeks to weld language and "direct" corporal-concrete reality, refuting the foundational distinction between presentation and representation, symbol and symbolized, language and body.

Dōgen's "Body and Mind Study of the Way",[2] comprises two intertwined facets of the relationship between body-mind experience and discursive thought:

1  The phenomenology of body-mind experience.
2  "Knowledge" stemming from a distinct body-mind scheme.

Their intertwining is invaluable in substantiating the contribution of "Zen language" to the constitution and expression of a non-dualistic 'body-mind-set'.

In what follows I shall expand on these themes.

## The phenomenology of a 'body-mind' consciousness

David Shaner is one of a handful of Buddhist-scholars specializing in a phenomenological account of Japanese Buddhism's body-mind scheme. In Shaner's phenomenological analysis, Dōgen's body-mind project engenders a *non-discriminative disposition* within which "a *non-privileged* horizon ... [is] ... an experiential verification of the notion of emptiness" (Shaner, 1985a, p. 134, my italics). Translated into psychotherapeutic terms, this points to the fact that an unfolding experience is a 'compound', not a discrete physical *or* mental phenomena. Empty of predetermined categories, how can we discern and define an experience as 'either/or', 'bodily' or 'mental'? A phenomenologically oriented psychotherapist might ask, for instance, if "lovingly receiving a caress" is a distinct 'bodily' or 'psychical' event. From this radical phenomenological perspective – using experience as our criterion for judgement – body and mind are not discretely experienced as object and subject, actional-performer and initiating agent. Instead Zen teacher and psychoanalyst Moncayo contends that non-dual – 'body-mind' – reality itself is "equivalent to a spiritual register of experience..." (1998, p. 355).

Shaner claims that meditative practice furthers this experiential mode, engendering a modus of consciousness – often termed "big mind" – that is immanently psyche-somatic, wherein "You hear dharma with complete power, complete mind, complete body, and complete way" (Tanahashi, 2010, p. 553). In this formulation the unitive practice of the psyche-soma constitutes both a facet of reality – meditative posture – and the mode in which reality is mentally investigated and exposed – a meditative mental mode: "just sitting" (Dōgen's *shikantaza*') thus describes and cements a holistic "somato-psychic" introspective-perceptual-anatomical position. This position, in turn, generates an unconventional, paralogical and paradoxical use of language.

Earlier in this chapter I mentioned relational psychoanalyst Sommers Anderson's – and my own – search for words within an embodied mode of "letting go". Zen's resolution is that, within this experiential position, verbal communication is part and parcel of an all-embracing reality, not a 'sign' referencing it: "Words are all-inclusive, mind is all-inclusive, things are all inclusive" (Tanahashi, 1985, p. 91). In contemporary psychoanalytical terms, Bollas (2013) depicts this as an articulation welding speech, sensation and image: "by avoiding discursive discourse speech becomes a thing, like the image ... as if both imaginary and symbolic orders have been subordinated to a different order of transmission" (pp. 78–79): things and words are not intrinsically different, he insinuates. For Bollas (ibid.), it behooves the therapist to cultivate a non-dualistic mode of discourse in order to retain and further this non-dual position. This is reminiscent of Dōgen's concept of presencing things *as they* are (Jap.: *Genjōkōan*): "When you see forms or hear sounds, fully engaging body-and-mind, you intuit dharma intimately" (Tanahashi, 2010, p. 30).

It is this form of epistemology – intuitive "knowledge" – which I shall now turn to.

## Body-mind knowledge: the intuitive epistemology of Zen

A few months into therapy, Offer, a top media worker, is recovering from a heart attack and surgical procedure, following his dismissal from a long-held position. His tension and his sadness are distinctly noticeable. However, as soon as I make reference to this, his gaze wanders off, avoiding my eyes.

"I wish I could go back to work" he muses. "I called the office yesterday and tried to urge S. to get Y. to contact me".

"How did that feel?" I ask.

"... I felt myself struggling", he responds, as if constricted.

As he motions across his chest I envisage his heart within. I am suddenly reminded of Antonio Damasio's theory of "background feelings". Different from full-fledged social emotions, these "background feelings" are partly generated and patterned by the "biochemical milieu" around the heart.

"Perhaps your heart was sensing that you would have liked to be approached, rather than feeling – as you now feel – that you are compelled to make the effort yourself."

He ponders over this for a moment and exclaims: "It feels as if I were conniving ... I would like to be able to talk to Y. directly."

As he pauses, his chest relaxes noticeably.

"With an open heart", he says.

We both sink into silence and, for the first time during the session, I notice the birds chirping outside.

"I wonder, what they are saying", he all but whispers, as if, by joint agreement we had both decided to listen to the birds.

What caught my attention was a little pause he made after the word "wonder". I exploratively suggest that perhaps his sense of 'wonder' has to do not with "what" the birds are saying but with "how" they are saying it.

"Perhaps you sense that it is with 'wonder', 'with heart open'". I propose.

He takes this in. We both resign to silence.

He then says, as if reciting:

> With open heart I listen to the birds
> chirping
> with open heart.

"You just wrote a haiku", I exclaim.

"*We* just wrote a haiku", he counters and I realize "we" may include both of us, and/or an 'analytic third'. And the birds outside.

Until recently, psychoanalytic literature identified acquisition of 'knowledge' with the 'mental-mind'. However, in the interface of psychoanalysis and philosophy, the corporal aspect of mind has re-emerged through the recognition of the subject's embodiment, substantiated by phenomenological contributions. This strain of thought has been supported by Lakoff and Johnson's (1999) major project of "Philosophy in the Flesh", and the psychoanalytic-Buddhist interface introducing "The Embodied Mind" (Varela et al., 1993). Within this understanding of epistemology – termed "embodied realism" – knowledge is acquired directly, born of experiential involvement, dependent on "the nature of our bodies, brains, and interactions with our environment" (Lakoff & Johnson, 1999, p. 96). This form of knowledge welds the concrete and the metaphysical, intuitively weaving a cohesive mesh, as Offer and I – unwittingly – did in welding physical movement, posture and emotion with a verbal narrative, unconsciously orchestrating a haiku Zen poem.

Long antedating western "embodied realism", direct acquisition of knowledge via somatic faculties has always been a hallmark of Buddhism's interdependent body-mind formulations. In Chapter 7, I stressed Buddhist body-minded epistemology. Zen, with its emphasis on actional and performative involvement underscores it; Dōgen validates the Buddha's embodied epistemological claim ("in this very body … are the world, its cessation and the path that leads to cessation of the world") with a blunt Zen counterpart: "To study the way … means to study the way with your own body. It is the study of the way using this lump of red flesh" (Tanahashi, 1985, p. 91). From this epistemological standpoint, physical reality and its verbal extrapolation are one and the same thing. Thus, Dōgen proclaims, "If you know the sūtras are bones but do not understand the bones are sūtras, it is not yet the Way" (in Kim, 2004, p. 78).

Adding another dimension to this conceptual trajectory, Nagatomo (1992) attributes the uniqueness of Dōgen's epistemological claims – as regards the body-mind – to his spiritual quest. Stemming from the transition from a mundane orientation to an 'awakened' (or 'enlightened') one, the body-mind, he argues, assumes a transformative potential. By 'just sitting' and following the breath so "that the circulation of energy activated by the bellows of breathing takes over from discursive consciousness" (Seo & Addiss, 2010, p. 9), a reciprocal co-origination ensues: 'just sitting' culminates in a state of 'being' termed "body and mind having been shed off". "Shedding off" engenders the 'oneness' of 'awakening' and 'practice', of 'enlightenment' and mundane reality, of mystical spirituality inseparable from a physical-sensational 'total exertion' (Jap.: *zenki*) in each and every aspect of involved action and interaction.

In psychoanalytic practice, the same "empirical-spiritual" common ground has long been ascribed to two contradictory formulations: 'primitive' mental states, on the one hand, or a supra-ordinate – 'spiritual' – category, on the other. In Dōgen's formulation, the two converge to attain an existential status in which a 'body-mind' unity serves as a means of recognizing reality, thus becoming an epistemological tool. This state is neither 'primitive' nor strictly 'spiritual' or 'transcendental'. Repudiating both 'pre-reflective' (primitive) and 'post-reflective' (transcendental) stances, 'awakened' experience is presented as "the way an experience … in total selfless openness" leads to a condition wherein "all things are experienced just as they are, apart from discrimination…" (Cook, 1989, p. 52). The emphasis here is that – within a stringently experiential mode of examination – *no "hyphenated" reality or essential interposition between "things"* can be made. Thus, instead of declaring "unity", Zen texts present a seemingly moderate claim which I shall now briefly present.

## *"Just simply say, when doubt arises: not two"*[3]

Buddhist thought is often beleaguered by the division between an allegiance to either a gnostic-based or a practice-based orientation. It thus echoes the mind-body dichotomy by transposing it on two distinct attitudinal modes, a mental one and a ritualistic-practical one. Poignantly aware of this problematic, Zen postulates the non-discriminating *meditative* mind to psyche-somatically subtend these positions which characterize 'ordinary thought'. This is experienced as a state wherein "sounds are simply heard, and thoughts simply occur and then they naturally disappear, just like the incoming and outgoing of breath" (Nagatomo, 1992, p. 119). In Dōgen's mind – we have seen – this 'without thinking' mode – *is authentic thinking.*

Note that the "without thinking" mode is not an arrest of thought processes, but one that conforms to the non-dualistic processes of mind described in Chapter 6. Kasulis (1989) succinctly summarizes this process by the following scheme:

- "Thinking" means either affirming or negating conceptualized objects.
- "Not thinking" relates to a position of negating thought (as encouraged in some meditative regimens).
- "Without thinking" refers to neither affirming nor negating both objects and thoughts.

But how then does this form of knowledge – this epistemology – apply to language, verbal communication and psychoanalytic methodology? Requiring its appropriate non-dualistic languaging, this unique non-discriminating mode of "minding" reality both necessitates and generates its particular vocabulary, syntax and semantics.

## Zen language

In a book entitled *The Buddha's Philosophy of Language*, Kalupahana (1999) demonstrates that "Buddhist language" – as part and parcel of Buddhist philosophy – vacillates between the 'phenomenal' and the 'absolute'. Mirroring this constant oscillation, verbal communication is paradoxically conceived of as:

1 "one of the means by which we gain experience of the world and share that experience with others" (ibid., p. 4).
2 part of a spiritual path wherein, "...[one]... can enter into the exalted state ... which is free from speech-discrimination" (Suzuki, 1932, p. 122).

Language and speech are thus exalted and berated, essential and contingent, useful but made redundant.

In Western phenomenology, Merleau-Ponty (2002) teaches that human beings are known "through their glances, their gestures, their speech" (p. 82). Similarly, within the wider perspective of non-dualistic propositions, one resolution to the above paradoxes is to contextualize language within an embodied semiotic sphere: "In some Buddha-lands ideas are indicated by looking steadily, in others by gestures, in still others by a frown, by the movement of the eyes, by laughing, by yawning..." (Suzuki, 1932, p. 79). Watts (1957) takes this point of view to its ultimate end, suggesting that an onomatopoeic *equation* exists between content (reality) and articulation. Reality-'suchness' – '*tathatā*' in Sanskrit is accordingly denoted by a quasi-infantile babble in the utterance "tat", which is the Sanskrit equivalent of the word "that". This position, argues psychoanalyst Michael Eigen (2011), is a far cry from the exalted position conventionally assigned in the West to "the Word, the creative Word, generator of the kind of life we have and can have" (p. 58).

In psychoanalytic terms, this debate echoes a foundational one represented by Lacanian thinking, on the one hand, Winnicottian, on the other: are we realized via signification, entering the world of communication via verbal communication, as Lacan would have it? Or are signs an "elaboration of bodily parts" (Winnicott, 1975, p. 244) – a "thatness", reflecting the psyche-soma and the relational matrix at large? Winnicott, it would seem, would have concurred with Watts: in the beginning there are babies, and mothers, infantile babble and 'primary maternal preoccupation'. The meaning of verbal communication is thus dependent on a wider contextual matrix, including the interlocutors' dispositions and their non-verbal and non-linguistic communications. Within the Zen teacher-disciple relationship this is congruent with the practice of conferring meaning through enacted communication.

In order to reconcile the two poles, Dōgen proposes his version of what I have, in previous chapters, termed a 'new ordering structure', embracing both the symbolic order and that of 'direct presentation'. This is typical of Zen and Daoist thinking. Rather than adopting dualistic propositions – thus contending with paradox as a given and trying to resolve it – Zen *posits language and reality within the same order, creating a conceptual horizon to embrace both*. Once language and reality are put on the same plane, no paradox arises.

Dōgen's project is predicated on one instance in the Buddha's sermons known as the "Sermon on Vulture Peak":

> Once, on Vulture Peak in India … Shakyamuni Buddha held up a … blossom and blinked. Mahakashyapa smiled. The Shakyamuni Buddha said, "I have the treasury of the true dharma eye, the wondrous heart of nirvana. I entrust it to Mahakashyapa"….
> (Tanahashi, 2010, p. 569)

The orthodox rendition of this fascicle maintains that Zen's "true Dharma" rests on the unique appropriation of the 'Dharma' directly – the Buddha blinks, Mahakshyapa smiles – without verbal or scriptural mediation. It thus constitutes the root of what is known as direct, 'face-to-face', or 'mind-to-mind' ('heart-to-heart') transmission. Dōgen is not, however, content with this interpretation, which privileges one form of transmission over another. Rather, he maintains that the truth of direct expression is not made manifest through wordlessness and silence and is not a translogical truth: there is nothing inherently valuable in direct (non-verbal) transmission, nor is there any intrinsic value in verbal transmission itself. Instead, he suggests that understanding is established through an 'intimacy', the mystery of which is realized through what he terms "expression" (Jap.: *dōtoku*).

Words, advises Buddhism, lack an 'independent' meaning. Within Zen's infrastructure "each and every word requires other words for its existence, and even more so – for its opposition, without which it will possess neither meaning nor existence..." (Raz, 2007, p. 21). Furthermore, the signifier is totally dependent *on the subject* for its elucidation. Within a spiritual context, this means that the deeper the practice and the involved exertion, the further the distance from the inevitable reductive rendition of the fullness of the signified. Meaning is embedded in the matrix of our experience "not isolatable ... from the mind and its environs" (Kim, 2004, p. 82): the more profound the experience, the richer the texts: texts, words and scriptures fulfil their potential when they are embodied in "upright sitting", in "wholesome restfulness", or in "still walking" of engaged involvement with life.

Experience, meditative practice and language thus maintain an interactive 'co-originative' matrix of procedural relationships which they ongoingly constitute. In line with this, Kalupahana (1999) suggests that the "Buddha's language" does not adhere to a strict representation of external reality. Rather, it is a language of 'becoming' and is consistently constituted by factual and practical aspects of daily life, making language and phenomena interconnected in a "mysticism of intimacy" (Kim, 2007, p. 60). It is this compound instrumental-mystical aspiration that motivates and enables Dōgen to anticipate psychoanalytic attempts at creating a unitive discursive-embodied language through utilizing the polysemous potentialities of both enacted communications and of words.

## *Dead words, live words*

During my internship I took part in a rehabilitation project of post-psychotic adolescents. Apart from my psychotherapeutic duties I undertook to facilitate a martial arts group, which appealed especially to the rougher boys. Aron was one such kid: brought up in an ultra-academic household, he was educated up to the chin, having done years of extra-curricular work at home throughout his childhood years. There was little in terms of "trivia" that he was ignorant about; he excelled at math and geometry.

Aron was diagnosed with an anxiety disorder, concurrently displaying what seemed to be schizoid features, gradually exposing underlying psychopathic features. In martial arts group-work, however, he proved to be helpful, resourceful and made immense progress in what my Winnocottian supervisor termed "being-there", i.e. embodied presence. Conversely, in individual and verbal group therapy, his disturbances showed up clearly. As other participants shared and communicated, Aron would watch them like a hawk, and, not infrequently, responded to the minutest hesitation in disclosure or reticence of expression with a snigger, his disgusted expression almost revealing his innermost thoughts: I don't trust you, and, moreover, I distrust your words, all the more so when you try to be accurate and objective.

I had an inkling of what Aron was about. His upbringing had engendered a deep-set suspicion of words; he was victim to what Laing had termed "a double-bind" – a confabulation in communication in which verbal and embodied-gestural messages stood painfully at odds, confusing him and making him feel unsure as to what communicative message to attend to. Inevitably – he confided in me – something would go wrong since he would – as always – "misunderstand" and was consequently reprimanded, punished, or, what was worse – ignored. Inevitably he was right, since his domineering academic father and his obsessive overly-anxious mother were extremely defensive in the process of exposing the rifts between their cultivated responses to him and their underlying dislike of – and aggression towards – him.

This state of affairs had persisted for almost a year when a new art teacher entered the scene. Nina was just out of teachers training and unprepared for the challenges in store for her in this particular school. With all good intentions she was attempting to come across clearly when a few of the delinquent kids toppled over her watercolour cart. She later recounted how, in what she perceived of as a very collected manner, she asked the kids to help her in collecting what was left of the colours, cleaning up and arranging the class for the consecutive lesson.

Under threat of suspension following previous instances of misconduct, Aron's account to me was strikingly different. He recounted: "She just stood there and said 'Aron, would you very kindly help clean up the mess?'" As I was still puzzled he said: "She didn't mean it. I could see she didn't. Why wasn't she angry? I am sure she was angry! She was hiding it. She was speaking, but the words she was using were not meant to say something to us. She wasn't really looking at us, even. Her words were dead."

Zen's response to the challenge of the relationship between reality and language depends on the "aliveness" of communication. This is dependent on embodied involvement, on 'total exertion' in non-discriminatory, participatory functions: the question as to the validity and reliability of verbal communication rests not on the content of words but on the context and the disposition of their issue. This means that it is not speech and verbalization itself that are disparaged. Rather, it is the obstructions – due to the speaker's inadequacy or loss of direct communion between speech and underlying reality – that are berated. Accordingly, Heine (1994) makes the distinction between "living words" and "dead words" in Zen: the former are "apropos of the moment ... ideally suited to an encounter ... because they reflect the interpenetration of universality and particularity and ... inseparability of subjectivity and objectivity" (ibid., p. 201); the latter "fall back on predictably and ineffectively logical responses to dynamic, translogical inquiries" (ibid.).

Zhuangzi – the Daoist sage – maintains that "words exist because of meaning. Once you have gotten the meaning, you can forget the words." But then he wonders: "Where can I find a man who has forgotten words, so I can have a word with him?"(Watson, 1968, p. 302). Zhuangzi's *ad absurdum* portrayal highlights the paradox, elucidating it at the same time: meaning subsumes words but is not derived from them: it is the aliveness of experience that is carried forth in human communication, presenting itself through words. Words are not arbitrary carriers of meaning. Rather – they are enlivened by true, involved and fully presenced meaning, without the experiential-embodied undercurrent of which they are "dead words", a signifier devoid of an experiential signified. The ineffable is communicable through the interplay of active participation, silence and language. *Its ineffability is a feature of the experienced world and not a reality, metaphysically set apart: in as far as language is not taken to define and delimit a conscious appraisal of the world, the world does not possess intrinsic incommunicable properties.*

In an attempt to clarify the relationship between the written text and non-dual body-mind experience, Eubanks (2011) queries: "How is it that Mahāyāna *sūtras come alive?*" (p. 23, my italics). Eubanks attributes this to the "heart-mind" (Jap.: *shin; kokoro*) and maintains that the 'heart-mind' "is embodied, firmly situated in the flesh" (ibid., p. 24). Consequently, she argues that "what the Mahāyāna sūtras seek is nothing short of a mutually beneficial symbiotic relationship with the human body" (ibid.). Eubanks's stipulations point to an unusual relationship between text and body, suggesting that the body and verbal contents can – potentially – *mutually interact* and that embodiment may be used as a vehicle for deciphering verbal contents. In a similar vein, Bollas, in his (2013) *With China on the Mind*, highlights the intimate relationship between language – Chinese ideographs used in Zen texts – and the 'sensual', pointing out that "each character is in itself a small poem ... [in which] ... image and sound unite with ... emotion ..." (p. 37). In sync with Zen and with contemporary psychoanalytic efforts, Bollas delineates an embodied conceptual and therapeutic language emerging from a non-dualistic nosology which uses "live words".

## Conclusion and dialogue

In this chapter I traced a particular trajectory within the evolution of psychoanalytic interpretative technique, which is gradually challenging the monopoly of verbal signification: privileging unmediated presentation, embodied presence and non-verbal communications, this trajectory has been instrumental in establishing an embodied conceptual and therapeutic language. Many psychoanalysts and psychotherapists adhering to this approach have long maintained an intuitive – although often reductive and misguided – affinity with Zen-Buddhist conceptualizations.

The Buddhist mirror image of the above psychoanalytic stratification – embodied participation versus verbal signification – takes the form of 'direct' (intuitive, unmediated, non-verbal) as opposed to 'scriptural' (textual, verbal) transmission. Zen is traditionally focused on the former: "not based in words and letters", it maintains that Buddhist precepts may not be grasped through verbal communication or by intellectual endeavour alone. Understanding the teachings entails practice. 'Oneness of practice and awakening' implies that true understanding is neither an intellectual nor a transcendental affair. Accordingly, in contemporary psychoanalytic-Buddhist dialogue, Zen provides an alternative epistemological proposition, suggesting that the compound body-mind – not just the cogitating mind – might serve as a mode for recognizing, knowing and relating to reality. Within this proposition, language and body are not essentially distinct.

Psychoanalytic "knowledge" that lies outside the precincts of intellectual awareness and verbal signification is represented by terms such as "unformulated experience" (Stern, 1983), "unthought known" (Bollas, 1989) or "preverbal, implicit, procedural knowing" (Beebe et al., 2003). Seeking to mitigate the seemingly inevitable bifurcation of experience in psychoanalysis, these formulations imply a revision of what comprises conscious thought. The revised postulate – in sync with Zen propositions – is a *"non-symbolic and extraverbal form of thought…"* (Arnetoli, 2002, p. 742, my italics), manifesting in non-dual relational formulations which take into account a "mind-body attuned with other mind bodies and with the world" (ibid.). In Zen terms, this conforms to the congruity of a 'without thinking' experience of actional oneness between the 'body-mind' and its surroundings. This is in stark contrast to the orthodoxy of "Cartesian dualism … that fragments the human body and divorces mind from body in way that make[s] the understanding of the analytic process more difficult…" (Meissner, 2003a, p. 294).

In Zen, 'undivided activity' is both prerequisite to – and synonymous with – the acquisition of understanding. In the intertwining of the spiritual acquisition of 'non-duality' with the somatic-physiological 'total exertion', the faculties of 'thinking' and 'meditative-praxis' merge. From within the psychoanalytic Buddhist dialogue, Brickman (1998) maintains that this gestalt of experience helps cultivate "an altered … perspective … a healthy … decapsulation or depolarization of self boundaries…" (ibid., p. 3) and of "boundaries with the social surround" (ibid., p. 4), furthering a non-intellectual mode of reverie: it is from within the profundity of this mode of reverie that Kulka (2003) communicates his empathic understanding of his bereaved patient by standing up beside her as the ambulance goes by.

The ongoing search for a non-representational view of the mind consistently recognizes the shortcomings of linguistic formulations which inevitably bear definitive, bifurcative aspects. Lacking in parsimonious meta-theory and appropriate nomenclature, psychoanalytic theories' innovations in the field of non-duality are hard put to formulate themselves: as psychoanalysis comes to acknowledge the fact that 'consciousness' does not coincide with verbal language, direct intuitions of the "unformulated" or "unthought known" imply a mode of consciousness, which is impervious to conventional verbal configurations and interpretative-communications; consequently, images and language originating in Buddhist and Daoist texts – such as "somato-psychic" experience (Alfano, 2005) – inevitably seep into psychoanalysis.

The present chapter thus suggests that Zen-Buddhism potentially supports non-dualistic frameworks and propositions in contemporary psychoanalysis. In "Zen eyes", unitive experience is not removed from the empirical and the existential, nor does it present as an aloof metaphysical or transcendental stance. Rather, it is deeply embedded in communication and interaction: within it the intersubjective sphere emerges as *a particular facet* of the indivisibility of reality, contained within the recognition that "the individual arises out of an extremely extensive environment of other individuals ... culture, soil, water, stone, mist..." (Cook, 1989, p. 24). This 'individual-environment' coalescence constitutes a unified field of 'inter-being' within which "to study the way with mind is this mountains-and-rivers-and-earth-mind itself thoroughly engaged in studying the way" (Tanahashi, 1985, p. 89).

Buddhist and Daoist-based psychotherapeutic practice derives its integrity from this position. Consequently, it constitutes a viable response to Anderson's queries presented in the beginning of this chapter as to the compatibility of embodied "unspoken dimension[s]" with psychoanalytic practice. A formative 18th-century Japanese medical text recommends: "If you hope to perfect your clinical art ... you will find clues ... in your daily activities – in walking in the mountains or in handling a tray", since "absorption is the way to the high art of medicine". In this body-mind mode of 'total exertion', the text goes on to say: "you should never use superfluous words nor rely on logic when trying to help neurotic people.... You should ... speak the words that come from within.... This attitude ... has a power that can penetrate a rock" (Matsumoto et al., 2001, p. 56).

Zen "interpretations" thus follow different pathways from those traditionally trodden by psychoanalytic interpretations; yet these pathways demarcate attributes closely compatible with contemporary foci in psychoanalysis, with an emphasis on aliveness, resonance and embodied relationality. It is via these pathways that new prisms are generated, through which psychoanalytic orthodoxy can be reviewed and classical "text-book" vignettes reconciled with more contemporary theorizations.

Consider the following – often quoted – interventions in this light: "A patient dug her nails into my hand at a moment of intense feeling. My interpretation was 'ow'. This ... meant to the patient that my hand was alive, that it was part of me, and that I was there to be used" (Winnicott, 1987, p. 83); or Kohut's self-revelation in his last lecture – "I suddenly had the feeling [and said]: 'How would you feel if I let you hold my fingers, for a little while now while you are talking?'" (Kohut, 2010, p. 130): both reflect the total compatibility and intertwining of verbal expression, absorption and action. Verily – these interventions show how 'body' and 'mind' may co-exist within a non-dual linguistic and conceptual ordering: Interchangeable in their use of words and gesture, welding symbolical and pre-reflective meaning, moulting representation and presentation, they make gestures communicative and the words that accompany them "live". Conceptually, they are the methodological-technical counterparts of "unformulated experience"; epistemologically they are counterparts of the "unthought known".

Emphasizing direct experience and actional involvement, Zen teachings have a long history of contending with the conundrum of using cogitations to redefine a 'non-thinking' reflection: Zen's language is not only that of constant flux-becoming – defying definitive sign-signified relations – it is also a language in which physical and textual reality are intermeshed. 'Suchness' (*tathatā*) and the expression of 'suchness' are semantically-onomatopoetically aligned; 'Expression' is not necessarily *either* verbal *or* non-verbal. Similarly – as the clinical vignettes show – rising in communion in response to an ambulance siren or silently co-authoring an "open-hearted" Haiku poem may both constitute "interpretations", although not spelt out as such. The intuitive affinity between gesture, bodily counter-transference and language is profoundly validated.

Reality and its communication thus subtend each other and serve as metonymic portrayals of each other at one and the same time. It is the body-mind disposition – rather than the pre-determined allotted meaning of the signified-signifier relationship – that confers meaning. It is the 'body-mind' reality – as Aron so poignantly reminded me – which turns "dead words" into "live words". In Chapter 9, these assumptions will be reviewed within the interactive context of psychoanalytic practice, focusing on the analyst's empathic body-mind presence and on the intersubjective intercorporal attunement between therapist and patient.

## Notes

1 This is an allusion to German and English etymology of "understanding", which includes the route "to stand".
2 Name of a *Shōbōgenzō* fascicle.
3 From Merzel's (1991) annotated version of "The eye never sleeps" ("Xin Xin Ming"), p. 109.

# Chapter 9

# A non-dualistic body-mind-set in psychoanalysis?

In what was, for a time, a formative pro-psychoanalytic text, French novelist, Marie Cardinal (1983) describes the predicament which brought her to seek psychoanalytic help: suffering from years of uterine bleeding Marie enters the clinic envisioning her prospective psychoanalytic session. She all but revels in the thought of describing her predilection as in the most evocative and provocative terms. Expecting sympathy and concern after years of concealment, she literally makes a point of giving the most physically – and metaphorically – explicit and demonstrative depiction of years of incessant humiliating and debilitating menstrual bleeding. Her analyst's sole response, however, is to suggest that she limit herself to content-matter that is not so obviously psychosomatic; he is all but indifferent to her detailed, flowery and heart-rending physical depictions.

However, even at the time of writing, the late 1970s, the tide was already beginning to turn: a contemporary of Cardinal, French psychoanalyst Didier Anzieu maintained that, in some instances, "the interpretative function ... must be preceded by the exercise of a pre-symbolic function which ensures intersensorial connections..." (1990, p. 66). The fact that "the analyst protects himself ... from any smells, affect or rhythms that might emanate from the patient", he warns, may determine the fate of psychoanalysis to be "shelved in the storehouse of obsolete accessories, that are no longer talked about, except in courses on the history of medicine..." (ibid., p. 69). For Anzieu, the analyst's capacity to perceive the patient not only as a bearer of ideas, thoughts, fantasies and dreams but as a "bodily container" is a significant fulcrum of the psychoanalytic encounter.

These excerpts from Cardinal and Anzieu bring to the fore questions regarding the analyst's capacity to engage psychosomatically, overcoming his own dissociative splits: how does the dynamically inclined psychotherapist – who prides himself on his empathic verbal response to verbal contents – relate to sensorial dimensions of interaction? What are the psychotherapeutic mindset and disposition required for such a mode of relating? And how might interpersonal-intersensorial connections – so evidently acknowledged in contemporary psychoanalysis – be furthered in the psychotherapeutic encounter?

Thus far, I have shown how the espousal of 'embodied' thinking in contemporary psychoanalytic psychotherapy may benefit from non-dualistic Zen body-mind paradigms. The present chapter refines this issue, pointing to the potential for a radically non-dual 'body-mind' analytical engagement. With the therapist's 'body-mind' functioning as a comprehensive epistemological vehicle, the unmediated grasp of psyche-somatic linkages provides an indispensable tool for furthering unitive experience. In line with this, I propose to draw guidelines demarcating the psyche-somatic disposition required of the analyst in recognizing and furthering body-mind integration. Moreover, I shall suggest that a comprehensive body-mind disposition – a 'body-mind-set' – generates a specific type of body-mind 'attunement', leading to a specific mode of empathic linkage. *This compound dispositional attitude, presence, mode of attunement and empathic linkage redefine the psychoanalytic encounter.*

In order to outline these guidelines and extricate the components of this compound state, I shall focus on Buddhist tenets, practices and injunctions that reflect and support embodied and non-dual modes of interaction. I propose to do this in three consecutive steps:

1 Consider Buddhist meditative practice as potentially enhancing the therapist's 'analytic' mindset, hence his capability of mental noting, introspection and introception.
2 Focus on the concept of 'attunement' in contemporary psychoanalytic literature and delineate Zen's particular contribution to psyche-somatic attunement.
3 Consider the relationship between attunement, interpretation and the therapist's empathic-compassionate role as constitutive of the patient's body-mind integration.

## Meditative practice and contemporary psychoanalysis

In an early contribution to the Buddhist-psychoanalytic interface Karen Horney (1952) described Buddhist meditation as enhancing the capacity of "being with all one's faculties in something…", a capacity she sees as tantamount to "the essence of living" (in Molino, 1998, p. 36). Implied is the notion that, in maintaining a meditative state of mind, a body-mind framework is established that alters perception. Lawner (2001) describes this as an involved "interdigitation with our bodies and material worlds…", furthering a mode of being and interaction in which the analyst is "as vital and present as possible [in order] to respond to the plenitude and marvel of the material and psychic/spiritual worlds…" (p. 548). This observation reinforces the clinical notion that "the mind-set of the analyst … regarding the integration of mind-body can have important reverberations … [on] … therapeutic intervention and management" (Meissner, 2007, p. 333).

### *The mindset of the analyst*

The mindset of the analyst or psychotherapist presents as a focal point in psychoanalytic-Buddhist dialogue. Engler (2003) describes this mindset as a "non-dual awareness in which we are unselfconscious but acutely aware, attuned to the realities of the moment … focused and engaged, but relaxed … at the same time" (p. 60). Engler equates this non-dual "unselfconscious" mode of experience with what Kohut presents as the stable and sustained experiential state of self-continuity, acquired through the outcome of successful therapy.

Elaborating on Kohut's formulations, Kulka (2012) leans on Buddhist theory to demonstrate the manner in which the therapist's transition into a "diffusive" mode of experience engenders un-cogitated attuned responses. These, he suggests, may reflect a mutual-restructuring of experience, eschewing the conventional 'body' versus 'mind' polarity. Rather, he proposes that *a matrix* displaying a 'body-mind' fluctuation between states of psyche-somatic "emergence" and states of non-dual "diffusion" is a more realistic portrayal of the analytic experience. *Separately 'body' and 'mind' alternately 'emerge'; non-dually 'body' and 'mind' diffusively, mutually intersect and converge.* Kohut's original formulations and Kulka's elaborations lend meta-theoretical validity to otherwise esoteric facets of psychoanalytical theory, initially based on clinical and intuitive claims to 'oneness', 'undifferentiation', 'fusion', 'interpenetration' and 'merger' (see Eigen, 1981, 1983, for some examples). In contemporary practice it highlights the notion of psyche-somatic 'presence' as conducive to furthering co-joint verbal-actional "now moments" which confer and define implicit "mind-bodied" knowledge (see Stern, 2004, pp. 143–147, on this issue).

From a relational perspective, Bromberg (2012) suggests that intersubjectivity includes non-verbal "body-to-body" experiential phenomena. These he attributes to a particular mode of communion termed "right brain to right brain communication" (ibid., p. 684). The relational perspective is thus embedded in neuro-psychological nomenclature, introduced by Allan Schore (2001, 2003), in regard to non-verbal modes of inter-personal attunement. Schore (2001) maintains that the clinician's intuitive right brain psychobiological 'attunement' to the moment-to-moment implicit communication is a prerequisite for a "vitalizing attunement to the patient..." (ibid., p. 313), providing empathic resonance, in and of itself. Akin to what Winnicott terms the chaotic state of "mix up" and "fusion", right brain to right brain communication precludes intellectual discernment, which characterizes left brain functions. Rather, it is global, a-modal and intuitive, "[pertaining to] the analyst's ability to experience the field as a process in which ambiguity, paradox, and sometimes even chaos are felt to be relationally valid elements in the growth of self" (Bromberg, 1991, p. 299).

The preceding statements pose a significant challenge to conventional psychoanalytic know-how. Verily they suggest that, rather than the therapist's interpretations being the ground on which mental and emotional growth is fostered, it is the therapist's *being* which constitutes the predominant factor. Moreover, they suggest that this mode of being is:

1  A compound psyche-somatic one.
2  Communicated non-verbally through modes of unconscious attunement and enactment.

## In dialogue

Psychoanalytic-Buddhist dialogue proliferates in professional literature examining the cultivation of the above states of being and their promotion within the therapeutic encounter. Psychoanalyst and Buddhist practitioner Will Adams (1995) stresses the advantages to the analyst's receptive mindset specifically derived from 'Mindfulness' (Pali: *Vipassanā*) meditation: in the seminal 'Mindfulness' sūtra – the 'Satipatthana Sūtra' – adepts are taught to pay attention to the 'four foundations of Mindfulness':

1 *Body: physical attributes* – such as 'breathing' and 'posture'.
2 *Sensations* – 'pleasant', 'unpleasant' or 'neutral'.
3 *Mental states* – such as 'love', 'hate', and 'distraction'.
4 *Contents of mind* – such as 'factors and hindrances of enlightenment'.

Regarding any and all of these experiential phenomena, the injunctions direct meditation-practitioners to be attentive, non-discriminating and non-judgemental: the outcome is an experience of a chain of 'notations' the practitioner makes as he "notices himself" (for example, shallow breath; love; unpleasant). Comprising distinct phenomena, they are not seen to be conceptually bound to each other by a cause and effect relationship (i.e. shallow breath *caused by* an unpleasant feeling such as anxiety). Ultimately, it is suggested, in mindful meditation, these transient foci of attention will appear and recede spontaneously, as they arise in retrogressive conscious attention: they come and go; they do not have intrinsic attributes; nor do they inhere as personal, objective states. Conversely, rigid mental states – *including psychological malaise and pathology* – are seen to arise from an 'attachment' to – and a causal and categorical valuation of – these otherwise neutral phenomena: these then conglomerate to appear as compound 'real' entities such as 'anxiety-shallow-breath-caused by...', 'shallow breathing caused by anxiety', etc.

## *Embodied awareness*

The practice of intricate mental noting was highly formalized and elaborated by the late S. N. Goenka, a 'Mindfulness' meditation teacher. In accord with 'state-of-the-art' neuro-psychological practice, Goenka asserts that "mind, in its innermost core, is primarily occupied with experiencing bodily feelings..." (quoted in Drummond, 2006, pp. 288–289). Accordingly, he urges his students to "be aware of all different sensations..." *since misery*, according to this notion, "*arises ... at the level of bodily sensations...*" (Goenka, 2000, p. 36, my italics), with the affective states known as anxiety, depression, etc. as concomitant sequelae. Consequently, he warns against assuming that cognitive understanding of unwholesome experience is the royal road to its resolution; rather, in sync with Buddhist orthodoxy, he reminds us that it is through embodied contemplation that volitional and emotive formations may be gradually eradicated. Pursuing this form of 'mindful' practice in a methodical manner imbues the adept practitioner with a thorough recognition of his *embodied sensational and emotive life*.

## Evenly hovering attention reconsidered

This mode of meditative mental noting seems to comply with what – from a psychoanalytical perspective – Adams (1995) terms "revelatory openness". It provides the methodology for indiscriminately noting a variety of psychic and somatic events, sidestepping evaluative and categorical prejudices. In a similar vein, Rubin (2009), a practising psychoanalyst, suggests that Buddhist "meditation fosters heightened attentiveness and equanimity, ... training one's capacity to notice ordinarily obscure phenomena – ranging from fleeting somatic sensations to subliminal thoughts, feelings and fantasies, ... creative images and insights" (p. 95). Consequently, he suggests "meditation offers ... techniques for accessing 'evenly hovering attention', which could facilitate psychotherapeutic listening" (ibid.). Rubin even goes as far as to suggest that "attempting to listen to someone without developing [this] heightened attentiveness is like taking a photograph with a wonderful lens held by an unsteady hand – the picture will be blurred" (ibid., p. 103). Thus, for Rubin, the "wonderful lens" of 'mindfulness' is tantamount – and yet superior – to the elusive sought-after quality of "freely hovering attention" advised by Freud.

## A Zen non-dualist perspective

But is the sought-after non-dualistic position – ultimately – one of meticulous mental notation? From within an intra-Buddhist discourse Bielefeldt (1988) and Kasulis (1989) critique this approach on two counts, presenting it as inherently dualistic:

1 "Engag[ing] the object actively, *contemplating it under the rubric of some Buddhist category...*" (Bielefeldt, 1988, p. 81, my italics) entails the presupposing of categories of experience prior to 'experiencing'. For Bielefeldt, employing four foundations of 'mindfulness' and their sub-categories is thus inherently a dualistic practice since it presupposes discrete and distinct categorizations of experience: either "body" *or* "sensations" *or* "mental states" *or* "contents of mind". Zen would therefore advise that experience be dealt with without predetermined categories, such as 'physical' versus 'mental' phenomena, for instance.

2 Moreover, this formulation presupposes a subject–object divide between subject and would-be-object of discrimination (i.e. "I" perceive "this"), based on discriminatory cognitive functions. Kasulis (1989) takes this presupposition to task by reminding us of Dōgen's concept of "without thinking". Within this disposition oneself does not stand as a discrete entity outside of the relational interaction with the object of engagement: "It is not that I do not think of self and other. Rather, *without thinking*, there is no self and other" (ibid., p. 92, my italics).

In order to fully take these two qualifications into account a Zen-oriented approach to body-mind inquiry is in order. In his seminal book, *The Body, Self-Cultivation and Ki-Energy* Yuasa (1993) surmises that a definitive determinant of Zen training is the embodiment of an undifferentiated disposition of 'body-mind-one' (Jap.: *shishin ichinyo*). Supportive of this train of thought, psychoanalyst and Zen-teacher Stuart Twemlow (2001) delineates the contribution of Zen practice to psychoanalytical procedure and to the training of psychotherapists. In a forceful argument Twemlow focuses on the incongruence between Freud's injunction for "evenly hovering attention" and his own perception of what 'attention' ought to include. Guided by contemporary psychoanalytic theorizing and Zen-inspired practices, he examines the terms 'attention' and 'mind'. While 'attention' is unequivocally a quality of the conscious mind, maintains Twemlow, the term 'mind' itself requires redefining. From within a Zen perspective, the 'psychoanalytic mind' – defined as "an apparatus for thinking thoughts..." (ibid., p. 4) – is deemed a restrictive concept for the requirements of contemporary psychoanalytical training. For Twemlow, the Zen concepts of 'embodiment', 'emptiness', 'impermanence' and 'paradox' should be used to redefine the requirements for the training of the psychoanalytical 'mind'. Rubin (1996) complements this by maintaining that "Freud's suggestions for removing the hindrances to listening..." need be refined by the "training and practice ... of Buddhist meditative praxis" (p. 110).

## Dōgen's contributions

Dōgen's theorizing – as we have seen – relates to the very essence of such a 'would-be' training, determining that 'mental mode' and physical 'practice' are indivisible: 'awakening' – a supposedly mental or spiritual attribute – does not exist separately from 'practice'; at the same time 'practice' is performed within a given, set, physical mode. For Dōgen, meditation is not defined by a mindful and discerning notation of specific mental objects. Rather, Dōgen states: "The zazen I speak of is not meditation practice [in the traditional Buddhist sense]. It is simply the practice-realization of totally culminated awakening" (Leighton & Okamura, 2004, p. 534). The "awakened", "realized" or "enlightened" disposition exists only within a psyche-somatic "practice" form, within a physical-actional posture or set of movements. In his eloquent language, Dōgen cements the seeming paradox thus: "because this is the realization of practice, there is no boundary in the realization; because this is the practice of realization, there is no beginning in practice" (Tanahashi, 1985, pp. 151–152). In plain words, Dōgen is suggesting the feasibility of abiding within an integrated 'body-mind-set'.

Is this paradox? Dōgen would reply in the negative: paradox entails the apparent incompatibility of two distinct semantic categories. Since body and mind, practical-concrete physical practice and mental-spiritual awakening are essentially inseparable, they do not constitute two such separate categories – QED. Rather, one might say that – in the above – Dōgen is clarifying Twemlow's position as to the concept of 'mind'. In this formulation the psychical-spiritual dimension of 'mind' is realized minute by minute via the physical-sensual-perceptual position, whereas the physical dimension of 'mind' is essentially enhanced by its continuous maintenance of a specific embodied-mental posture, designed to facilitate a non-dualistic mode of "evenly hovering attention". As body and mind moult to sediment a 'without-thinking' mode of awareness, "man ... unaware of his own person ... constitutes one body with the process of change" (Ames, 1993, p. 172). It is this "oneness" that provides the vehicle for attunement with existents at large. As Dōgen proposes: "When actualized by myriad things, your body and mind, as well as the body and mind of others drop away" (Tanahashi, 1985, p. 70). It is this laboriously attained-pristine state[1] of body and mind that is coincidental with seeing "forms or hear[ing] sounds fully engaging body and mind..." (ibid., p. 70), eliciting the capacity of intuition in which "you grasp things directly" (ibid.).

## Attunement

In the late 1980s, I visited Japan to meet, study with and pay homage to some of my Zen, Eastern medicine and martial arts teachers. Mornings would be dedicated to study and clinical attendance; afternoons and evenings to martial arts classes and martial arts demonstrations.

One such demonstration started out with advanced students displaying their skills. The rough and tumble display was often impressive, obviously physically demanding, always ending with a declared winner, the opponents courteously acknowledging their respective statuses.

After a while the ambience began to change: the displays seemed to be more subdued, more to do with the 'presence' of the competitors and less with their physical prowess. Finally, the previous competitors vacated the floor, and two older masters took the stage. Both seemed to be in their seventies, obviously highly trained and well versed in the intricacies of the art they were performing – that of Bōjutsu – long staff combat. Slowly they stood up, eloquent in their long robes; facing each other they gracefully brought their staffs up above their heads, holding and maintaining them in combat positions. The hall seemed alive with subdued tension; it was obviously replete with energy, exuding from the two masters' presence. Then, very slowly and deliberately, as if by common accord, both men declined their staffs, ceremoniously positioned them by their sides, bowed to each other with respect and reclined in their respective seats, on both sides of the hall. To all present, it was as clear as could be that combat had already taken place, had reached its peak and subsided, ending in an obvious draw.

But how could this interaction – no words exchanged, no gestures performed – be conceptualized and interpreted?

An *inclusive, responsive and attuned 'body-mind' interpersonal field* within psychoanalysis invokes the problematic known as that of "other minds", closely linked to Cartesian dualism:

Arising from Descartes's bifurcation of people into two distinct parts, mind and body, ... and our own lack of direct sensory contact with other minds, we cannot infer from the mere presence of the body of the other any conclusion that a mind is "housed" within.

(Reis, 1999, p. 374)

With no "other mind" to relate to, reciprocity falters; empathy has no recipient. Reis's depiction emphasizes the fact that *an interlaced-compounded psyche-somatic relationality* requires some variant of the unorthodox, empathic-relational mindset manifested by the elderly martial artists in attuned 'presence', 'attention' and 'reverie'.

Freud's original construct of 'empathy' as a *"feeling-in"*[2] (Freud, 1921, p. 108) provided the baseline for the analytic mindset, in which empathy is considered a prerequisite for the curative agent of analysis, interpretation of patients' communications. But what about the unverbalized dimensions of the psychotherapeutic encounter? Unless we can relate to modes of psyche-somatic non-verbal communications, the ambiguous connection between the analyst's "feeling-in" – or empathy – to the *patient's unverbalized modes of being* remains unaccounted for. The question of empathic attention and attunement to the unverbalized realm of experience thus rests on the capacity and capability of the analyst to embrace and develop a distinct, specialized mode of attunement. Reis (1999) describes this as an embodied transposition, a "regrounding [which] ... allows for the introduction of the analyst's pre-reflective and sensuous experience through reverie" (p. 371).

What does this regrounding comprise? Although counter-transference seems an obvious solution, it hardly accounts for the full scope of mutually experienced mental-sensual-cognitive-physical aspects evinced and acknowledged within 'intersubjectivity'. Some alternative suggestions were examined in Chapters 4 and 5: a 'fusion', a 'mix-up' or an 'interpenetration'. Interpenetration, in particular, is a conceptually rich and evocative formulation. An elusive term – elicited by Marion Milner (1969) – it presupposes a pre-reflective ability to merge with an-other. It entails the capability for an archaic sense of attunement and thus, potentially, forms the substrate for a presymbolic "regrounding" of empathic sensibility.

Currently, however, it is clear that the huge impact of these concepts on psychoanalytic thinking far transcends their conventional role as pertaining to regressive positions, defined by their "pre" "prefixed" qualities (as in 'pre-reflective', 'presymbolic', 'preverbal', etc.). In fact, the intertwining of somatic, affective and mental attributes, described as "affect contagion ... resonance ... and attunement" (Arnetoli, 2002, p. 749) *seems to redefine empathy* as an incorporation of a 'mind-body' mode of attentive registration and attunement, such as would suggest "a mind-body attuned with other mind-bodies..." (ibid., p. 744). Thus Arnetoli's claim demonstrates how, in certain contexts, *the process of non-verbal attunement* usurps the traditional role of interpretation based on an empathic "feeling-in", redefining the historical core of psychoanalytic practice: rather than stressing the effect of psychoanalytic procedure on physical symptomatology, it demonstrates that psyche-somatic empathic attunement comprises the new, revised sine qua non of psychoanalysis.

The revised theory and its methodological counterparts are distinctly recapitulated in a number of contemporary psychoanalytic schools. From a Relational point of view, Knoblauch (1999) describes attunement as comprising processes of "continuous ... exchanges between dyadic partners ... [that] ... occur as nonverbal process[es] ... such as volume, tone, rhythm, tempo, gestural patterning, and muscular shifts ... [are] bidirectional[ly] ... [and] *simultaneously shaping and shaped...*" (p. 42, my italics). From a neuro-psychoanalytic standpoint, Rand (2002) makes a similar point, suggesting that only once a therapist practises postural mirroring in a conscious manner, will she know in her own body what the other person is feeling. Finally, Wrye (1996) – from a compound relational-feminist-Buddhist stance – warns that the bodily experience required for such an undertaking is "absent from analytic exploration in the consulting room, and absent from our theories...", since it encompasses "the whole range of somatosensory phenomena: our breath, pulse, posture, muscle strength, fatigue, clarity and speed of thought, sense of boundedness; our skin, mucous membranes, bodily tension, facial expression, taste, smell, pulse, vitality" (ibid., p. 287). Little wonder then that Knoblauch (1999) soberly summarizes: "this is difficult to conceive because it requires a level of observational attention atypical of daily discourse" (pp. 42–43).

## *Zen-minded interpenetration-attunement*

In an indirect response to the challenges brought up by Arnetoli, Knoblauch, Rand and Wrye, Brickman (1998) maintains that the gestalt of experience furthered by Zen practice makes Zen's contribution to empathic-embodied relating indispensable. In cultivating "an altered ... perspective ... illuminat[ing] a healthy need for a generic decapsulation or depolarization of self boundaries..." (ibid., p. 3) *it furthers a non-intellectual mode of reverie*. From a purely Zen perspective, similar sentiments are voiced: the mode of being 'attuned to' or 'uniting with' is not a cognitive "ability to read the minds of others". In Dōgen's words, it is, rather, a matter of a "decapsulated" practice: the ability to see into others' minds, "the art of seeing others' bodies, and the art of seeing others' eye[s]" (ibid.) is concomitant with "the art of seeing through the mind of the self and the art of seeing through the body of the self" (ibid.). In this way, Zen emphasizes the position that attuned empathy and inter-being – bridging the gap between one's body-mind and those of others – is a gradual outcome of a sustained and fruitful introspective body-mind meditative practice.

Stambough (1990) suggests that the form of 'inter-being' mentioned above warrants the term 'interpenetration'. Zen 'interpenetration' is a broader term than that employed in psychoanalysis, since it is not delimited by a specific relational matrix. Rather, it denotes a wider unitary matrix, the unitive experience of which manifests in "simultaneous-mutual-causation within an all-merging field of suchness" (Odin, 1982, p. 99), encouraging an intuitive, comprehensive paralogical grasp of reality, which, in turn affirms one's sense of 'being'. Dōgen terms this experience, in which selfhood is affirmed by the "suchness" of reality and environment – "authentication". This mode of interactive inter-being-authentication provides the basis for non-intellectual intuition of the totality of "being", leading to instances of attunement between self and environment.

Thus, in respect to the analyst-analysand interaction, Zen envisages a wider scope than that of an exclusive interpersonal counter-transferential state leading to purported 'interpenetration'. Dōgen's view implies that it is not a case of mutually dependent – but exclusive, distinct – subjectivities coming together through interpenetration. Rather, 'interpenetration' as a precursor to 'attunement' is an inevitable outcome of 'practice-authentication' leading to the perception of the immersion of the body-mind, through its total engagement, in a communion of being with whatever stimulus or facet of reality presents itself. As such, this mutuality of engagement is a total one, inherently embodied, incorporating somatic, incarnate consciousness. Within this reading *"Dōgen's world may be characterized as 'intercorporeal' in contrast to the intersubjective"* (Nagatomo, 1992, pp. 101–102, my italics). Such, for example, is the case of the two elderly martial artists described earlier in this chapter. Within this intercorporeal mode, subjectivity and intersubjectivity are transformed into a state which Nagatomo terms "trans-subjectivity".

## A Zen-minded attuned presence: the practice-wisdom of empathy

What comprises this trans-subjective intercorporeality and how may it be attained?

Shigenori Nagatomo is a modern Japanese scholar focusing on mind-body issues from the standpoint of depth psychology and meditative experience. Largely based on Zen conceptualizations, Nagatomo expounds on trans-subjective intercorporeality in his *Attunement through the Body*, propounding an integrative mind-body theory. The following traces Nagatomo's line of thinking.

Dōgen postulates: "The Zazen [meditation] of even one person at one moment imperceptibly *accords with all things and fully resonates through all time*" (Tanahashi, 1985, p. 147, my italics). The meditative process of introspection-introception enables "the entire body [to] become ... an affective sensorium ... simultaneously accompanied by a transformation of the body image" (Nagatomo, 1992, p. 153). The newly-acquired body image, rather than being delineated by the skin "is changed into a lived experiential feeling which expands beyond ... to embrace the ... world" (ibid.).

We consequently note then, that Zen attunement is tantamount to interpenetration. It is not an idealistic mental or spiritual attainment; it is attainable via a physical-mental meditative stance which precludes words and intellectual distinctions: transcending temporal and spatial impediments it leads, potentially, to an interpenetrative "mix up" (borrowing Milner's, 1969, term) with the external world. Nagatomo describes this as a "non-tensional" disposition allowing an inter-corporal "tao of action" manifest in "feeling-judgement without forming an intellectual judgement" (1992, p. 256).

Viewed through a psychoanalytic prism it is easy to see that Dōgen's embodied, engaged and interactive attunement stands in direct contradistinction to "the Cartesian paradigm [which] is individualistic ...

conceives of the universe as formed of particles; ... defines movement as mechanistic ... is dualistic and ... stresses the analytic methodology" (Rendon, 1986, p. 498). Rather, it rests on the basic Buddhist premise that "self-realization" is attainable only through "other-realization". In Dōgen's words: "To carry the self forward and experience ... things is delusion. That ... things come forward and experience themselves is awakening" (Tanahashi, 1985, p. 69). 'Realization' is tantamount to a non-dualistic, involved and attuned comportment, fostering a mental disposition in which the ego refrains from "coming forward", thus allowing entities to "come forth" and reveal themselves. Hammer describes the equivalent – more prosaic – analytical disposition as a transition from "leaning forward to catch the [verbal] clues ... [to a] leaning back to ... listen to the music behind the words" (quoted in Schore, 2002, p. 24). The therapist thus attunes to the patient who, in turn, comes forward to realize himself through the therapist's presence.

## Attunement, interpersonal engagement and the "original face"

Sue is a 60-year-old lady with multiple diagnoses – including a bipolar disorder and PTSD following sexual abuse – whom I have been seeing for over ten years. Functional and highly intelligent, she is often besotted by mood fluctuations and finds it difficult to consistently pursue a line of thought. Her physical demeanour is restrained; she ordinarily enters a session with a vociferous sigh, complaining of physical discomfort. Her physical dis-ease is manifest in her tense shoulders, held high, with her chest caving in as if it were shielding something and her stiff upper back muscles holding her whole thorax rigidly in place.

As she recounts episode after episode of what she perceives of as betrayal, abuse and exploitation, I find myself tensing up. I can hardly resist giving vent to my feelings which – if I were to sum them up – would comprise one almost mono-syllabic utterance: "Enough".

"Enough." I pronounce quietly but sternly.

As the word I thought I was patiently bearing in my mind finds its way out – without my having fully accounted for its formulation and utterance – Sue seems shocked by my atypical behaviour.

"Why are you shouting at me?" She enquires, nearly in tears.

In a state of some shock myself, I search for the internal space within which I can reflect. Realizing that my unconscious *and* my conscious appraisal are both nucleusly compressed in the utterance she found so hurtful, I am still not totally clear to myself: was my utterance a collusion with what she perceived of as constant perpetration? An outcry against the injustice she was suffering? A misguided protest against her way of coping? An attuned, echoed reiteration of her own sigh of "enoughness" as she enters the room?

As I relax my shoulders and resign myself to contemplation, I internally "sink", drawing the focus of my attention down and into the belly, finding refuge in the intima of my own body; the words are formed, and I utter them as they configure, deep from within my current psyche-somatic state: "I don't feel as if I was shouting at you – I think I was protesting."

As if mirroring my own contemplative, somewhat subdued state, Sue's posture relaxes. She reclines on the couch and "emerges" after a few minutes of what seems to be silent – and tranquil – contemplation. She hesitantly and shyly says:

> At first, it felt as if – yet again – there is a man menacing me and I must retreat in order to protect myself. Now it feels as if I am not myself and yet ... it feels as if I have peeled off a layer – maybe even layers – and under them is something that is 'more me' but which is unfamiliar to me.

She then adds words which have lingered with me since: "I feel that maybe you were shouting for me."

In reflecting upon this episode myself – and in supervision – I found Nagatomo's viewpoint extremely helpful. From a Zen perspective, Nagatomo (1992) elucidates the transition from the somatic-meditative posture of 'just sitting' – contemplation – to attuned engagement. 'Just sitting' – sinking into the "centre-belly" – the body – initially "a supportive framework within which thoughts take place" (ibid., p. 102) – acquires a potency of intercorporeal involvement, which furthers realization and objectification of experience. It facilitates the conditions of knowledge via which an "intuition of essence" evolves as "the body and mind will naturally drop off and the original face will presence itself" (ibid., p. 113). (This latter term is reminiscent of Sue's words: a sense of being "more me" but "unfamiliar to me".)

Attunement thus perceived is a conglomerate of mind-bodied communications and physio-mental states of engagement and withdrawal, within implicit and explicit intersubjective exchanges. The attuned mindset is – momentarily – of a different order from that operant in everyday awareness, implying a *"trans-descend[ence] into the source out of which both the mind and body appear"* (ibid., p. 129, my italics), intuitively unravelling and exposing hitherto unfamiliar levels of psyche-somatic being. 'Realization-awakening' and 'attunement' are thus not only inextricably intertwined, but stand as nearly synonymous terms: 'attuned' one 'realizes'; in 'realization-awakening' one is 'attuned'.

In elucidating Zen's spiritual enterprise, Steven Heine (1994) shows it to anticipate contemporary psychoanalysis in maintaining that an existential, sensed, presenced wedding of "concrete lived experience" and "mutual ... verbal and non-verbal exchange between two existentially dynamically engaged persons" (p. 47) is tantamount to 'realization': this he equates with Zen teacher-student dialogical relationship – '*Kannōdōkō*'. Encoded within Kan-nō-dō-kō – the four characters comprising it being "feeling-response-paths-intersect" – is a new ordering of subjectivity, defined by attuned psyche-somatic mutuality. Almost uncannily resembling the concept of relational 'interpenetration' in its psychoanalytic formulation, within this mode of consciousness, "there occurs an interfusion or interpenetration of animating energy, which arises as an instance of felt inter-resonance..." (Nagatomo, 1992, p. 161): in a bilateral confluence of mutual constitution "that which engages and that which is engaged *no longer takes place between two ... things ...*" (ibid., p. 239, my italics). In Nagatomo's project, 'attunement' and 'interpenetration' are thus seen as arising simultaneously, as being dependent on dynamic engagement and as being a mutually "animated" and "animating" experience for the parties involved.

These stipulations are an obvious affront to the divisive-Cartesian predicament of psychoanalysis: they obviate the *recognition of other minds through intercorporeal interpenetration*, eschewing the quest for recognition of other minds through cognitive reflection. In a way, they seem to state the – intuitively – obvious: one doesn't think "Oh, there's a body, a mind must be within." Rather, one recognizes the existence of other selfhoods via mutual interpenetration that transcends the exclusivity of both a physical "self" and a mental-subjective "selfhood", elucidating the fact that awareness of "other minds" is not an intellectual enterprise. In Zen terms, empathic attunement so defined amounts to an "inter-resonance ... a mutual *responding* ... in respect of both the explicit and the implicit dimensions of ... being ..." (ibid., p. 240, italics in the original). The hazardous transition from the perception of empathy as an introspective process, to conceiving of empathy as a dual form of active attunement – between the intra and inter-psychic, and between one psyche-soma and another – is thus completed.

## *Empathy reconsidered: from interpretation to transmutation*

From their distinct perspectives (relational and neuro-psychoanalytical, respectively), psychoanalysts such as Reis (1999, 2006) and Meissner (2007) seek a response to a basic phenomenological query: "How can my ego, within his peculiar ownness, constitute under the name 'experience of something other,' precisely something other?" (Husserl, quoted in Reis, 2006, p. 94). Contemporary psychoanalysis contends that it is the therapist's attuned-empathic 'mindset' that determines the grasp, construal and constitution of that "something" – or someone – "other". The Zen counterpart adds its particular perspective, suggesting that the condition of trans-subjectivity – realization – is tantamount to a state wherein "the entire body is hands and eyes", traversing the "path of ... going beyond, encountering reality" (Tanahashi, 2010, pp. 382–383). Having cast off body and mind, the 'body-mind' that reveals itself brings 'practice' – hands – and 'wisdom' – eyes – together. For Buddhists, this integrative – body-mind, physical-mental – function evokes the image of Kannon (or Avalokiteshvara) – a deity whose body is "all hands and eyes" – the embodiment of compassion, partaking in the sorrows and suffering of humanity and all sentient beings. Inasmuch as 'Kannon' is synonymous with 'empathy', empathy is defined by the capability of immersing the 'body and mind' – "hands and eyes" – in an attuned-empathetic response.

Idealized in the image of Kannon, Zen-empathy connotes 'practice-realization', 'hands-eyes', 'action-non-action' matrices of interpersonal communion. Describing the Zen-inspired teacher-student encounter, Kasulis (1989) emphasizes the underlying meditative stance, as giving rise to such psyche-somatic "communions": "Without thinking ... the Zen master merely 'lets be' [the] encounter, in its prereflective form" (ibid., p. 135). However, the student's presence and behaviour are bound to "subsequently activate some response from the master ... [and] ... the master will do what the situation evokes – whether ... encouragement ... instructions, *or a slap in the face*" (ibid., my italics). This evocative description directly challenges the axiomatic breach between the seemingly exclusive categories of action versus mentation, and verbal interaction versus 'enacted' or 'procedural' interpretation.

The closure to the present discussion thus complements issues dealt with in the previous chapter, delineating the attitudinal disposition in which 'body and mind', acting as a co-joint unit, confer meaning and determine a 'body-mind-set' empathetic attunement. Pointedly, Zen maintains that inclinations, thoughts and tendencies alone – unless coupled with action – do not suffice. The testimony to cultivation and acquisition of a compassionate disposition *is its active manifestation*. Dōgen defines this dispositional mindset in terms such as "identity action", denoting a state of "no difference from self, no difference from others", manifest in action. In a similar vein, Suler (1993) proposes that, in contemporary psychoanalysis "clinicians have ... recognized the powerful condensation of meaning ... embodied even in the simplest ... behavioral patterns and somatic reactions" (p. 115), thus attaining an "interpersonal fit", or an "optimal overlap" of subjectivities. Psychotherapeutic effect is therefore enhanced – rather than compromised – when cross-coded, welding verbal concepts, images and enactments: a multi-dimensional and cross-modal patient-therapist communication – utilizing verbal concepts, images and enacted communication – *implies that the communication of an interpretation is one possible variant of actional attunement.*

The fact that this multifaceted communion is highly dependent on an internal attuned-empathetic position makes the therapist's 'presence' an essential aspect of effective intervention. Allowing for the possibility of "silent interpretations" (Sponitz, 1969), and "procedural interpretations" (Herzog, 2011), contemporary psychoanalysis now recognizes this; in sync with Zen conceptualizations, it is becoming gradually accepted that the communication of an interpretation comprises a specific mode of attunement through involved participation. From this perspective, interpretation and empathic involvement complement each other in conferring meaning through an ongoing constitution of one body-mind by another, through 'attunement', 'interpenetration' and, at times, 'fusion'. I would suggest that it is the compassionate presence, thus perceived and presented, that serves as a vehicle for a fundamentally mutual, essentially reciprocal process of change and transformation, as Dōgen proposes:

> To study the buddha way is to study the self. To study the self is to forget the self. To forget the self is to be actualized by myriad things. When actualized by myriad things, your body and mind as well as the bodies and minds of others drop away.... At the moment when dharma is correctly transmitted, you are immediately your original self.
>
> (Tanahashi, 1985, p. 69)

How are these represented in psychoanalytical theoretical conceptualizations? In an early allusion to the manner in which the parent's embodied presence becomes the substrate for the toddler's future well-being, Kohut and Wolf write:

> However grave the blows may be to which the child ... is exposed, ... the proud smile of the parents will keep alive a ... nucleus of ... self-confidence and inner security.... Their ... tranquility, [transmitted] via their calm voices or via our closeness with their relaxed bodies ... will be retained by us as the nucleus of ... strength ... and ... calmness....
>
> (1978, p. 417)

Supplementing this, Knox (2009) maintains that psyche-somatic attunement is paramount in times of severe emotional distress, when the very use of "words convey[s] the separateness of one mind from another [and] ... may be unbearable" (p. 9). He suggests that, "in these situations, the analyst's ... instinctive ... *modulation of affect ... is an integral part of analytic understanding*" (ibid., pp. 9–10, my italics). Finally, in a contemporary contribution from neuro-psychology, Gallese, Eagle and Migone (2007) point to the fact that patient and therapist – mutually and unconsciously – modify each other's reactions and responses, gradually encouraging the formation of specific neural circuits within each other's brains. *Relationally this is a revolutionary proposition: the patient's 'psyche-soma' and the therapist's 'psyche-soma' interact so as to mutually constitute and configure each other, independently of the verbal contents of interaction.* Therapeutic presence and inter-being are, in and of themselves, a curative and transformational agent: interpretation is replaced by transmutation.

From an integrated psychoanalytic Zen-Buddhist approach, Alfano (2005) underscores this. She typifies these interlocking attitudinal interactions as constituting a mode of mutual, reciprocal "somato-psychic", "transcendent attunement[s] ... a fluid state of being in which there occurs a transient suspension of duality between self and other ..." (ibid., p. 225). It is this suspension that leads from the concept of empathic interpretations to enacted empathy, culminating in attunement, manifest in psyche-somatic presence and "inter-being". More radically yet: this is also the mode whereby 'meaning formation' inextricably intertwines with psyche-somatic transformation: ultimately, it is the analyst's attuned presence in its totality that constitutes what Durban (2011) – a staunch Kleinian analyst – terms "total interpretations".

## Conclusion and dialogue

In Chapters 4 and 5, I outlined disparities regarding body-mind relations that seem to be inherent within current psychoanalytical theory and practice. Briefly recapitulated in the beginning of the present chapter, the problem stands thus: "Cartesian ontology and epistemology form a dualist conception that splits off the mind from the body ..." (Reis, 1999, p. 374). Since awareness and recognition of others are restricted to cognitive appraisal and "reflection is equated with being ... to the exclusion of sensuous experience ..." (ibid.), this split determines the analyst's disposition and mindset, *inhibiting the therapist's ability to respond adequately*. Hence – in order to avoid perpetuation of pathological splits in the patient's psyche – "the doctor's own dissociations need to be considered along with the dissociations in the personalities of the patients" (as Winnicott, 1966, so poignantly reminds us): it behooves the analyst to overcome his own dissociative inclinations – as regards the psyche-soma – in order to further the patient's body-mind integration.

As contemporary psychoanalysis vies with the shadow of dualistic 'Cartesianism', intersubjective, mystical-religious, developmental and neuro-psychoanalytic approaches converge in seeking alternative paradigms. A dominant feature within these configurations is one of 'attunement', perceived as an axis of interaction and a current yardstick for both implementation and evaluation of modern psychoanalytic technique. Reliant on unitive experiences and pre-verbal modes of awareness and interaction, attunement – as perceived within these theoretical formulations – is not monopolized by verbal communication and interaction. Rather, it stresses relational aspects of non-verbal responsiveness and accommodation, dyadic 'right brain to right brain' regulation, sensual and bodily reverie, interpenetration and diffusion. Non-duality takes its place as underlying psychoanalytic endeavours which attempt "*to overcome any* dualism by proposing *a unitary picture* of the human being..." (Lombardi, 2002, p. 369). Within this framework, Buddhist theory is used as a fertile theoretical substrate for non-dualistic approaches to the body-mind question.

How does the analyst's disposition reflect, engender or enhance this purported Buddhist-informed non-dual picture? Initially I showed how mindful meditation – 'Mindfulness' – provides an aid in responsively and non-judgementally noting a multitude of psyche-somatic happenings. The impact on the analyst's attentiveness to the non-verbal realms of his own experience and that of his patients seems invaluable. Noting 'sensations', one arrives at the bed-rock of emotional life. Noting their vicissitudes, one arrives at a comprehensive picture of the body-mind substrate of mental and psyche-somatic life. Making use of this comprehensive picture is a valuable tool in transforming Freud's 'feeling-in' empathy to an attuned empathetic attitude, coordinated with another's unverbalized internal milieu, inhabited by sensations, images and emotions, along with their physiological corollaries.

I then went further, tracing the implications of Zen – a declaratively non-dualistic approach – to a psyche-somatic mode of intersubjective, immersed interaction. In this context, Buddhist philosophy forms a conceptual and practical bridgehead, a suture which overcomes seemingly inherent breaches between the mystical and the concrete, transcendental faith and sensual-sensuous reality. In harnessing Buddhist "revelatory openness" to psychoanalytic procedure, Adams (1995) demonstrates this, drawing on Bion's seminal texts. Adams suggests that Bion's plea for suspension of "memory, desire, and understanding ..." is tantamount to a "quality of awareness ..." termed "'faith' – faith that there is an ultimate reality and truth – the unknown, unknowable, 'formless infinite'" (ibid., p. 31).

Zen-Buddhism's position outlines the psyche-somatic demarcations of such a "formless infinitude" – a lived experience of an overarching infinite, interpenetrating form of inter-being. Within this conceptualization, interaction is tantamount to a mode of presencing things which does not conform to the notion of distinct selfhoods. Rather, it connotes a radical and distinct non-dual mode of relating, attained only "when the mind and object perish ..." (Bokusan, 2011, p. 51), thus leading to a selfhood wherein "everything is the contents of the 'self' and whatever we encounter is a part of ourselves" (Uchiyama, 2011, p. 183). Consequently, relational psychoanalyst and Zen teacher Magid describes Zen practice as a practice in "forgetting the self in the act of uniting with something" (2002, p. 134). Within this paradigm Leavy's (1995) notion of "unitive experiences" (see Chapter 5) and Gates's (1959) mysterious "leaps" from mind to body, from body to mind, from mind to mind, and from body to body (see Chapter 3) coincide.

According to Bokusan's (2011) commentary, Dōgen arrived at these intuitions by "open[ing] up his body and mind" (p. 12), utilizing Buddhist practices. In the present chapter I showed how a host of Buddhist-inclined psychotherapists and psychoanalysts demonstrate these practices to generate and reflect a revised approach to "evenly hovering attention", evincing a mode of intuitive intimacy with one's own psyche-soma and the intuitive linkage between two psyche-somatic subjects. Conversely, conventional "evenly hovering", "discrimination-by-thinking-attention" ultimately causes 'mind' and 'body', 'subject' and 'object' to be perceived as discrete phenomena, causing a level of intra and inter-personal alienation, and consequently, an "unheimliche" feeling, an estrangement between self and environment.

An epithetical saying claims that "Zen person is Zen action". Zen-Buddhism maintains that body-mind integration applies, by and large, to "expressing the Buddha mudra [form] in the three *activities* [body, speech, and thought]" (Tanahashi, 2010, p. 5, my italics): in Zen practice, having "shed-off body and mind", one's 'body-mind-speech' is attuned to those of others. Actions performed within this mode stem from a trans-subjective, non-dual perception of self and other so that "my body-mind, and the body mind of the other person is a single, complex entity. ... I and the ... [other person] ... are ... responding to each other's movements in a completely spontaneous and non-reflective manner", commensurate with an attuned-spontaneous response "to the compassionate intuition of another's suffering" (Kasulis, 1989, p. 91): if "Zen action is Zen person", then, *rather than precluding meaningful-empathetic intervention, enactment enriches it*: It is my hope and conviction that patients such as Sue, described in this chapter, often respond to spontaneous attunements as manifestations of empathic resonance with their unconscious psyche-somatic states.

Consequently, the configurations presented in the present chapter offer a direct response to queries as to the feasibility of a non-Cartesian interpersonal psychotherapeutic endeavour; similarly, they address the queries raised in Chapters 3–5 as to the concrete determination of one 'body-mind' by an-other. The interpersonal world promoted by Zen-psychoanalytic dialogue is constituted via direct and spontaneous attunement, commensurate with the triune presence of potential merger, interpenetration and unitive experience. In Nagatomo's (1992) evocative language, this is accompanied by an empathic presence-attunement, a "lived feeling within ... [the] ... body-image that reveals that [the] internal world envelops and extends to the entire ... world of ... things, with the intrinsic qualities of this lived feeling fulfilling the gap between them" (p. 149). Within this radical conceptual trajectory, the body-mind is not only observed and sensed by another's body-mind in a heightened form of sensual-affective reverie: through enhanced 'presence' and compassionate 'attunement', it is also reciprocally constituted and co-determined by the 'body-minds' of others.

A significant lineage within psychoanalysis has long recognized that "what ... [is] said [is] often less important than [the] body-mind state of being in ... sessions" (Milner, 1969, p. 43). In a specific and direct allusion to the contribution of 'being' and 'attunement' to the empathic disposition in psychoanalysis, Kakar suggests that:

> a significant enhancement of the ... empathic capacity through meditative practices, and its communication to the patient/seeker through other channels besides the verbal one, can make an important contribution to the discussion on the role of empathy in psychoanalytic discourse and ... to a place for meditative practices in psychoanalytic education.
>
> (2003, p. 659)

In this chapter I have sought to further this line of thinking via Adams's (1995), Rubin's (1996, 2009) and, Twemlow's (2001) recommendations regarding psychoanalytical training incorporating particular modes of attention, reverie and attunement. Adams, Rubin, Twemlow and Kakar are among the psychoanalysts who delineate the guidelines for their acquisition: a progression from the conscious cultivation of a heightened sense of perceptual awareness, to its psyche-somatic suffusion, leading to a broadening of attentive capacities. Its culmination is in an "unselfconscious" mode of awareness, leading to a non-dualistic perception of body-mind selfhood which is concomitant with empathic presence and attunement, is born of an ethical stance, and becomes manifest in attuned verbal, procedural or 'enacted' action-interpretation.

## Notes

1 Shunryū Suzuki translates this as "freedom of body and mind": the acquisition of an experiential state devoid of differentiated categories of 'body' versus 'mind' engenders a sense of freedom emerging from within the non-dual perception of body and mind (see Suzuki, 2011, p. 106).
2 The original German term for empathy, employed by Freud, is "Einfühlung", literally meaning "feeling-in".

Chapter 10

# From duality to oneness
Zen contributions to psyche-soma meta-theory in contemporary psychoanalysis

## Point of departure

Reclining on the psychoanalytic sofa I wait for myself – the patient – to begin the session, vaguely recognizing the paradox inherent in realizing I am waiting for myself. I am aware of my bodily contours against the sofa, aware of the sofa's support, deeply aware of the beckoning to let go, both mentally and physically, allowing myself to surrender. I am reminded of the time, some 25 years ago, when I heard Yael Ofarim – a staunch Freudian analyst in Jerusalem's Psychoanalytic Institute – describing her first experience of a Zen shiatsu session: "If anything, it resembled a good psychoanalytic session," she had said.

At the time I was puzzled by her remark: psychoanalysis had then seemed to be so much at odds with anything tactile, sensual, manual. After all, Freud (1904) devised his technique most particularly so as to avoid any physical exertion, any physical sensation, anything purely of the soma. Little did he think of autistic-contiguity, of vitality, of holding and support, or of the need – seen to by mother-earth – to provide a substitute for the mother's support of the individual on his life's path.

Lying back, I feel myself supported, surrounded by an infinite space. It is neither a mental nor a physical sensation and yet it is both. Dōgen says:

> What is inseparable from mind is not limited to one, two ... realms.... It is conceived by consciousness, and yet it is not conceived by [discriminating] consciousness.... It is mountains, rivers, and the great earth. Mind is skin, flesh, bones, and marrow.
> (Tanahashi, 2010, Sangai Yuishin fascicle, p. 490)

On the sofa I perceive, ultimately "not two" or "as one".

In Chapter 1, I suggested that "the sensation of two as one-ness" is tantamount to vitality itself since "when you feel oneness, there is life" (Masunaga, 1976, p. 50). Stemming from this stipulation, this book is about the fusion of horizons, an interweaving leading to a 'bodymind' proposition: within it 'body' does not *pre*-cede 'mind' in human development; primitive positions do not exist as distinct categories divorced from mind-consciousness, from reference, from reflection, from sophistication. Bodymind formulates itself in vitality since body and mind inhabit the same time; they coexist, coincide, fuse, interpenetrate. Gadamer teaches us that the process of understanding "always involves rising to a higher universality that overcomes not only our own particularity, but also that of the other" (1991, p. 305). So, yes – as Gadamer says – we must rise high to perceive all this. Then we must sink low to embody what we have seen. Finally – I propose – we may centre and – moulting body and mind – find body-mind-as-one through our body-mind-as-one.

The point of departure for this flight of ideas is the long-standing conceptual lacunae pertaining to mind-body relations in psychoanalysis: an intra-psychic one, the notorious "leap from the mind to the body" and an inter-psychic one – the means by which the analysand's body-mind is affected by the analyst's, transduced via the "talking cure". Freud's seemingly parsimonious explanatory model simply failed to coherently account for the clinical reality of this dual unitive experience; contemporary theories have not fared much better in reaching an accord as to psychoanalytic meta-theory.

This ineptitude is nourished and supported by long-standing cultural and philosophical heritages, within which dualism has seemed to be indubitably intrinsic: even monism itself is defined by an "either-or" ("bodily" or "spirit-psyche") determination. This has suffused and invaded our clinical thinking. In the clinic it remains unclear: are the psychoanalytic 'body' and 'mind' presentation or metaphor, biology or hermeneutics, causative apparatuses or models of meaning formation? Since a canonical meta-theory has not emerged, divergent theories have been inconclusive, leading to divisive vocabulary and an unclear methodology. Currently the predominant view is that the 'mind-body question' remains 'the hard question' since "traditional dualistic and monistic resolutions ... [are] ... insufficient" (Meissner, 2009, p. 369).

## The basic premise

Theory construction always occurs in some intellectual community, which involves conceptual, factual, ideological and ontological worldviews, affecting epistemological presuppositions and methodological procedures. As evidence accumulates, presuppositions are reviewed and new findings are accommodated within preexisting structures until these structures no longer serve their original purpose. This leads, often unexpectedly, to what Kuhn (2012) has termed "a paradigm shift". In sync with this, positivistic presuppositions in psychoanalysis have – over the years – been complemented and at times substituted by post-modern influences on psychoanalytic thinking.

Investigating post-modern contributions to psychoanalytic theory-formation, Chessick (1995) cites Foucault to suggest that in "cultural postmodernity … non-discursive language … transgress[es] … into the space of discourse" (p. 397). From a cultural studies sociological perspective, Lash (1990) underscores this, suggesting that one of the defining features of postmodern thinking is non-discursive corporeal involvement. These contentions dovetail with phenomenological convictions: revising Cartesian philosophy, phenomenologically oriented theories concur as to the growing import of the body and of somatic experience as a formative and forceful vector in the formation and elucidation of being, of selfhood and of subjectivity. They consequently seek to integrate the body into meaning formation structures. In stressing experience in lieu of discursive logic, phenomenology has been paramount in generating "a new ordering structure" which delineates a new hierarchy between the sensuous and the non-sensuous. Within this new ordering structure, there is no a priori distinction between the seemingly apodictive categories of mind and body. Rather, for a phenomenologist, unified psyche-somatic manifestations are seen as being "neither psychical nor somatic" (Boss, 1979, p. 21).

The phenomenological turn towards the concreteness of subjective experience was synchronically matched by a cultural turn upholding the ineluctable importance of the body as a fulcrum of participatory and performative "being" in the world (Csordas, 1994). Within this cultural strain, corporality as a definitive component in the philosophy of psychology is reflected in Merleau-Ponty's phenomenological psychology of perception. Merleau-Ponty's psychology is based on physical and perceptual involvement as a direct – rather than subsidiary or secondary – modus of meaning creation. Merleau-Ponty's pioneering project consequently provides a fertile ground for theoretical innovation, impacting upon seemingly inveterate presuppositions of 'psyche' and 'soma' predication within the psychoanalytic endeavour. Assuming both corporeal involvement and non-discursive communication, it challenges the defining pillar of the psychoanalytic project as a positivistic study of the 'unconscious as object' by 'analyst-subject' via the use of verbal communication – a "talking cure". Rather, it embraces notions pertaining to multifaceted "leaps from mind to body, from body to mind, from mind to mind, and from body to body" (Gates, 1959, p. 15).

## A unitary turn

With the growing emphasis on the patient's involved 'psyche-somatic' experience – rather than on his 'thoughts-ideas' – the Cartesian paradigm has been, by and large, replaced by phenomenological ones. Due to the forceful sway of the psychoanalytic phenomenological project initiated by Atwood and Stolorow (1984), the espousal of phenomenology by Relational psychoanalysis, self-psychology, and – to a large extent – Object Relations theory – has engendered novel categorizations. Eschewing positivistic 'subject' to 'object' predications, phenomenological propositions entailed the dual pathway of hypothesizing the substantial existence of a 'psyche-soma' or even a 'psychesoma', and its multifaceted interactions with other 'psychesomas'. As a corollary of this, the sphere of 'subjectivity' and 'intersubjectivity' expanded so as to include the somatic sphere.

The forceful sway of this dual intra/inter-psychic 'unitary turn' is saliently represented in three distinct – yet complementary – psychoanalytic strains: intersubjectivity (with Relational and self-psychology offshoots), neuro-psychoanalytic and mystical-religious. The psychoanalytic rigour of intersubjectivity is supported by the scientific rigour of neuro-science; both are supplemented by the forceful debut of spirituality into psychoanalysis and its espousal of unitive experiences. All three maintain reciprocal conceptual dialogue with Developmental and Object Relations theorizing. With the advent of supportive conceptualizations of the psyche as a multi-track coding experiential system maintaining 'complex' 'connectionist' and 'systems' relations between its somatic and mental constituents, the 'unitary turn' was all but declared.

## The reformation of language and categories

From a philosophy of language perspective, Johnson (1993) suggests that "mind body dualism is ... deeply embedded in our philosophical and religious traditions, in our shared conceptual systems and in our language..." (p. 2). These reflect Cartesian–Platonic presuppositions, which defer body to psyche in a way that maintains their discrete existence, delineating the developmental and hierarchical progression from body to mind, from soma to psyche, from unmodulated affect to cortical self-regulation. Thus psychoanalysis's deeply ingrained recalcitrant dualism is inextricable from the language and cultural prejudices in which it is embedded: in an inevitable conceptual "loop", language is constitutive of meaning, which is then disseminated by our everyday use of language so as to construe the "metaphors we live by" – the title of Lakoff and Johnson's famous (1980) book. One such metaphor is that "higher is better", reflecting assumptions pertaining to body topology (head higher than heart and belly-centre), neuro-psychology – equating brain and psyche – and cultural convention. Post-modern philosophy has shown these metaphorical fulcrums to be derived from knowledge-power discursive relations. Thus, if we aspire to amend these prejudices, we must also reform the language used to formulate and explicate it, welcoming novel, overarching, more 'unitary' categorizations.

The tacit reformation of body-mind non-dualistic terminologies becomes obvious when we investigate the blurring of dividing lines between categories of bodily and the mental faculties. Formerly considered monopolies of the 'mind', mental attributes such as memory and awareness have been supplemented by body memory, and body awareness. Concurrently, a full panoply of nomenclature denoting overarching categories, such as 'rhythmicity', 'aliveness', 'vitality' and 'intensity' has entered psychoanalysis. Pointedly, these terms do not adhere to the conservative exclusivity of 'mind' to 'body' predication but, rather, form overarching terms that incorporate – and thus straddle – both. What appeared to Freud to be the definitive aspect of psychoanalysis – "the presence of the body in language" (Gliserman, 1996, p. 1), has now become the presence of compound 'psyche-somatic' categories in language, accompanied by a matching amendment in the language of psychoanalysis itself.

A similar progression pertains to analyst-analysand relations. Concepts such as 'harmonious interpenetrating mix-up' (Balint, 1968/1979) represent compound 'psyche-soma' to 'psyche-soma' relationships between therapist and patient. Representing a "revolt against Cartesianism" (Eigen, 1983 p. 420), "terms such as union, permeability ... interweaving, and the like" (ibid.) denote a benignity of primary fusion. Together they reflect a revision of subject–object relations (in both their philosophical and psychoanalytic denotations) in regard to the evaluative-developmental sphere and, accordingly, impact on clinical procedure. In intra-psychic terms, this reflects a view of "mind ... [as] an emergent property of ... interaction in relation to sensory and motor processes..." (Meissner, 2003a, p. 293). In Relational terms, Lewis Aron (1998) describes analyst and patient interactions in which "each gets under the other's skin, ... is breathed in and absorbed by the other" (pp. 25–26).

## *The Zen of unitive experience and unitary paradigms*

In 1903, while lecturing at Harvard University, William James beckoned a Buddhist monk sitting in the audience saying, "Take my chair ... you are better equipped to lecture on psychology than I" (Bricklin, 2015, p. 5). James – inadvertently – anticipated the fact that Buddhism may provide an alternative conceptual framework for psychology so as to accommodate paradigm shifts and create new, integrated parsimonious meta-theoretical structures. Leaning on almost a century of psychoanalytic-Buddhist dialogue, I suggest Zen-Buddhism may provide psychoanalysis with an overarching conceptual body-mind infrastructure with ontological, epistemological, phenomenological and even clinical ramifications. These – I suggest – may aid psychoanalysis in generating the missing links towards the formulation of a unitary, non-dualistic, psyche-soma meta-theory.

## *Venturing forth*

David Loy's (1998) project of establishing non-duality as an axis for comparative philosophy demarcates three characteristics pertaining to non-duality: (1) the negation of dualistic thinking; (2) the non-plurality of the world; and (3) the non-difference of subject and object. The full-fledged revision of categories required for a coherent paradigm shift in psychoanalysis is greatly aided by this comparative and provocative extra-cultural input, since "in Eastern paradigms ... dualism has ... been shown to be nonexistent ... [and] ... the body mind fissure rarely arises (Shaner, 1985a, p. 188). Consequently, I used it as a point of departure for Part II.

Initially construed specifically as a response to Western society's spiritual crisis, the prolific infiltration of Eastern concepts into psychoanalysis increasingly influences the study of the mind, consciousness and psyche-soma relations. Specifically, I propose that the *"differences in the basic premises of thought and in the very methods of thinking"* (Watts, 1957, p. 24, my italics), are particularly pertinent to the field of mind-body relations. Buddhist propositions fundamentally counter the Western Platonic and Cartesian presuppositions as to what 'mind' is, what 'body' is and what, accordingly, comprises 'body-mind': what is considered 'the hard question' of Western philosophy is thus dealt with in much milder terms in Eastern paradigms.

On these grounds, even Western phenomenology is taken to task. Zen-Buddhism argues that the Husserlian-Heideggerian underpinnings on which Western phenomenology stands retain a basic Cartesian opposition in espousing "a world view worked out by the intellect that ... exercise[s] its function only when there is a distinction made between ego and alter" (Izutsu, 1977, p. 19). Similarly, Kuang-Ming (1997) takes Merleau-Ponty's 'phenomenology of the flesh' to task, contending that in Merleau-Ponty's philosophy, the body is reduced to the role of a signifier, a stratum for a "systematic (logical), external point of view" (p. 319). Finally, Nagatomo (1992) and Kuang-Ming (1997) both point to the fact that Western phenomenology relies on perception rather than on the capacity to somatically, introceptively, intimately and intuitively relate and attune to reality.

## The Zen of 'body-mind'

Izutsu (1977) suggests that, from a comparative philosophy perspective, Zen is unique in generating an "ability to look at things not in terms of a culturally preconditioned pattern ... [or] ... preconditioned categories of cognition, but in terms of limitless ontological possibilities..." (p. 142). How so? In the present work I have drawn attention to four features within Zen-Buddhist formulations potentially furthering the constitution of a non-dualistic body-mind meta-theoretical paradigm:

1 Potentiality of existence as a predicate which precedes substantial manifestation.
2 Constant change as a substantial position.
3 Recognition of the inevitable limitations and constraints on language and discursive logic as means of elucidating reality.
4 The meditative state as enabling a presence within, and a non-judgemental recognition of, a non-dualistic psyche-somatic state.

## *Potentiality and 'pre' prefixes*

Cartesian theory is based on the premise that matter and spirit stand as discrete categories standing in paradoxical opposition to the obvious psyche-soma interaction. From an Eastern philosophical perspective, Li (1999) offers a resolution to this paradox, suggesting that Western philosophies' bane is the axiomatic assumption that, having transformed, a substance loses its original characteristics and becomes another. Kasulis (1989) tackles the same question by demonstrating the Daoist and Zen-Buddhist interplay between 'potentiality' and coming into 'being' as a temporal synchronicity. In this context, 'existence' connotes a perpetual potentiality, fundamentally empty of any essential defining characteristic. I demonstrated this through Nāgārjuna's notion of "emptiness": Within this construal, things may *conventionally* be defined as either of the body or of the mind, while still adhering to an emptiness of essential nature. Another example is the Zen rendition of the term '*garbha*' (Skt.), within which potentiality and manifestation are interchangeably designated by the same word as both "womb" and "germination". Kulka's Buddhist-inspired psychoanalytic notions of complementarity as an oscillation between body-mind states of consciousness – indifferent to whether these manifest somatically or mentally – are in sync with this.

In the Pali Canon, the Buddha makes a profound and compound epistemological-ontological claim: "I declare that in this very fathom-long carcass, ... lies the world, ... the cause of the world, ... the cessation of the world and course of action that leads to the cessation of the world" (Rhys, 1993, p. 86). Dōgen's notions follow on from this, refuting the conventional equation of subjectivity with mental attributes such as cognition. His epistemology is an experiential 'psyche-somatic' undertaking rather than a removed intellectual one. Consequently Dōgen's soteriological-philosophical project consistently maintains that it is via the body-mind that the 'way' is studied, and the 'way' thus studied is the potential for the formation of the body mind. This is further indicated by the concept of a 'without thinking' potentiality of body-mind consciousness, responsive to and "authenticated" by the "myriad things".

Nagatomo (1992) takes this idea to an extreme: in his rendition of Dōgen's teachings "studying the way with one's body ... the body comes from studying the way ... [and] becomes the true human body" (p. 166). Dōgen does not of course literally mean that the physical body is metaphysically constituted. Rather, Dōgen upholds the conviction of 'practice-realization', the indivisibility of intellectual and spiritual realization and the performative physio-mental posture conducive to its acquisition. The positing of a composite-fluctuating-indivisible psyche-soma unit corresponds to psychoanalytic concepts of potentiality such as an underlying "idiom", the phenomenology of "unformulated" experience and, even more generally, to 'pre' and 'proto' prefixes.

## Constant change and body-mind systems

Traditional Buddhism stipulates an interdependent relationship between body and mind that refutes their seemingly discrete nature and categorization. The model of the 'aggregates' – especially – stresses the fact that, when carefully monitored, every experience is an essentially 'psyche-somatic' event. This is further accentuated by the fact that, using the notion of 'dependent origination'/'co-arising', the flow of experience is intrinsically a body-mind one, noted-experienced by an indivisible body-mind system. Experience thus perceived is recast as an ongoing, ceaseless series of psyche-somatic 'events'; ontology of 'self' thus perceived is inextricable from body-mind phenomena. The 'mind' thus perceived is a mental-physical apparatus, interdependently 'co-arising' with its surroundings. Adhering to the concept of a psyche-somatic 'being' which is a constant experiential stream, the individual self is seen as comprising an incessant stream of "mental elements and ... physical ones as well ... as far as they constitute the experience of a given personality" (Stcherbatsky, 1923, p. 26).

From within a radically non-dualist paradigm, Dōgen redefines the constantly and intrinsically fluctuating relations between mental-physical selfhood and world as constituting 'being-time'. This is the constant *and synchronous* intrinsically inseparable arising of a co-joint body-mind consciousness seeking its object and objects seeking their subjects: "Mind is the moment of actualizing the fundamental point" (1985, p. 82), which is accomplished through "fully engaging body and mind ..." (ibid., p. 70). The fullness of the body-mind experience is radically hinged on the concept of emptiness-potentiality of both experience and conceptualization. This Dōgen describes as a state wherein "body and mind ... drop away" (ibid.). Within this scheme, the ontology, epistemology and phenomenology of body-mind are immanently intertwined.

In her study, "Tibetan 'wind' and 'wind' illnesses: A multicultural approach to health and illness", Yoeli-Tlalim (2010) investigates the relationship between Buddhist practices and their attendant medical systems. She asserts that in therapeutic projects based on Buddhist teachings, the "method of investigation, in this case meditation, leads to the nature of knowledge attained ... [and that] the method is also intertwined with the goal" (ibid., p. 321): the perspective of flux-change acquired via meditation is indivisible from the knowledge attained – i.e. that there is constant flux – which is again indivisible from the therapeutic goal of the practice – embracing change through 'non-attachment'. From within a kindred perspective, psychoanalyst and Zen-Buddhist practitioner, Barry Magid (2002) notes that seeing a symptom as "*either* biological or psychological in nature" (p. 135, my italics) is a culturally laden assumption. Ultimately, he summarizes, "we have to recognize that we are dealing with ... constantly changing complex systems (i.e. displaying dependent co-origination)..." (ibid.).

Nowhere is the interchangeability of body and mind – both conceptually and substantially – so pronounced as when defining the dynamics of 'aliveness' or 'energy' within Buddhist-derived medical systems. In Daoist and Zen-Buddhist-based therapeutic systems, "body and mind [are] not seen as a mechanism (however complex) but as a vortex of energy and vital substances interacting ... to form an organism" (Maciocia, 1989, p. 35). This is essentially a 'systems'-'connectionist' physiomental paradigm. Key to this notion is the concept of 'qi'. In Occidental terms, qi constitutes the equivalent of both the material and the immaterial foundation of body-mind vitality that "broadens to ... embrace properties which we would call psychic, emotional, spiritual ... mystical; ... sentiment, and attitudes ... moods and tastes ..." (Lidin, 2006, p. 21). From a cross-cultural and comparative philosophy perspective the concept of 'qi' is unique inasmuch as it has no equivalent in traditional philosophy. Emphasizing its culturally indigenous nature, Kuang-Ming (1997) maintains that "such ... thinking reflects the ... contrastive flow of contraries ... ready to turn themselves one into the other" (p. 157).

Since it is neither material nor metaphysical, neither fully a concept nor an entity in the ordinary sense of the word, 'qi' does not conform to the triune dichotomies of essentialist philosophy: body-mind, sign-signifier, subjective-objective. Rather, it represents both constant change and persistent potentiality, the spirit of embodied presence and the embodied spiritual aspects of selfhood. Clinically, I tend to think of it as given to an "inter-objective" observation: two clinicians assessing a patient's 'qi' will concur as to the level of vitality and energetic-sensual-perceptive-mental properties of their patient which are determined by 'qi'; which are 'qi'; they will say things such as "his qi is tight", or "his qi is slippery". Yet their objective accord is totally determined by their subjective assessment of it. Thus, the diagnostics of 'qi' validate psycho-analytic postulations of overarching categorizations – such as 'vitality', 'patterning', etc. straddling body and mind – determined within the embodied intersubjective relationship. Within it "brain and body, self and other, nervous system and environment ... riff ... off each other as jazz musicians do" (Carrol, 2014, p. 12).

## The body-mind vocabulary of unitary articulation and unitive experiences

Contemporary psychoanalysis progressively recognizes the 'psyche-soma' experience as a conceptual reality, hesitantly generating the vocabulary required for its incorporation. In this context I referred to two distinct but connected issues: 'unitive experience' and 'unitary formulations'. The former denotes an experiential 'psyche-somatic' modus; the latter denotes descriptive categories defining the 'psyche-soma' entity. Together they reflect an attempt to create a congruous relationship between psychoanalytic procedure and theory and the growing recognition that the psychoanalytic dyad – as so many of the clinical vignettes in the book demonstrate – comprises two 'psyche-somatic' entities interacting with each other.

From a Marxist-linguistic vantage point, Voloshinov (1986) suggests that we can gain a perspective on our own language only through linguistically inhabiting another; from a cultural-studies point of view, Shaner

(1985a) maintains that conceptual and terminological innovation is aided by stepping outside the precincts of a given culture. Implicitly embracing Rorty's contention that philosophical problems may be solved by reformulating language, Shaner (1985a) suggests the accommodation and integration of a non-dualistic body-mind model require "devising a new rationale, rules of logic, definitions, etc." (p. 26). From a psychoanalytic-Zen dialogical perspective, Suler (1995) subscribes to a similar notion, stipulating that "language is tightly woven into the cognitive-affective schemata of self structure which shapes, perhaps inaccurately, our experience of the self" (p. 411).

Buddhist ideas as to the place of discursive thinking and language stem from notions of inter-dependence and thus of radical contextuality. Since "each and every word requires other words, ... without which it will possess neither meaning nor existence ..." (Raz, 2007, p. 21), words do not stand as discrete categorizations of discrete entities. Consequently the "Buddha's language" is a language of 'becoming' and of continuous procedural inter-connection, and maintains an inter-dependence with factual and practical aspects of daily life. The signifying function of words is thus provisional, constantly fluctuating according to context, relational matrices and praxis.

Zen culture provides an infrastructure for the promotion of embodied cognizance furthered by body-mind 'cultivation' (Jap.: *shugyō*), and for embodied interaction, enhancing attunement and interactive regulatory patterns. Emerging from within these practices, novel modes of perception and communication arise. In sync with contemporary psychological research pointing to the fact that "living beings ... actively generate and maintain their ... psychological identities ... enact[ing] their cognitive domains through their activities" (Schmalzl, Crane-Godreau & Payne, 2014, p. 2), these procedures structure and direct communication on a cross-modal spectrum. This is confirmed by contemporary psychoanalytic reappraisal of embodied selfhoods and mutual intersubjective configuration: the resultant mode of interaction is described as "a state of enhanced connectivity referred to as 'resonance'" (ibid., p. 6).

Unitary categorizations are generated by clinical experience pointing to unitive 'psyche-somatic' reciprocal experience. Inasmuch as unitive experiences require a corollary 'unitary' nomenclature in contemporary psychoanalysis, they tend to generate idiosyncratic linguistic innovations: concepts, such as "at one-ment" (Bion, 1970), or "inter-corporeality"

(Lombardi, 2009). A hermeneutic circle ensues wherein unitive experiences further a paradigm shift, necessitating unitary categorizations in order to clarify and conceptualize unitive experiences within the psychoanalytic encounter. Zen vocabulary shows promise in supplementing psychoanalytical unitary formulations and presenting a more cohesive and parsimonious nomenclature. After all, it has confronted the challenge of generating a non-dualistic vocabulary for almost two millennia.

Zen teachings have a long history of contending with the conundrum of using cogitations to define a 'non-thinking' reflection, thus using words in the instruction of the ineffable. Emerging from the notion of radical inseparability between 'self' and 'world' and, consequently, 'self' and 'other', one of Zen's original contributions is a reformulation of what comprises communication and what communication entails. Hence Zen distinguishes between "dead" and "live" words. Heine (1994) defines "living words" as "apropos of the moment ... ideally suited to an encounter ... because they reflect interpenetration ... and ... inseparability of subjectivity and objectivity" (p. 201). This is opposed to "dead words" which "fall back on predictably and ineffectively logical responses to dynamic, translogical inquiries" (ibid.).

Within this context Dōgen's unique approach to non-duality is a radical yet comprehensive attempt at integrating unitive experience, enacted communication and unitary formulations. Dōgen considers the relation between language and reality as totally dependent on an internal cognitive-emotional "realist-mystical" disposition. On top of this, Dōgen's stress is radically on the performative-actional aspects of expression, and is thus *indifferent as to whether this expression is conveyed verbally or otherwise*. He thus waives the conventional opposition of language and action, verbal and performative expression. Whereas – from within psychoanalytic theory – Leavy (1995) maintains that "language is intrinsically divisive of experience" (p. 355), Dōgen proposes that unitary categories may define unitive experience and reality, provided that they are derived from "body-mind oneness" and are based on the "indivisibility of practice and realization". He thus diverges from the conventional "discursive/verbal" to "enacted" opposition. Instead, he proposes that both verbal and embodied expressive articulations be evaluated along an axis pertaining to the internal-performative state of their issue. Contemporary Zen-Buddhist teacher Shunryū Suzuki (2011) describes this state thus: "To stop the mind ... means your mind pervades your ... body" (p. 25).

As the posture of body within this performative state is perfected, "psyche-somatic" form is transformed into a specific communication. Within *this* framework, 'representation' and 'presentation' are indivisible, since communication – language and silence included – does not stand apart from reality and experience. This framework, in turn, engenders a comprehensive and parsimonious body-mind vocabulary, supporting unitary 'psyche-somatic' nomenclature which broadens the scope, viability and the validity of unitive categories.

## The meditative state as a non-dualistic psyche-somatic state

Within contemporary psychoanalysis it is clear that "the mind-set of the analyst ... regarding the integration of mind-body ... can dictate decisions for therapeutic intervention and management" (Meissner, 2007, p. 333). Verbal interventions are inevitably mediated by the analyst's – conscious or unconscious – mindset as to 'mind' and 'body' relations. Accordingly – as Winnicott (1966) teaches – "The doctor's own dissociations need to be considered along with the dissociations in the personalities of the patients" (p. 510). This, teaches relational analyst Knoblauch (1999), is accomplished through attention to "volume, tone, rhythm, tempo, gestural patterning, and muscular shifts of the face or other body regions" (p. 43); not an easy feat since these "require ... a level of observational attention atypical of daily discourse" (ibid.).

Enhancing attention to each and every facet of experience, Buddhist "observational attention" – meditation – focuses on the complementary aspects of 'concentration', and 'mindfulness'. Their integration "fosters heightened attentiveness ... training one's capacity to notice ordinarily obscure phenomena – ranging from fleeting somatic sensations to subliminal thoughts, feelings and fantasies..." (Rubin, 2009, p. 95). However, enhanced attention, notation and a richer spectrum of categorization alone do not suffice to engender and sustain 'unitive experience' and attendant unitary conceptualizations. Accordingly, psychoanalyst and Zen teacher Twemlow (2001) suggests that non-dualistic "observational attention" may be highly enhanced specifically by Zen-Buddhist meditative mindsets, embracing 'emptiness', 'impermanence' and 'paradox'.

Twemlow's position as regards a joint body-mind perceptual field is in sync with Dōgen's. Dōgen's philosophy points to the fact that, in the meditative posture, a distinct 'psyche-somatic' state is implicated. Within this disposition, the all-inclusive experience of 'bodymind as one' is paramount; within this experiential mode, linguistic, conceptual and perceptual categories are essentially inseparable from experience, both moulding it and adding a symbolical surplus to it. Rather than either enhancing or obscuring meaning-construction and significance, well-founded practice – within a 'body-mind cast off' mode – is conceived of as a means of attaining direct insight. In meditative praxis, precise instructions as to bodily form are a prerequisite for 'studying the way', and, in studying the way one experiences "dharma with ... complete mind, complete body, and complete way ..." (Mujō Seppō fascicle, Tanahashi, 2010, p. 553). Thus, Dōgen preaches a distinctive mode of being in which the 'empirical-experiential' and the 'subjective' converge in 'undivided activity' (Jap.: *Zenki*), tantamount to the – seemingly – paradoxical claim that meditation *is* thinking.

Uchiyama (2011) maintains that this conveys the radical import of Dōgen's message. Adding a surplus to Buddhist 'concentration' and 'mindfulness' practice, it circumvents the temporal and spatial lapse between 'thought' and 'object' entailed in purely discursive thinking and cognitive 'notation'. Rather – Uchiyama proposes – Dōgen preaches the indivisibility of the category of "life" itself. Temporally and spatially undivided, communion with life and sentient beings takes place in an unmediated interpenetrative manner, articulated and articulating, conveying and being conveyed by all life-expressions. It is in this particular dispositional body-mind-set mode, welding unitive experience and its unitary conceptualization, that Dōgen's project reaches its highest distillation, enhancing psychoanalytic concepts such as 'empathy', 'regulation', 'attunement', 'attention', 'reverie' and 'resonance'.

## Conclusion and future directions

The mysterious connection between the human mind and the human body was revealed to Freud through his studies of hypnosis. The fact that mental induction is instrumental to creating and alleviating physical symptoms was also clear. What remained unclear was the mode via which this transition was possible: neither monistic nor dualistic theorems or models fully accounted for this "leap". However, traversing the leap, ridding itself of it, has become crucial to psychoanalytic integrity: one of the hallmarks of contemporary psychoanalysis's evolutionary progression is the contention of inseparability of mind and its environs. One of the implications of this notion is the inseparability of one 'psyche-somatic' array from the other, the reciprocal manner in which a multitude of "leaps" take place, not only between 'body' and 'mind' but between two 'psyche-somas'. It is inconceivable to think of psychoanalysis without it. It has not been – as yet – fully conceived with it: the leap has beleaguered psychoanalysis since Freud's times; the leap was the trigger for writing this book.

In this book, I propose that contemporary psychoanalysis has embraced a dual inter/intra-psychic 'new ordering system'. This dual inter/intra-psychic 'new ordering system' revises entrenched views as to the relative role of body and mind as categorically, developmentally and hierarchically distinct. As *Zeitgeist*, presuppositions and prejudices change, novel – at times idiosyncratic – terminology was created to accommodate them. I suggest that the wedding of a new ordering system and its concomitant terminological revision constitutes a paradigm shift. I have termed this paradigm shift the 'unitary turn'. The 'unitary turn' – I have shown – enables us, finally, to comprehensively re-evaluate Freud's initial intuition as to the inseparability of mental state and the soma. This re-evaluation, however, requires its own terminology and often proves futile without an appropriate philosophical substrate. This, I have shown, may be adopted from Eastern philosophies which have infiltrated psychoanalytic thinking along two distinct pathways: as part of the counter-culture and post-modern *Zeitgeist* and as an integral part of the interdisciplinary psychoanalytic-Buddhist dialogue. In this dialogue, Freud's initial intuition as to the inseparability of mental state and the soma was re-evaluated, reconfirmed and recast within a new paradigmatic conceptual mould.

These initial conclusions define the course for future research as regards the hypotheses of radical intra- and inter-psychic 'psyche-soma' non-duality, unitive experiences and unitary terminology.

1   Sheets-Johnstone (2002), Alfano, (2005), Ogden, (2008), Rick (2013) and other authors have mentioned the therapist's corporeality as a matrix for deep analytic work. In urging the therapist to pay consistent attention to the body, these authors point to the use of the body as a register of the analysand's mental state, thus emphasizing the

'doubly-dual' reciprocal resonance of 'mind' to 'body' and 'psyche-soma' to 'psyche-soma'. The implication is that supplementing 'freely hovering attention' and 'reverie' with close notation of somatic processes is crucial to ameliorating the analyst's all-but-inevitable dissociations in regard to psyche-somatic integration. The implementation of a meditative-introspective study of consciousness is an obvious extension of this. Forming the basis of all Buddhist contemplative disciplines, the potential theoretical and clinical integration of a contemplative study of the 'psyche-soma' and its attendant relational matrices in psychoanalysis seems fertile ground for future research.

2   Directly following on from this is the question of appropriate training. Currently, as this book shows, psychoanalysis and Buddhist studies constitute two discrete conceptual and methodological domains, each maintaining its own distinct disciplines, praxis and training formats. Thus, while dialogue has been long, rife and fruitful, it remains to be seen if specific Buddhist practices and terminologies – affecting mindsets, dispositions and attendant interventions – can be usefully integrated into the emerging field of non-dualistic formulations in psychoanalysis within psychoanalytic training institutes. Fromm (2000), and more specifically Twemlow (2001) Rubin, (2009) "and the visionary proposal of psychoanalytic-Buddhist training" (Gabrieli-Rehavi, Green & Kulka, 2014) have pointed out the potential. However, they have not yet applied this potential directly to the emerging study of 'psyche-somatic' non-duality in psychoanalysis. Future research is required to determine the effect of specific-focused training methods derived from Buddhist and Zen models on training outcomes as pertains to issues such as embodied capacities, psyche-somatic integration, etc.

3   Emerging from the psychoanalytic-Buddhist dialogue, Buddhist, Zen and Daoist terms have seeped into psychoanalysis (Eigen, 1995). This seems to reflect the fact that, while non-dualistic formulations have implicitly and explicitly infiltrated psychoanalysis, indigenous non-dualistic *terminology* is still lacking. Especially, psychoanalysis lacks a concept such as 'qi', which straddles psyche and soma in a congruous way, forming the infrastructure for an integrative psyche-soma theory. Attempts such as Stern's *Forms of Vitality*, representing the inseparability of "movement, time, force, space and intention …"

(Stern, 2010, p. 4) have yet to stand the test of time, and prove robust enough to be accommodated and integrated into psychoanalytic mainstream. It thus seems that researching the conceptual interface of Eastern and psychoanalytical 'systems' and 'connectionist' paradigms and the attendant inter-disciplinary confluence of terms such as 'vitality' and 'qi' may prove a promising avenue for future research and a contribution to the emerging field of unitary conceptualizations.

4   Finally, the question of what constitutes an intervention or an interpretation is another potential focus for future studies. Spotnitz (1969) has described "silent interpretations" long hence and Little (1993) has referred to "direct presentation". Whereas physical action and bodily interactive responsiveness in psychoanalysis have long been considered a bane and tantamount to misconduct, more recently enacted and procedural interventions have become accepted. In a pioneering model, Suler (1993) has suggested integrating Zen's active, attuned participation and psychoanalytic procedure, proposing psychotherapeutic effect is enhanced when cross-coded, utilizing verbal concepts, images and enactments. In this context, interpretation is one possible variant of actional attunement. Based on these premises, future research may explore how psychoanalytic therapy might potentially expand the concept of interpretation. This would include providing the dual-track conceptualization of psyche-somatic expression and attunement, manifest in both non-verbal exchanges, and in verbal exchanges comprising "live" as opposed to "dead" words.

# References

Aarts, B., Chalker, S. & Weiner, E. (2014). *The Oxford dictionary of English grammar*. Oxford: Oxford University Press.

Abe, M. (1992). *A study of Dōgen: His philosophy and religion*. New York: SUNY Press.

Adams, W. (1995). Revelatory openness wedded with the clarity of unknowing. *Psychoanalysis and Contemporary Thought, 18*, 463–494.

Aisenstein, M. (2006). The indissociable unity of psyche and soma. *International Journal of Psychoanalysis, 87*, 667–680.

Aisenstein, M. (2008). Beyond the dualism of psyche and soma. *Journal of the American Academy of Psychoanalysis and Dynamic Psychiatry, 36*(1), 103–123.

Aisenstein, M., & De Aisenberg, E. R. (2010). *Psychosomatics today: A psychoanalytic perspective*. London: Karnac.

Alexander, F. (1998). From Buddhistic training as an artificial catatonia (1931). In A. Molino (Ed.), *The couch and the tree: Dialogues in psychoanalysis and Buddhism* (pp. 12–25). New York: North Point.

Alexander, F., French, T. M. & Pollock, G. H. (1968). *Psychosomatic specificity: Experimental studies and results*. Chicago: University of Chicago Press.

Alfano, C. F. (2005). Traversing the caesure. *Contemporary Psychoanalysis, 41*, 223–247.

Ames, R. (1993). The meaning of body in classical Chinese philosophy. In T. Kasulis, R. Ames & W. Dissanayake (Eds.), *Self as body in Asian theory and practice* (pp. 157–178). New York: State University of New York Press.

Ammon, G. (1979). *Psychoanalysis and psychosomatics*. New York: Springer.

Anderson, C. A. (2001). Heat and violence. *Current Directions in Psychological Science, 10*, 33–38.

Anderson, F. S. (2008). *Bodies in treatment: The unspoken dimension*. New York: The Analytic Press.

Anzieu, D. (1989). *The skin ego*. New Haven, CT: Yale University Press.

Anzieu, D. (1990). *A skin for thought: Interviews with Gilbert Tarrab on psychology and psychoanalysis*. London: Karnac.

# References

Arieti, S. (1981). Presidential address: Psychoanalytic therapy in a cultural climate of pessimism. *Journal of the American Academy of Psychoanalysis, 9*, 171–184.
Armstrong, D. (1999). *The mind-body problem: An opinionated introduction.* Sydney: Westview Press.
Arnetoli, C. (2002). Empathic networks: Symbolic and subsymbolic representations in the intersubjective field. *Psychoanalytic Inquiry, 22*(5), 740–765.
Aron, L. (1998). The clinical body and the reflexive mind. In L. Aron & F. S. Anderson (Eds), *Relational perspectives of the body* (pp. xiv–xviii, 3–37). London: The Analytic Press.
Atwood, G. E., & Stolorow, R. D. (1984). *Structures of subjectivity: Explorations in psychoanalytic phenomenology.* London: The Analytic Press.
Babakin, M. M. (1978). The history of psychotherapy: From healing magic to encounter. Ed. by Jan Ehrenwald: A review. *Psychoanalytic Review, 65*, 659–662.
Balint, M. (1968/1979). *The basic fault: Therapeutic aspects of regression.* London: Routledge.
Basch, M. F. (1976). Psychoanalysis and communication science. *Annals of Psychoanalysis, 4*, 385–421.
Battersby, C. (1998). *The phenomenal woman: Feminist metaphysics and the patterns of identity.* Cambridge: Polity Press.
Becker, E. (1961). The psychotherapeutic meeting of East and West. *American Imago, 18*(1), 3–20.
Beebe, B., Knoblauch, S., Rustin, J. & Sorter, D. (2003). Introduction. *Psychoanalytic Dialogues, 13*, 743–775.
Beebe, B., & Lachmann, F. M. (1994). Representation and internalization in infancy: Three principles of salience. *Psychoanalytic Psychology, 11*(2), 127–165.
Beebe, B., & Lachmann, F. M. (1998). Co-constructing inner and relational processes: Self- and mutual regulation in infant research and adult treatment. *Psychoanalytic Psychology, 15*(4), 480–516.
Beebe, B., & Lachmann, F. M. (2002). Organizing principles of interaction from infant research and the lifespan prediction of attachment: Application to adult treatment. *Journal of Infant, Child, and Adolescent Psychotherapy, 2*(4), 61–89.
Berger, L. S. (1996). Psychoanalytic neonate models and non-Cartesian frameworks. *Psychoanalytic Review, 83*(1), 49–65.
Bernstein, R. (1971). *Praxis and action: Contemporary philosophies of human activity.* Philadelphia: University of Pennsylvania Press.
Besmer, K. M. (2007). *Merleau-Ponty's phenomenology.* London: Continuum.
Biancoli, R. (1995, April). "Center-to-center" relatedness between analyst and patient. *International Forum of Psychoanalysis, 4*(2), 105–110.

Bick, E. (1968). The experience of the skin in early object-relations. *The International Journal of Psychoanalysis, 49*, 484–486.
Bielefeldt, C. (1988). *Dōgen's manuals of Zen meditation.* Berkeley: University of California Press.
Binswanger, L. (1962). *Grundformen und Erkenntnis: Menschlichen Daseins.* Munich: Ernst Reinhardt Verlag.
Bion, W. R. (1952). Group dynamics: A review. *International Journal of Psychoanalysis, 33*(2), 235–247.
Bion, W. R. (1962). *Learning from experience.* London: Tavistock.
Bion, W. R. (1970). *Attention and interpretation.* London: Tavistock Publications.
Black, D. M. (2006a). The case for a contemplative position. In D. M. Black (Ed.), *Psychoanalysis and religion in the 21st century: Competitors or collaborators?* (pp. 63–79). New York: Routledge.
Black, D. M. (Ed.). (2006b). *Psychoanalysis and religion in the 21st century: Competitors or collaborators?* New York: Routledge.
Black, D. M. (2011). *Why things matter: The place of values in science, psychoanalysis and religion.* Hove: Routledge.
Bloefeld, J. (1962). *The Zen teachings of Hu Hai: On sudden illumination.* New York: S. Weiser.
Blomfield, O. H. (1982). Interpretation: Some general aspects. *International Review of Psycho-Analysis, 9*, 287–301.
Bodhi, B. (1995). *The middle length discourses of the Buddha.* Boston: Wisdom Publications.
Bokusan, N. (2011). Nishiari Bokusan. In E. Dōgen Zenji, N. Bokusan, S. Okamura, S. Suzuki, K. Uchiyama, S. M. Weitsman, K. Tanahashi & D. M. Wenger (Eds), *Dōgen's Genjō Kōan: Three commentaries* (pp. 5–91). Berkeley, CA: Counterpoint.
Bollas, C. (1989). *The shadow of the object: Psychoanalysis of the unthought known.* New York: Columbia University Press.
Bollas, C. (1991). *Forces of destiny: Psychoanalysis and human idiom.* London: Free Association Press.
Bollas, C. (1999). *The mystery of things.* New York: Routledge.
Bollas, C. (2013). *With China on the mind.* Hove: Routledge.
Boss, M. (1963). *Psychoanalysis and daseinsanalysis.* New York: Basic Books.
Boss, M. (1979). *Existential foundations of medicine and psychology.* Northvale, NJ: Jason Aronson.
Bowlby, J. (1969/1997). *Attachment and loss* (Vol. 1, *Attachment*). London: Random House.
Bricklin, J. (2015). *The illusion of will, self, and time: William James's reluctant guide to enlightenment.* New York: SUNY Press.

Brickman, H. R. (1998). The psychoanalytic cure and its discontents: A Zen perspective on "common unhappiness" and the polarized self. *Psychoanalysis and Contemporary Thought*, *21*(1), 3–32.

Briggs, A. (Ed.). (2002). *Surviving space: Papers on infant observation*. London: Karnac.

Broadie, S. (2007). *Aristotle and beyond: Essays on metaphysics and ethics*. Edinburgh: University of St Andrews.

Brodsky, A. (2007). Realizing the self – What it means to be real. *International Journal of Psychoanalytic Self Psychology*, *2*(2), 163–186.

Bromberg, P. M. (1991). Artist and analyst. *Contemporary Psychoanalysis*, *27*, 289–299.

Bromberg, P. M. (2012). *The shadow of the Tsunami and the growth of the relational mind*. New York: Routledge.

Brousse, M. H. (2007). Art, the avant-garde and psychoanalysis, *Lacanian Compass: Psychoanalytic Newsletter of Lacanian Orientation*, *1*(11), 4–13.

Bucci, W. (1997). *Psychoanalysis and cognitive science: A multiple code theory*. New York: Guilford Press.

Bucci, W. (2012). Is there language disconnected from sensory/bodily experience in speech or thought? Commentary on Vivona. *Journal of the American Psychoanalytical Association*, *60*, 275–228.

Burckhardt, J. (1999). *The Greeks and Greek civilization*. New York: St Martin's Griffin.

Campbell, K. (1970). *Body and mind*. Norwich: Fletcher and Son Ltd.

Cardinal, M. (1983). *The words to say it*. Cambridge, MA: Van Vactor & Goodheart Publications.

Carrol, R. (2014). Four relational modes of attending to the body in psychotherapy. In K. White (Ed.), *Talking bodies: How do we integrate working with the body in psychotherapy from an attachment and relational perspective?* (pp. 11–41). London: Karnac.

Cassirer, E. (1945). *An essay on man: An introduction to a philosophy of human culture*. New Haven, CT: Yale University Press.

Chaney, E. (2007). A compulsion for antiquity: *Freud and the Ancient World* by Richard H. Armstrong. *Psychoanalysis and History*, *9*(1), 123–130.

Chessick, R. D. (1980). The problematical self in Kant and Kohut. *The Psychoanalytic Quarterly*, *49*(3), 456–473.

Chessick, R. D. (1995). The application of postmodern thought to the clinical practice of psychoanalytic psychotherapy. *The Journal of the American Academy of Psychoanalysis*, *24*(3), 385–407.

Chomsky, N. (1968). *Language and mind*. New York: Harcourt, Brace & World.

# 238 References

Clancier, A., & Kalmanovitz, J. (1987). *Winnicott and paradox: From birth to creation.* London: Tavistock Publications.

Cleary, T. (Trans.). (1998). *The Sūtra of Hui-Neng, grandmaster of Zen.* Boston: Shambhala Publications.

Cohen-Shabot, S. (2008). *Ha-guf Ha-groteski* [On the Grotesque Body]. Tel-Aviv: Resling.

Cook, F. H. (1977). *Hua-Yen Buddhism: The jewel net of Indra.* Pennsylvania: Pennsylvania State Press.

Cook, F. H. (1989). *Sounds of valley streams: Enlightenment in Dōgen's Zen: Translation of nine essays from Shōbōgenzō.* New York: SUNY Press.

Cooper, J. W. (1989). *Body, soul and life everlasting: Biblical anthropology and the monism-dualism debate.* Grand Rapids, MI: William B. Federman.

Cooper, P. C. (2010). *The Zen impulse and the psychoanalytic encounter.* New York: Routledge.

Crayne, T., & Patterson, S. (Eds). (2000). *History of the mind-body problem.* New York: Routledge.

Csordas, T. J. (1994). *Embodiment and experience: The existential ground of culture and self* (vol. 2). Cambridge: Cambridge University Press.

Damasio, A. (1994). *Decartes' error: Emotion, reason and the human brain.* London: Papermac.

Damasio, A. (1999). *The feeling of what happens: Body and emotion in the making of consciousness.* London: Harcourt Brace and Company.

Damasio, A. (2003). *Looking for Spinoza: Joy, sorrow and the feeling brain.* London: Harcourt Incorporated.

De Bianchedi, E. T., Antar, R. Bianchedi, M., Cortinas, L., Kaplan, A., Neborak, S., Oelsner, R. & Saenz, M. (2002). Prenatals/postnatals: The total personality. In S. Alhanati (Ed.), *Primitive mental states: Psychological and psychoanalytical perspectives on early trauma and personality development* (pp. 99–110). New York: Karnac.

Demos, V. (1984). Empathy and affect: Reflection on infant experience. In J. Lichtenberg, M. Bernstein & D. Silver (Eds), *Empathy* (pp. 9–34). Hillsdale, NJ: Erlbaum.

Derrida, J. (2005). *On touching – Jean-Luc Nancy.* Stanford, CA: Stanford University Press.

Descartes, R. (1641/1989). *Meditations on first philosophy* (Y. Or, Trans.). Jerusalem: Magnes.

De Silva, P. (1979). *An introduction to Buddhist psychology.* London: Macmillan.

Detrick, W., & Detrick, S. P. (1989). *Self-psychology: Comparisons and contrasts.* Hillsdale, NJ: Lawrence Erlbaum.

Deutsch, H. (1959a). Psychoanalytic therapy in the light of follow-up. *Journal of the American Psychoanalytical Association, 7*, 445–458.

Deutsche, F. (1959). *On the mysterious leap from the mind to the body: A workshop study on the theory of conversion.* New York: International Universities Press.

Dillon, M. (1971). Gestalt theory and Merleau-Ponty's concept of intentionality. *Man and World, 4*, 436–459.

Dimen, M. (1996). Bodytalk. *Gender and Psychoanalysis, 1*, 385–401.

Drummond, M. (2006). Western science meets eastern wisdom to experience bodily feelings. In D. K. Nauriyal, M. Drummond & Y. B. Lal (Eds), *Buddhist thought and applied psychological research: Transcending the boundaries.* London: Routledge.

Dumoulin, H. (1989). *Zen Buddhism: A history* (Vol. 1: *India and China with a new supplement on the northern school of Chinese Zen*). New York: Macmillan.

Durckheim, K. (1962). *Hara: The vital center of man.* London: George Allen and Unwin.

Durban, J. (2011). Shadows, ghosts and chimaeras: On some early modes of handling psycho-genetic heritage. *International Journal of Psycho-Analysis, 92*(4), 903–924.

Eigen, M. (1981). The area of faith in Winnicott, Lacan and Bion. *The International Journal of Psycho-Analysis, 62*(4), 413–433.

Eigen, M. (1983). Dual union or undifferentiation? A critique of Marion Milner's view of the sense of psychic creativeness. *International Review of Psycho-analysis, 10*, 415–428.

Eigen, M. (1995). Stones in a stream. *Psychoanalytic Review, 82*, 371–390.

Eigen, M. (2011). *Contact with the depths.* London: Karnac.

Eisenberg, D., & Wright, L. (1995). *Encounters with qi: Exploring Chinese medicine.* New York: Norton and Company.

Elisha, P. (2011). *The conscious body: A psychoanalytic exploration of the body in psychotherapy.* Washington, DC: American Psychological Association Press.

Ellman, S. J., & Moskowitz, M. B. (1980). An examination of some recent criticisms of psychoanalytic "Metapsychology". *Psychoanalytic Quarterly, 49*, 630–662.

Engler, J. (2003). Being somebody and being nobody: A reexamination of the understanding of self in psychoanalysis and Buddhism. In J. D. Safran (Ed.), *Psychoanalysis and Buddhism: An unfolding dialogue* (pp. 35–79). Boston: Wisdom Publications.

Epstein, M. (2005). The structure of no structure: Winnicott's concept of unintegration and the Buddhist notion of no-self. In D. M. Black (Ed.), *Psychoanalysis and religion in the 21st century: Competitors or collaborators?* London: Routledge.

Eubanks, C. (2011). *Miracles of book and body: Buddhist textual culture and medieval Japan* (Vol. 10). Berkeley: University of California Press.
Fast, I. (2006). A body-centered mind: Freud's more radical idea. *Contemporary Psychoanalysis, 42*(2), 273–295.
Foucault, M. (1970). *The order of things: Archaeology of the human sciences.* London: Tavistock Publications.
Frank, A. (1983). Id resistance and the strength of the instincts: A clinical demonstration. *Journal of the American Psychoanalytic Association, 31*, 375–403.
Freud, S. (1900). The interpretation of dreams. *Standard Edition, 4*, 9–627.
Freud, S. (1904). Freud's psycho-analytic procedure. *Standard Edition, 7*, 249–254.
Freud, S. (1909). Notes upon a case of obsessional neurosis. *Standard Edition, 10*, 155–318.
Freud, S. (1912). Recommendations to physicians practicing psychoanalysis. *Standard Edition, 12, 111–120.*
Freud, S. (1915). Observations on transference-love: Technique of psycho-analysis. *Standard Edition, 12*, 159–171.
Freud, S. (1916). Introductory lectures on psycho-analysis. *Standard Edition, 15*, 1–240.
Freud, S. (1920). Beyond the pleasure principle. *Standard Edition, 18*, 7–64.
Freud, S. (1921). Group psychology and the analysis of the ego. *Standard Edition, 18*, 69–143.
Freud, S. (1923). The ego and the id. *Standard Edition, 19*, 12–66.
Freud, S. (1927). The future of an illusion. *Standard Edition, 21*, 5–56.
Freud, S. (1930). Civilization and its discontents. *Standard Edition, 21*, 57–146.
Freud, S. (1933a). New introductory lectures on psycho-analysis. *Standard Edition, 22*, 5–182.
Freud, S. (1933b). The question of a Weltanschauung. *Standard Edition, 22*, 158–184.
Freud, S. (1940). An outline of psycho-analysis. *Standard Edition, 23*, 144–207.
Frie, R. (Ed.). (2003). *Understanding experience: Psychotherapy and postmodernism.* New York: Routledge.
Frie, R. (2007). The lived body: From Freud to Merleau-Ponty in contemporary psychoanalysis. In J. P. Muller & J. P. Tillman (Eds), *The embodied subject: Minding the body in psychoanalysis* (pp. 55–67). Plymouth: Jason Aronson.
Friedman, L. (1988). *The anatomy of psychotherapy.* London: The Analytic Press.
Fromm, E. (1960/1998). Extract from "Psychoanalysis and Zen Buddhism". In A. Molino (Ed.), *The couch and the tree: Dialogues in psychoanalysis and Buddhism* (pp. 65–71). New York: North Point.

Fromm, E. (2000, January). Dealing with the unconscious in psychotherapeutic practice: 3 lectures. In *International Forum of Psychoanalysis* (9(3–4), 167–186). London: Taylor & Francis Group.

Fromm, E., Suzuki, D. T. & De Martino, R. (1974). *Zen-Buddhism and psychoanalysis*. London: Souvenir Press Ltd.

Gabrieli-Rehavi, I., Green, A. & Kulka, R. (2014, February). Human spirit: Psychoanalytic-Buddhist training. Collaboration between Israel Association for Self Psychology and the Study of Subjectivity and Lama Tzong Khapa Institute, Pomaia, Italy, member of the Foundation for the Preservation of the Mahayana tradition. Retrieved from: www.selfpsychology.org.il.

Gadamer, H. G. (1976). *Philosophical hermeneutics* (D. E. Linge, Trans. and Ed.). Berkeley: University of California Press.

Gadamer, H. G. (1991). *Truth and method* (J. Weinsheimer & D. G. Marshall, Trans.). New York: Continuum.

Gallese, V., Eagle, M. N. & Migone, P. (2007). Intentional attunement: Mirror neurons and the neural underpinnings of interpersonal relations. *Journal of the American Psychoanalytical Association*, 55, 131–176.

Gallesse, V., & Goldman, A. (1998). Mirror neurons and the simulation theory of mind-reading. *Trends in Cognitive Sciences*, 2, 493.

Galton, G. (2006). *Touch papers: Dialogues on touch in the psychoanalytic space*. London: Karnac.

Garfield, J. (Trans.). (1995). *The fundamental wisdom of the middle way: Nāgārjuna's Mūlamadhyamakakārikā*. Oxford: Oxford University Press.

Gates, F. (1959). Is the term "the mysterious leap" warranted? In F. Deutsche (Ed.), *On the mysterious leap from the mind to the body: A workshop study on the theory of conversion* (pp. 11–27). New York: International Universities Press.

Gazzaniga, M. S. (1985). *The social brain: Discovering the networks of the mind*. New York: Basic Books.

Gellman, J. I. (2005). Mysticism and religious experience. In W. J. Wainwright (Ed.), *The Oxford handbook of philosophy of religion* (pp. 138–167). Oxford: Oxford University Press.

Gerzi, S. (2005). Trauma, narcissism and the two attractors in trauma 1. *International Journal of Psycho-Analysis*, 86(4), 1033–1050.

Gill, M. M. (1976). Metapsychology is not psychology. In M. Gill & P. Holzman (Eds), *Psychology versus metapsychology: Psychoanalytic essays in memory of George S. Klein* (pp. 71–105). New York: International Universities Press, Inc.

Gliserman, M. J. (1996). *Psychoanalysis, language, and the body of the text*. Gainesville: University Press of Florida.

Goble, A. (2011). *Confluences of medicine in medieval Japan: Buddhist healing, Chinese knowledge, Islamic formulas and wounds of war.* Honolulu: University of Hawaii Press.

Goenka, S. N. (2000). *The discourse summaries of S.N. Goenka.* Washington, DC: Pariyatti publications.

Gordon, P. E. (2010). *Heidegger, Cassirer, Davos.* Cambridge, MA: Harvard University Press.

Greenspan, S. I. (1982). Three levels of learning: A developmental approach to "awareness" and mind-body relations. *Psychoanalytic Inquiry, 1,* 659–694.

Griffiths, P. J. (1986). *On being mindless: Buddhist meditation and the mind-body problem.* Chicago: Open Court.

Grotstein, J. S. (2002). Projective identification and its relation to infant development. In S. Alhanaty (Ed.), *Primitive mental states: Psychological and psychoanalytical perspectives on early trauma and personality development* (pp. 67–99). New York: Karnac.

Grunbaum, A. (1984). *The foundations of psychoanalysis: A philosophical critique.* Oakland: University of California Press.

Gundert, B. (2000). Soma and psyche in Hippocratic medicine. In J. P. Wright, & P. Potter (Eds), *Psyche and soma: Physicians and meta-physicians on the mind-body problem from antiquity to Enlightenment* (pp. 13–37). Oxford: Oxford University Press.

Hakeda, Y. (Trans.). (2006). *The awakening of faith in the Mahāyāna.* New York: Columbia University Press.

Hall, D., & Ames, R. (1998). *Thinking from the Han: Self, truth and transcendence in Chinese and Western culture.* New York: State University of New York Press.

Hallett, M., Fahn. S., Jankovic, J., Lang, A., Cloninger, R. & Yudofsky, S. (2006). *Psychogenic movement disorders: Neurology and neuropsychiatry.* New York: AAN Press.

Hanh, T. N. (2009). *The heart of understanding: Commentaries on the Prajnaparamita Heart Sūtra.* Berkeley, CA: Parallax Press.

Hanna, R., & Maiese, M. (2009). *Embodied minds in action.* Oxford: Oxford University Press.

Hannay, A. (1979). The what and the how. In D. F. Gustafson & B. L. Tapscott (Eds), *Body, mind and method: Essays in honor of Virgil C. Aldrich* (pp. 17–37). Dordrecht: D. Reidel.

Hegel, G. W. F. (1807/1977). *Phenomenology of spirit.* Oxford: Oxford University Press.

Heidegger, M. (1962). *Being and time.* London: Blackwell.

Heine, S. (1994). *Dōgen and the Kōan tradition: A tale of two Shōbōgenzō texts*. New York: State University of New York Press.
Herder, J. (2002). *Herder: Philosophical writings* (M. Forster Trans. and Ed.). Cambridge: Cambridge University Press.
Herzog, B. (2011). Procedural interpretation: A method of working between the lines in the nonverbal realm. *Psychoanalytic Inquiry, 31*, 462–474.
Holt, R. R. (1967). Beyond vitalism and mechanism: Freud's concept of psychic energy. In J. Masserman (Ed.), *Science and psychoanalysis* (Vol. XI: *The Ego*, pp. 1–41). New York: Grune & Stratton.
Holt, R. R. (1997). *Psychoanalysis and the philosophy of science: Collected papers of Benjamin B. Rubinstein*. Madison, WI: International Universities Press.
Horney, K. (1998). Extract from "Free associations and the use of the couch". In A. Molino (Ed.), *The couch and the tree: Dialogues in psychoanalysis and Buddhism* (pp. 35–37). New York: North Point.
Humphreys, C. (1971). *A western approach to Zen: An inquiry*. London: George Allen and Unwin.
Husserl, E. (1931). *Ideas II: General introduction to pure phenomenology*. London: George Allen and Unwin Ltd.
Husserl, E. (1965). *Phenomenology and the crisis of philosophy: Philosophy as a rigorous science, and philosophy and the crisis of European man* (Q. Lauer, Trans). New York: HarperCollins.
Hutten, E. H. (1961). An interpretation of the mind-body problem. *American Imago, 18*(3), 269–277.
Irwin, J. W. (1996). Science or hermeneutics? Psychoanalysis in search of self-definition. *Modern Psychoanalysis, 21*(1), 61–89.
Izutsu, T. (1977). *Toward a philosophy of Zen Buddhism*. Tehran: Imperial Iranian Academy of Philosophy.
James, S. (2000). Emergence of the Cartesian mind. In T. Crayne, & S. Patterson (Eds), *History of the mind-body problem* (pp. 111–130). New York: Routledge.
Jaspers, K. (1913/1963). *General psychopathology* (J. Hoenig, & W. H. Hamilton, Trans.). Chicago: The University of Chicago Press.
Johnson, M. (1987). *The body in the mind*. Chicago: University of Chicago Press.
Johnson, M. (1993). *The meaning of the body*. Chicago: University of Chicago Press.
Jones, J. W. (1992). Knowledge in transition: Toward a Winnicottian epistemology. *Psychoanalytic Review, 79*, 223–237.
Kakar, S. (2003). Psychoanalysis and Eastern spiritual healing traditions. *Journal of Analytical Psychology, 48*(5), 659–678.

Kalupahana, D. (1999). *The Buddha's philosophy of language*. Ratmalana: Vishva Lekha Publications.
Kant, I. (1787/1999). *Critique of pure reason* (W. Pluhar, Trans.). Indianapolis: Hackett Publications.
Kasulis, T. P. (1989). *Zen action, Zen person.* Honolulu: University of Hawaii Press.
Kasulis, T. P., Ames, R. & Dissanayake, W. (Eds). (1993). *Self as body in Asian theory and practice*. New York: State University of New York Press.
Kavaler-Adler, S. (2011). In memorium: A tribute to Dr. Joyce McDougal, who passed away in August 2011. The Object Relations Institute for Psychotherapy and Psychoanalysis. Retrieved from: www.orinyc.org/index.html.
Kelman, H. (1960/1998). Psychoanalytic thought and Eastern wisdom. In A. Molino (Ed.), *The couch and the tree: Dialogues in psychoanalysis and Buddhism* (pp. 72–80). New York: North Point.
Kim, H. J. (2004). *Eihei Dōgen – Mystical realist*. Boston: Wisdom Publications.
Kim, H. J. (2007). *Dōgen on meditation and thinking: A reflection on his view of Zen*. New York: State University of New York Press.
Kirsner, D. (1986). The other psychoanalysis. *Psychoanalysis & Contemporary Thought, 9*, 299–330.
Klein, D. (1970). *A history of scientific psychology: Its origins and philosophical backgrounds*. New York: Basic Books.
Knoblauch, S. H. (1999). Absorbing maternal erotics. *Gender and Psychoanalysis, 4*, 35–46.
Knoblauch, S. H. (2001). Chapter 7 Nonverbal implicit dimensions of interaction. *Progress in Self Psychology, 17*, 79–86.
Knoblauch, S. H. (2005). Body rhythms and the unconscious: Toward an expanding of clinical attention. *Psychoanalytic Dialogues, 15*(6), 807–827.
Knoblauch, S. H. (2011). Contextualizing attunement within the polyrhythmic weave: The psychoanalytic Samba. *Psychoanalytic Dialogues, 21*, 414–427.
Knoblauch, S. H. (2014). The centrality of the analyst's vulnerability to interactive regulation and therapeutic movement: Discussion of paper by Paolo Stra. *Psychoanalytic Inquiry, 34*, 288–294.
Knox, J. (2009). The analytic relationship: Integrating Jungian, attachment theory and developmental perspectives. *British Journal of Psychotherapy, 25*(1), 5–23.
Kohavi. T. (2009, May). Bodily knowledge: Anthropological practice as a corporeal praxis. Paper presented at the Department Seminar of the Department of Sociology and Anthropology, Ben Gurion University of the Negev, Be'er Sheva, Israel.

Kohut, H. (1959). Introspection, empathy, and psychoanalysis: An examination of the relationship between mode of observation and theory. *Journal of the American Psychoanalytical Association, 7*, 459–483.

Kohut, H. (1966). Forms and transformations of narcissism. *Journal of the American Psychoanalytic Association, 14*, 243–272.

Kohut, H. (1977). *The restoration of the self.* Chicago: University of Chicago Press.

Kohut, H. (1984). *How does analysis cure?* Chicago: University of Chicago Press.

Kohut, H. (2010). On empathy. *International Journal of Psychoanalytic Self Psychology, 5*(2), 122–131.

Kohut, H., & Wolf, E. S. (1978). The disorders of the self and their treatment: An outline. *International Journal of Psychoanalysis, 59*, 413–425.

Kolod, S. (2012, Jan.). The thinking body, the moving mind: What I learned from Merce Cunningham about psychology. Psychological reflections on the end of the Merce Cunningham Dance Company. *Psychology Today.* Retrieved from: www.psychologytoday.com/magazine.

Køppe, S., Harder, S. & Væver, M. (2008). Vitality affects. *International Forum of Psychoanalysis, 17*(3), 169–179.

Kripal, J. J. (2007). *Esalen: America and the religion of no religion.* Chicago: University of Chicago Press.

Krueger, D. (2002). *Integrating body self and psychological self: Creating a new story in psychoanalysis and psychotherapy.* New York: Brunner-Routledge.

Kuang-Ming, W. (1997). *On Chinese body thinking: A cultural hermeneutic.* Leiden: Koninklijke Brill.

Kubie, L. S. (1947). The fallacious use of quantitative concepts in dynamic psychology. *Psychoanalytic Query, 16*, 507–518.

Kuhn, T. S. (2012). *The structure of scientific revolutions* (4th ed.). Chicago: University of Chicago Press.

Kulka, R. (2003). Between emergence and diffusion: A psychoanalytic Kōan of body-mind. Paper presented at The Body in Psychotherapy – Occidental and Eastern Perspectives symposium (Collaboration of the department of psychology and the department of East-Asian studies), Tel Aviv University, Tel Aviv, Israel.

Kulka, R. (2012). Between emergence and dissolving: Contemporary reflections on greatness and ideals in Kohut's legacy. *International Journal of Psychoanalytic Self Psychology, 7*(2), 264–285.

Kuriyama, S. (1999). *The expressiveness of the body and the divergence of Greek and Chinese medicine.* New York: Zone Books.

Lacan, J. (1975/1988). *The seminars of Jacques Lacan: Book I. Freud's papers on technique 1953–1954* (J. Forrester, Trans.; J. A Miller, Ed.). New York: Cambridge University Press.

Lachmann, F. M., & Beebe, B. (1992). Representational and selfobject transferences: A developmental perspective. In A. Goldberg (Ed.), *Progress in self psychology* (Vol. 8, pp. 3–15). Hillsdale, NJ: The Analytic Press.

Lakoff, G., & Johnson, M. (1980). *Metaphors we live by*. Chicago: University of Chicago Press.

Lakoff, G., & Johnson, M. (1999). *Philosophy in the flesh: The embodied mind and its challenge to western thought*. New York: Basic Books.

Lash, S. (1990). *Sociology of postmodernism*. London: Routledge.

Lawner, P. (2001). Spiritual implications of psychodynamic therapy: Immaterial psyche, ideality, and the "area of faith". *Psychoanalytic Review, 88*, 525–548.

Lazar, R. (2001). Subject in first person – subject in third person: Subject, subjectivity, and intersubjectivity. *The American Journal of Psychoanalysis, 61*(3), 271–291.

Leavy, S. (1995). Roots of unitive experience. *Psychoanalytic Review, 82*, 349–370.

Leder, D. (1990). *The absent body*. Chicago: University of Chicago Press.

Leder, D. (1999). Flesh and blood: A proposed supplement to Merleau-Ponty. In D. Welton (Ed.), *The body: Classic and contemporary readings* (pp. 200–210). Oxford: Blackwell.

Leibowitz, Y. (2005). *Mind and brain: Fundamentals of the psycho-physical problem*. Bnei-Brak: Hakibbutz Hameuchad Publishing House.

Leighton, D., & Okumura, S. (Trans.). (2004). *Dōgen's extensive record: A translation of the Eihei Kōroku*. Boston: Wisdom Publications.

Levin, F. (2011). *Psyche and brain: The biology of talking cures*. London: Karnac.

Lévi-Strauss, C. (1973/1989). *The savage mind* (A. Gildin, Trans.). Tel Aviv: Sifriyat Poalim.

Li, C. L. (1999). *The Tao encounters the West: Explorations in comparative philosophy*. Albany, NY: State University Press.

Lidin, O. (2006). *From Taoism to Einstein: Ki and Ri in Chinese and Japanese thought*. Folkestone: Global Oriental.

Little, M. (1993). *Transference neurosis and transference psychosis*. New York: Jason Aronson.

Lobel, T. (2014). *Sensation: The new science of physical intelligence*. New York: Atria.

Loewald, H. W., & Meissner, W. W. (1976). New horizons in metapsychology: View and review. *Journal of the American Psychoanalytic Association, 24*, 161–180.

Lombardi, R. (2002). Primitive mental states and the body: A personal view of Armando B. Ferrari's concrete original object. *The International Journal of Psychoanalysis, 83*(2), 363–381.

Lombardi, R. (2009). Body, affect, thought: Reflections on the work of Matte Blanco and Ferrari. *The Psychoanalytic Quarterly*, *78*(1), 123–160.
Lopez, D. S. (1988). *The Heart Sūtra explained: Indian and Tibetan commentaries*. New York: State University of New York Press.
Loy, D. (1998). *Nonduality: A study in comparative philosophy*. Atlantic Highlands, NJ: Humanities Books.
Lyons-Ruth, K. (1999). The two-person unconscious. *Psychoanalytical Inquiry*, *19*(4), 576–617.
Maciocia, G. (1989). *The foundations of Chinese medicine*. London: Churchill Livingstone.
Mackay, N. (1986). Freud, explanation, and the mind-brain problem. *Psychoanalysis and Contemporary Thought*, *9*(3), 373–404.
Magid, B. (2000). The couch and the cushion. *Journal of the American Academy of Psychoanalysis and Dynamic Psychiatry*, *28*, 513–526.
Magid, B. (2002). *Ordinary mind: Exploring the common ground of Zen and psychotherapy*. Sommerville, MA: Wisdom Publications.
Mahrer, A. R. (1978). *Experiencing: A humanistic theory of psychology and psychiatry*. Hove: Brunner/Mazel.
Mancia, M. (1994). Eclipse of the body: A psychoanalytical hypothesis. *International Journal of Psycho-Analysis*, *75*, 1283–1286.
Masunaga, R. (Trans.). (1971). *A primer of Soto Zen. A translation of Dōgen's Shōbōgenzō Zuimonki*. Honolulu: University of Hawaii Press.
Masunaga, S. (1976). *Zen-Shiatsu: Harmonizing Yin and Yang for better health*. Tokyo: Japan Publications.
Matsumoto, M., Inoue, K. & Kajii, E. (2001). Words of Tohkaku Wada: Medical heritage in Japan. *Journal of Medical Ethics*, *27*, 55–58.
McDougal, J. (1989). *Theatres of the body*. London: Free Association Books.
Meissner, W. W. (2003a). Mind, brain, and self in psychoanalysis: I. Problems and attempted solutions. *Psychoanalysis and Contemporary Thought*, *26*(3), 279–320.
Meissner, W. W. (2003b). Mind, brain, and self in psychoanalysis: II. Freud and the mind-body relation. *Psychoanalysis and Contemporary Thought*, *26*(3), 321–344.
Meissner, W. W. (2003c). Mind, brain, and self in psychoanalysis: III. Psychoanalytic perspectives after Freud. *Psychoanalysis and Contemporary Thought*, *26*(3), 345–386.
Meissner, W. W. (2007). Mind, brain, and self in psychoanalysis: Therapeutic implications of the mind-body relation. *Psychoanalytic Psychology*, *24*, 333–354.
Meissner, W. W. (2009). Mind-brain and body in the self: Psychoanalytic perspectives. *The Psychoanalytic Review*, *96*(2), 369–402.

Meltzer, D. (1986). Discussion of Esther Bick's paper "Further considerations on the function of the skin in early object relations". *British Journal of Psychotherapy*, 2(4), 300–301.
Merkur, D. (1989). Unitive experiences and the state of trance. In M. Idel & B. McGinn (Eds), *Mystical union and monotheistic faith.* New York: Macmillan.
Merleau-Ponty, M. (1945/1962). *Phenomenology of perception* (C. Smith, Trans.). London: Routledge.
Merleau-Ponty, M. (1964). Eye and mind. In J. Edie (Ed.), *The primacy of perception* (pp. 159–190). Evanston, IL: Northwestern University Press.
Merleau-Ponty, M. (1968). *The visible and the invisible.* Evanston, IL: Northwestern University Press.
Merleau-Ponty, M. (2002). *The world of perception.* London: Routledge.
Merzel, D. (1991). *The eye never sleeps: Striking to the heart of Zen.* Boston: Shambhala Publications.
Milner, M. (1969). *The hands of the living god: An account of a psychoanalytic treatment.* London: The Hogarth Press.
Milner, M. (1987). *The suppressed madness of sane men: Forty-four years of exploring psychoanalysis.* London: Tavistock Publications.
Mitchell, S. A. (1993). *Hope and dread in psychoanalysis.* New York: Basic Books.
Molino, A. (Ed.). (1998). *The couch and the tree: Dialogues in psychoanalysis and Buddhism.* New York: North Point Press.
Moncayo, R. (1998). True subject is no-subject: The Real, Imaginary, and Symbolic in psychoanalysis and Zen Buddhism. *Psychoanalysis and Contemporary Thought*, 21, 383–422.
Muller, J. P., & Tillman, J. G. (Eds). (2007). *The embodied subject: Minding the body in psychoanalysis* (Vol. 68). Plymouth: Jason Aronson.
Nagatomo, S. (1992). *Attunement through the body.* New York: New York State University Press.
Nagatomo, S., & Leisman, G. (1996). An East Asian perspective of mind-body. *Journal of Medicine and Philosophy*, 21(4), 439–466.
Nagel, T. (1986). *The view from nowhere.* Oxford: Oxford University Press.
Natsoulas, T. (1984). Freud and consciousness. *Psychoanalysis & Contemporary Thought*, 7, 195–232.
Nauriyal, D. K., Drummond, M. & Lal, Y. B. (Eds). (2006). *Buddhist thought and applied psychological research: Transcending the boundaries.* London: Routledge.
Ng, M. L. (1985). Psychoanalysis for the Chinese – applicable or not applicable? *The International Journal of Psychoanalysis*, 12, 449–460.
Odin, S. (1982). *Process metaphysics and Hua-Yen Buddhism: A critical study of cumulative penetration vs. interpretation.* Albany, NY: State University of New York Press.

Ogden, T. H. (1989). On the concept of an autistic-contiguous position. *The International Journal of Psychoanalysis, 70,* 127–140.
Ogden, T. H. (1992). *The primitive edge of experience.* New York: Jason Aronson.
Ogden, T. H. (2008). Reminding the body. In T. H. Ogden (Ed.), *Conversations at the frontiers of dreaming* (pp. 153–175). London: Karnac.
Oh, K. N. (2000). The Taoist influence on Hua-yen Buddhism: A case of the sinicization of Buddhism in China. *Chung-Hwa Buddhist Journal, 13,* 277–297.
Opatow, B. (1993). On the drive-rootedness of psychoanalytic ego psychology. *The International Journal of Psychoanalysis, 74,* 437–457.
Opatow, B. (1999). Affect and the integration problem of mind and brain. *Neuro-Psychoanalysis, 1,* 97–110.
Orange, D. M. (2000). The Chicago Institute Lectures: Heinz Kohut. *Psychoanalytic Psychology, 17*(2), 420–431.
Orange, D. M. (2009). Toward the art of the living dialogue: Between constructivism and hermeneutics in psychoanalytic thinking. In R. Frie & D. Orange (Eds), *Beyond postmodernism: New dimensions in clinical theory and practice.* New York: Routledge.
Orange, D. M. (2010). *Thinking for clinicians: Philosophical resources for contemporary psychoanalysis and the humanistic psychotherapies.* New York: Routledge.
Park, Y. J., & Kopf, G. (Eds). (2009). *Merleau-Ponty and Buddhism.* Plymouth: Lexington Books.
Parkes, G. (1987). Dōgen/Heidegger/Dōgen. *Philosophy East and West, 37*(4), 437–454.
Pelled, E. (2005). *Psychoanalysis and Buddhism: About the human capacity to know.* Tel Aviv: Resling.
Phillips, J. (1991). Hermeneutics in psychoanalysis. *Psychoanalysis and Contemporary Thought, 14,* 371–424.
Pickering, J. (2006). The first person perspective in postmodern psychology. In D. K. Nauriyal, M. S. Drummond & Y. B. Lal (Eds), *Buddhist thought and applied psychological research* (pp. 3–19). London: Routledge.
Proimos, C. (2001). Martin Heidegger on mimesis in Plato and Platonism. In A. Alexandrakis, & N. J. Moutafakis (Eds), *Neoplatonism and western aesthetics* (pp. 153–163). New York: State University of New York Press.
Pytell, T. (2006). Transcending the angel beast: Viktor Frankl and humanistic psychology. *Psychoanalytic Psychology, 23*(3), 490–503.
Rahula, W. (1974). *What the Buddha taught.* New York: Grove Weidenfeld.
Rand, M. L. (2002). What is somatic attunement? *Annals of the American Psychotherapy Association, 5*(6), 30.

Rapaport, D., & Gill, M. M. (1959). The points of view and assumptions of metapsychology. *International Journal of Psycho-Analysis, 40*, 153–162.

Raz, J. (2007). *Zen Buddhism: Philosophy and aesthetics*. Tel Aviv: The Broadcasted University (The Ministry of Defense Publishing).

Redfearn, J. W. (1966). The patient's experience of his 'mind' 1. *Journal of Analytical Psychology, 11*(1), 1–20.

Reich, W. (1933/1972). *Character analysis* (V. R. Carfagno, Trans.). New York: Farrar, Straus and Giroux.

Reis, B. (1999). Thomas Ogden's phenomenological turn. *Psychoanalytic Dialogues, 9*(3), 371–393.

Reis, B. (2006). Even better than the real thing. *Contemporary Psychoanalysis, 42*(2), 177–196.

Reis, B. (2007). Sensing and (analytic) sensibilities: Some thoughts following Eyal Rozmarin's "An Other in Psychoanalysis". *Contemporary Psychoanalysis, 43*(3), 374–385.

Rendon, M. (1986). Philosophical paradigms in psychoanalysis. *Journal of the American Academy of Psychoanalysis, 14*, 495–505.

Rhys, D. (Trans.). (1993). *The book of the kindred sayings (Sanyuytta Nikaya)*. Oxford: The Pali Text Society.

Rick, M. (2013, Mar.). The body of knowledge: The therapist's corporeality as a matrix for deep analytic work. Paper presented at the Winnicott Study Center, Tel Aviv, Israel.

Ricoeur, P. (1970). *Freud and philosophy: An essay on interpretation*. (D. Savage, Trans.). New Haven, CT: Yale University Press.

Rist, J. M. (1970/1988). Parmenides and Plato's Parmenides. *The Classical Quarterly, 20*: 2. In J. M. Rist (Ed.), *Man, soul and body: Essays in ancient thought: From Plato to Dionysus* (pp. 221–229). Aldershot: Variorum.

Roos, E. (1982). Psychoanalysis and the growth of knowledge. *The Scandinavian Psychoanalytic Review, 5*(2), 183–199.

Rorty, R. (1967). *The linguistic turn: Essays in philosophical method*. Chicago: University of Chicago Press.

Rorty, R. (1970). Mind-body identity, privacy and categories. In C. V. Borst (Ed.), *The mind-brain identity theory* (pp. 187–214). London: St. Martin's Press.

Rorty, R. (1979). The unnaturalness of epistemology. In D. Gustaphson & B. Tapscott (Eds), *Body, mind and method: Essays in honor of Virgil C. Aldrich* (pp. 77–93). Dordrecht: Springer.

Ross, N. (1975). Affect as cognition: With observations on the meanings of mystical states. *International Review of Psychoanalysis, 2*, 79–93.

Roszak, T. (1969). *The making of a counter culture*. New York: Anchor Books.

Rubin, J. B. (1996). *Psychotherapy and Buddhism: Toward an integration*. New York: Plenum Press.

Rubin, J. B. (2009). Deepening psychoanalytic listening: The marriage of Buddha and Freud. *American Journal of Psychoanalysis, 69*, 93–105.

Rubinstein, B. B. (1965). Psychoanalytic theory and the mind-body problem. In N. S. Greenfield & W. C. Lewis (Eds), *Psychoanalysis and current biological thought*. Madison: University of Wisconsin Press.

Safran, J. (Ed.). (2003). *Buddhism and psychoanalysis: An unfolding dialogue*. Somerville, MA: Wisdom Publications.

Safran, J. (2006). Before the ass has gone, the horse has already arrived. *Contemporary Psychoanalysis, 42*, 197–211.

Salzman, L. (1953). The psychology of religious and ideological conversion. *Psychiatry, 16*, 177–187.

Sasaki, P. (1996). Foreword. In C. Beresford-Cooke, *Shiatsu theory and practice: A comprehensive text for the student and professional*. Edinburgh: Churchill Livingstone.

Sawyier, F. H. (1973). Commentary on Freud and philosophy. *Annals of Psychoanalysis, 1*, 216–228.

Scalzone, F. (2005). Notes for a dialogue between psychoanalysis and neuroscience 1. *The International Journal of Psychoanalysis, 86*(5), 1405–1423.

Schafer, R. (1970). An overview of Heinz Hartmann's contributions to psychoanalysis. *The International Journal of Psychoanalysis, 51*, 425–446.

Schafer, R. (1975). Psychoanalysis without psychodynamics. *The International Journal of Psychoanalysis, 56*(1), 41–55.

Scharff, D. E., & Birtles, E. F. (1997). From instinct to self: The evolution and implications of W. R. D. Fairbairn's theory of object relations. *International Journal of Psychoanalysis, 78*, 1085–1103.

Scheper-Hughes, N. &. Lock. M. M. (1987). The mindful body: A prolegomenon to future work in medical anthropology. *Medical Anthropology Quarterly, 1*, 6–41.

Schmalzl, L., Crane-Godreau, M. A. & Payne, P. (2014). Movement-based embodied contemplative practices: Definitions and paradigms. *Frontiers in Human Neuroscience, 8*.

Schore, A. N. (1994). *Affect regulation and the origin of the self: The neurobiology of emotional development*. Hillsdale, NJ: Lawrence Erlbaum Associates.

Schore, A. N. (1997). A century after Freud's Project: Is a rapprochement between psychoanalysis and neurobiology at hand? *American Journal of Psychoanalysis, 45*, 807–840.

Schore, A. N. (2001). Minds in the making: Attachment, the self-organizing brain, and developmentally-oriented psychoanalytic psychotherapy. *British Journal of Psychotherapy, 17*, 299–328.

Schore, A. N. (2002). Clinical implications of a neuropsychobiological model of projective identification. In S. Alhanati (Ed.), *Primitive mental states: Psychological and psychoanalytical perspectives on early trauma and personality development* (pp. 111–140). New York: Karnac.

Schore, A. N. (2003). *Affect regulation and the repair of the self* (Vol. 2). New York: WW Norton & Company.

Sella, Y. (2009). Forgetting the self, remembering our selves: A Buddhist-informed perspective of relational psychotherapy in areas of trauma and death. Paper presented at IARPP Conference, The Shadow of Memory.

Sella, Y. (2013). There is a body, a mind, a bodymind, there is suffering: what the therapist must remember, what the patient cannot forget. Opening lecture given at 'Haminfgash' ('The Encounter') lecture series, integrative East–West Psychotherapy Programme, School of Social Work, Tel Aviv University.

Sella, Y. (2015). The sense of sense: a revised perspective on the schizoid dilemma in light of Winnicott's concept of the true self and Merleau-Ponty's phenomenology of the body. *Maarag: The Israel Annual of Psychoanalysis*, 5, 213–238.

Sellers, S. (2010). *The Cambridge companion to Virginia Woolf*. Cambridge: Cambridge University Press.

Seo, A., & Addiss, A. (2010). *The sound of one hand: Paintings and calligraphy by Zen master Hakuin*. Boston: Shambala Publications.

Shaner, D. E. (1985a). *The bodymind experience in Japanese Buddhism*. New York: State University of New York press.

Shaner, D. E. (1985b). The bodymind experience in Dōgen's "Shōbōgenzō": A phenomenological perspective. *Philosophy East and West*, 35, 17–35.

Shapiro, B. (2003). Building bridges between body and mind: The analysis of an adolescent with paralyzing chronic pain. *The International Journal of Psychoanalysis*, 84(3), 547–561.

Shapiro, S. A. (1996). The embodied analyst in the Victorian consulting room. *Gender and Psychoanalysis*, 1(3), 297–322.

Sheets-Johnstone, M. (2002). Taking Freud's "bodily ego" seriously: Commentary by Maxine Sheets-Johnstone. *Neuropsychoanalysis*, 4(1), 57–61.

Shibayama, Z. (2000). *Gateless barrier: Zen comments on the Mumonkan*. Boston: Shambala Publications.

Siegel, R. (2010). *The mindfulness solution: Everyday practices for everyday problems*. New York: Guilford Press.

Simmonds, J. G. (2006). The oceanic feeling and a sea change: Historical challenges to reductionist attitudes to religion and spirit from within psychoanalysis. *Psychoanalytic Psychology*, 23(1), 128–142.

Smith, J. H. (1986). Dualism revisited: Schafer, Hartmann, and Freud. *Psychoanalytic Inquiry*, 6(4), 543–573.
Sorenson, R. (2004). *Minding spirituality*. Hillsdale, NJ: Analytic Press.
Sperry, L. E., & Shafranske, E. P. (Eds). (2005). *Spiritually oriented psychotherapy*. Washington, DC: APA Publications.
Spitz, R. A. (1965). *The first year of life: A psychoanalytic study of normal and deviant development of object relations*. New York: International Universities Press.
Spotnitz, H. (1969). *Modern psychoanalysis of the schizophrenic patient*. New York: Grune and Stratton.
Stambough, J. (1990). *Impermanence is Buddha nature: Dōgen's understanding of temporality*. Honolulu: University of Hawaii Press.
Stcherbatsky, T. (1923). *The central conception of Buddhism and the meaning of the word Dharma*. London: Royal Asiatic Society of Great Britain and Ireland.
Stern, D. B. (1983). Unformulated experience and transference. *Contemporary Psychoanalysis*, 23(3), 484–491.
Stern, D. N. (1985). *The interpersonal world of the infant: A view from psychoanalysis and developmental psychology*. New York: Basic Books.
Stern, D. N. (2004). *The present moment in psychotherapy and everyday life*. New York: W.W Norton & Company.
Stern, D. N. (2010). *Forms of vitality: Exploring dynamic experience in psychology, the arts, psychotherapy, and development*. Oxford: Oxford University Press.
Stern, D. N., Sander, L. W., Nahum, J. P., Harrison, A. M., Lyons-Ruth, K., Morgan, A. C., Bruschweilerstern, N. & Tronick, E. Z. (1998). Noninterpretive mechanisms in psychoanalytic therapy: The "something more" than interpretation. *International Journal of Psychoanalysis*, 79(5), 903–921.
Stolorow, R. D. (2005). Prereflective organizing principles and the systematicity of experience in Kant's critical philosophy. *Psychoanalytic Psychology*, 22(1), 96–100.
Stolorow, R. D. (2011). *World, affectivity, trauma: Heidegger and post-Cartesian psychoanalysis*. New York: Routledge.
Stone, C. (2005). Opening psychoanalytic space to the spiritual. *The Psychoanalytic Review*, 92(3), 417–430.
Suler, J. (1993). *Contemporary psychoanalysis and eastern thought*. New York: State University of New York.
Suler, J. (1995). In search of the self: Zen Buddhism and psychoanalysis. *Psychoanalytic Review*, 82, 407–426.
Suzuki, D. T. (1908). *Outlines of Mahayana Buddhism*. Chicago: Open Court Publishing Company.

Suzuki, D. T. (Trans.) (1932). *The Lankavatara Sūtra*. London: Routledge & Kegan Paul, 270, 73–85.
Suzuki, D. T. (1956). *Zen Buddhism*. New York: Doubleday.
Suzuki, D. T. (1970). *Zen and Japanese culture*. Princeton, NJ: Princeton University Press.
Suzuki, S. (2011). *Zen mind, beginners' mind: Informal talks on Zen meditation and practice*. London: Shambala Publications.
Tanahashi, K. (Ed.). (1985). *Moon in a dewdrop: Writings of Zen master Dōgen*. New York: North Point Press.
Tanahashi, K. (Ed.). (2010). *Treasury of the true dharma eye: Zen master Dōgen's Shobo Genzo*. Boston: Shambala.
Thandeka, T. (1995). *The embodied self: Fredrich Schleiermacher's solution to Kant's problem of the empirical self*. New York: New York State University Press.
Trevarthen, C. (1980). The foundations of intersubjectivity: Development of interpersonal and cooperative understanding in infants. In D. R. Olsen (Ed.), *The social foundations of language and thought* (pp. 316–342). Stanford, CA: Stanford University Press.
Tustin, F. (1978). Psychotic elements in the neurotic disorders of children. *Journal of Child Psychotherapy*, 4(4), 5–17.
Twemlow, S. (2001). Training psychotherapists in attribute of "mind" from Zen and psychoanalytic perspectives, part 1: Core principles, emptiness, impermanence and paradox. *American Journal of Psychotherapy*, 55, 1–21.
Uchiyama, K. (2011). Kosho Uchiyama. In E. Dōgen Zenji, N. Bokusan, S. Okamura, S. Suzuki, K. Uchiyama, S. M. Weitsman, K. Tanahashi & D. M. Wenger (Eds), *Dōgen's Genjō Kōan: Three commentaries* (pp. 127–223). Berkeley, CA: Counterpoint.
Van Buren, J. (2002). Thoughts without a thinker. In J. Van Buren & S. Alhanati (Eds), *Primitive mental states: A psychoanalytic exploration of the origins of meaning* (pp. 112–121). New York: Routledge.
Van Peursen, C. A. (1966). *Body, soul, spirit: A survey of the body-mind problem*. London: Fernando Vidal.
Varela, F. J., Thompson, E. & Rosch, E. (1993). *The embodied mind: Cognitive science and human experience*. London: The MIT Press.
Veith, I. (1972). *The yellow emperor's classic of internal medicine*. Berkeley: University of California Press.
Voloshinov, V. N. (1986). *Marxism and the philosophy of language*. Cambridge, MA: Harvard University Press.
Voss, S. (2002). Descartes: Heart and soul. In J. P. Wright & P. Potter (Eds), *Psyche and soma: Physicians and metaphysicians on the mind-body problem from antiquity to Enlightenment*. Oxford: Clarendon Press.

Wachtel, P. (2013). The non-talking cure. Paper presented at International Association of Relational Psychotherapy and Psychoanalysis, Internet colloquium. 6–19 May.

Waldron, W. (1994). How innovative is the Alaya vijnana? *Journal of Indian Philosophy*, *22*(3), 199–258.

Wallace, E. R. (1992). Freud and the mind-body problem. In T. Gelfano & J. Kerr (Eds), *Freud and the history of psychoanalysis* (pp. 231–270). London: The Analytic Press.

Watson, B. (Trans.). (1968). *The complete works of Chuang Tzu.* New York: Columbia University Press.

Watson, G. (2008). *Beyond happiness: Deepening the dialogue between Buddhism, psychotherapy and the mind sciences.* London: Karnac.

Watts, A. (1957). *The way of Zen.* London: Penguin.

Watts, A. (1975). *Psychotherapy east and west.* New York: Vintage Books.

Wilhelm, R., & Jung. C. (commentary). (1984). *The secret of the golden flower. A Chinese book of life.* London: Arkana.

Winnicott, D. W. (1954). Mind and its relation to the psyche-soma. *British Journal of Medical Psychology*, *27*(4), 201–209.

Winnicott, D. W. (1956). On transference. *The International Journal of Psychoanalysis*, *37*, 386–388.

Winnicott, D. W. (1960). Ego distortion in terms of true and false self. In D. W. Winnicott, *The maturational process and the facilitating environment* (pp. 140–153). London: Karnac.

Winnicott, D. W. (1966). Psycho-somatic illness in its positive and negative aspects. *The International Journal of Psychoanalysis*, *47*, 510–516.

Winnicott, D. W. (1968). Communication between mother and infant and infant and mother, compared and contrasted. In D. W. Winnicott, R. Shepherd & M. Davies (Eds.). (1987). *Babies and their mothers.* London: Free Association Books.

Winnicott, D. W. (1975). Through paediatrics to psycho-analysis. *International Psycho-Analytical Library*, *100*, 1–325. London: The Hogarth Press and the Institute of Psycho-Analysis.

Winnicott, D. W. (1982). *Playing and reality.* London: Tavistock Publications.

Winnicott, D. W. (1986). Holding and interpretation. *International Psychoanalytic Library*, *115*, 1–194. London: The Hogarth Press and the Institute of Psycho-Analysis.

Winnicott, D. W. (1987). Dependence in child care. In C. Winnicott, R. Shepherd & M. Davis (Eds), *Babies and their mothers* (pp. 83–89). London: Free Association Books.

Wittgenstein, L. (1953). *Philosophical Investigations.* London: Basil Blackwell Publishing.

Wittgenstein, L. (1922/1999). *Tractatus Logico-Philosophicus*. (C. K. Ogden, Trans.). London: Routledge & Kegan Paul.

Wittgenstein, L., & Rhees, R. (1968). Conversations on Freud. *Psychoanalytic Review*, *55*, 376–386.

Woodward, F. L. (Trans.). (1993). *The book of the kindred sayings* (Sanyuytta Nikaya). Oxford: The Pali Text Society.

Woolf, V. (1925). *Mrs Dalloway*. London: Hogarth Press.

Wright, J. P., & Potter, P. (Eds). (2000). *Psyche and soma: Physicians and metaphysicians on the mind-body problem from antiquity to Enlightenment.* Oxford: Oxford University Press.

Wrye, H. K. (1996). Bodily states of mind: Dialectics of psyche and soma in psychoanalysis. *Gender and Psychoanalysis*, *1*(3), 283–296.

Wu, J. C., Wu, J., Merton, T. & Kraft, K. (2003). *The golden age of Zen: Zen masters of the T'ang dynasty*. Bloomington, IN: World Wisdom, Inc.

Yoeli-Tlalim, R. (2010). Tibetan 'wind' and 'wind' illnesses: Towards a multicultural approach to health and illness. *Studies in History and Philosophy of Biological and Biomedical Sciences*, *41*, 318–324.

Yuasa, Y. (1987). *The body: Toward an Eastern mind-body theory*. New York: New York State University Press.

Yuasa, Y. (1993). *The body: Self-cultivation and Ki-energy*. New York: New York State University Press.

Zeller, E. (1955). *Outlines of the history of Greek philosophy*. London: Routledge & Kegan Paul.

# Index

abstinence 31, 52
Adams, W. 6, 196–7, 212, 214
aggregates (*skandhas*) 149–51, 224; physical and mental 77, 98n5
Aisenstein, M. 46, 107
Alfano, C.F. 6, 36, 94, 145–6, 171, 176, 189, 210, 231
Ames, R. 36, 61, 199
Ammon, G. 17, 47, 74
Anderson, F.S. 1–2, 104, 169–70, 178, 189
Anzieu, D. 6, 57, 59n4, 71, 75, 77, 79, 171, 192
Aristotelian theory 19
Aristotle 7, 19–20; dualism 41n1
Arnetoli, C. 188, 202
Aron, L. 40, 73, 84, 108, 171, 184–5, 190, 221
at one-ment/at-one-ment 6, 89–90, 120, 126n2, 174, 227
attunement 11, 106, 112, 200, 203, 205–7, 227, 230; actional 209, 233; active 208; body-mind 193; empathic 202, 207, 209, 214–15; intersubjective intercorporal 190; non-verbal 195, 202; psyche-somatic 11, 193, 202, 210, 233; specialized mode 201; spontaneous 213–14; transcendent 145, 176, 211; Zen 204; *see also* awakening, enlightenment, realization
Atwood, G.E. 30, 40, 42, 73, 84, 219

authentic 181; authenticity 161
authentication 203; authenticated 224
autistic children 131
autistic-contiguity 216
autistic-contiguous position 52, 58, 86
awakening 134, 157–8, 180, 187, 199, 205; psychology of 129; realization-awakening 157, 207
*Awakening of Faith in the Mahāyāna* 127, 141, 146n5
Awakening of Faith sūtra 143

Balint, M. 41n6, 58, 72, 81, 155, 164, 220
Basch, M.F. 2, 21, 171
Battersby, C. 65, 100
Becker, E. 121, 126n3
Beebe, B. 4, 30, 92–3, 95, 106, 188
being 33, 35, 41n5, 49, 90, 123, 131, 140–1, 145, 174, 180, 203, 214, 223–4; belief in unity of 98; communion of 203; dimensions of 208; formation and elucidation of 218; order of 139, 176; pre-being 141; pre-verbal and non-verbal forms of 173; psyche-somatic 49, 207; reflection equated with 211; sense of 203, 206; time 224; totality of 81, 141; welding of 156
being, aspects of 130; integration of 159; psychical 171

## Index

being: inter-being 203, 210–12; interactive 203; unified field of 189
being in the world 69, 218
being, modes of 194–5, 230; attuned 203; embodied 36; interactive inter-being 203; preconceptual 89; pre-reflective 145; transitional 101; unverbalized 201
being, states of 89, 195; body-mind 214; fluid state 145, 211
being-there 185
being with all one's faculties 77, 194
beings 65; human 18, 33, 85, 90, 125, 182, 212; living 19, 227; sentient 146n5, 208, 230
Berger, L.S. 33, 113–14
Besmer, K.M. 35, 85
Biancoli, R. 107, 115
Bielefeldt, C. 147n10, 156, 176, 197–8
big mind 177
biologistic 8, 143; hermeneutic-biologistic oppositions 97; positivistic-biologistic 76
Bion, W.R. 1, 6, 30, 33, 49, 53, 58, 62, 89–91, 96, 120, 126n2, 145, 174, 212, 227
Black, D.M. 2, 4, 16, 30, 88
Bodhi, B. 136, 151
Bodhidharma 154, 167n2
body-mind 4, 115, 119, 125, 134, 138, 143, 149, 157, 163, 176, 208–9, 214, 217, 224, 226; actional aspects of 156; alternative model of 156; antinomy and bifurcation 127; attunement 193; breach 28; cast off mode 230; conceptual infrastructure 221; connections, reciprocal 3; cultivation 227; debate 8, 18, 39; dialectics 50; dichotomies 38; dilemma 24; disposition 190, 193; distinctions 135; divide 111; Dōgen's project 139, 177; Eastern philosophies 77; empathic presence 190; entity 148; epistemology 159; framework 194; inseparability 154; integration 10–11, 193, 211, 213; interactions 26, 106; interweaving 123; knowledge 178–81; meditative practice 203; mode of total exertion 189; modes of differentiation 77n1; model of 43; oneness 228; phenomena 27, 224; predication 165; problem 18, 21, 23; question 3–4, 25, 28–9, 91, 117, 130, 139, 145, 212; scheme 163–4, 177; substrate of mental and psyche-somatic life 212; system 10, 165, 224; theory 43; unitary paradigms 99; unitary protocol 109; vitality 225; vocabulary 226, 229
body-mind, Buddhist 150; epistemology 180; paradigms 135; scheme 177; theorem 153
body-mind, compound 6, 63, 117, 135, 144, 187; consciousness 135; potential 144
body-mind consciousness 135, 224–5; compound 135; states of 223; unified contribution 131
body-mind dualism 17, 22–3; contradiction to 50; hypostasis of 30; in psychoanalysis 113, 118; Western 18
body-mind experience 7, 77, 83, 135, 225; of discontinuity 162; flow of 224; non-dual 186; unitive 83, 167
body-mind field: interpersonal 200; joint perceptual 229; unified 169
body-mind-language relationships 173; body-mind-speech 213
body-mind meta-theoretical paradigm 222; meta-theory 1, 7–8, 121; theory 7, 17, 121, 155
body-mind, non-dualistic 155, 227; Eastern disciplines 55; matrix, transposition into 83; meta-theoretical paradigm 222; perception of selfhood 214;

proposed framework 40; terminologies 220
body-mind-one/body-mind-as-one 9–11, 158, 166, 198, 217
body-mind relations 4, 6, 22, 122, 125; alternative ordering 8; body contribution to 54; contemporary schools of 24; disparities in psychoanalysis 211; in psychoanalysis 2–3, 5, 28–9, 37–8, 40, 51; subverted by Cartesian dualism 21; in therapeutic practice 36; trajectories of 10
body-minds 136, 214
body-mind-set 177, 193; dispositional mode 230; empathetic attunement 209; integrated 199
body-mind states 106, 166; of being 214; of consciousness 223; fluctuation between 194; self 164
body-mind, unified matrix 50; consciousness contribution 131; field 169
body-mind, Zen 222; approach 122, 198
Bokusan, N. 212–13
Bollas, C. 81, 88, 90–1, 95, 103, 114, 120, 173, 178, 187–8
Boss, M. 34, 65, 218
Bowlby, J. 63, 122
brain 44, 180; bi-hemispheric interaction 93; bodily aspect of psyche-soma 69, 76; connecting to environment 94; equation with consciousness 48; head-brain-higher faculties credo 75; mind 49, 70, 91; neural circuits 210; pre-frontal cortex 20; processes 28, 66; right 195; skin and 71, 77; tissue 68
brain 226; equating with psyche 220; right 211
brain functions 69; highest 20; left 195; neurological 69
Brickman, H.R. 188, 202

Brodsky, A. 144–5
Bromberg, P.M. 195
Bucci, W. 52–3, 93, 105, 149
Buddhist-psychoanalytic 194; discourse 125; research 123
Burckhardt, J. 20

Cardinal, M. 61, 192
Carrol, R. 91, 226
Cartesian 32–3, 38–9, 73, 96; analytic approach 57; bifurcative psychology 80; body and mind dichotomy 34; divisive psychoanalysis 207; dualism 7, 20–1, 50, 62–3, 91, 100, 188, 200; framework 99; heritage 8; individualistic paradigm 204, 219; intellectual traditions 62; mind-body duality 102; models 41n1; ontology 211; opposition 222; philosophy 218; psyche-soma bifurcation 97; substance 176; theory 223
Cartesianism 20–1, 40, 49, 57, 97, 211; revolt against 83, 221
Cartesians 100, 102
Cartesian–Lockean–Kantian subject 33
Cartesian–Platonic presuppositions 220, 222
Cassirer, E. 65
categorical 8, 33, 100, 105; delineations 57, 71, 92, 94; differentiations 36; distinctions 39, 57, 79, 166, 231; evaluative hierarchy 58; position 119; prejudices 197; standpoint 17; valuation 196
chaos 54, 91, 100, 195; theory 114
Chessick, R.D. 104, 218
ch'i *see* qi
cogitans *see res cogitans*
cogito 21; *see also res cogitans*
complementarity 9, 55, 87–8, 100, 102, 111, 112, 121, 143; Buddhist-inspired psychoanalytic notions of

complementarity *continued*
223; dual-process 103; dual reversibility-complementarity of functions 71; of undivided activity 154
connectionist 9–10, 105, 111, 114, 143, 165, 219, 225, 233; cross-modal synthetic-connectionist 92; Eastern and psychoanalytical 233; formulations 114; models 104–6; networks 105; organizing principles in psychoanalysis 143; physio-mental paradigm 225; somatic-mental relations 219; systems-oriented theorizing 106; theorems 10; theories 119; theorizing 111
consciousness (*Vijñāna*) 9, 48, 63, 68, 70–1, 73, 77, 93, 95, 98n5, 100, 112, 118, 124, 127, 133, 138, 141, 144, 150–1, 164–5, 172, 174, 176, 188, 216, 222, 232; act aspect of 78n3; awareness 153–4; biological substratum 60; body 96; contents of 31, 49, 120, 132; corporal 123; discursive 180; Eastern traditions of 94; ego 160; embodied 69, 134; equating with psyche 80; existential experience of 57; higher spiritual 156; incarnate 204; localization of 70, 147n13; manifestations of 62; mind-consciousness 53, 176, 217; mind-consciousness-head trio 69; mode of 62, 89, 188, 207; pre-conceptual mode of 89; pre-conscious holistic infra-structures 90; pre-verbal 85; primary 140; reflective 87; reinscribe 73, 104, 139; self as potentiality of 91; six consciousnesses 133, 159, 163; substrate of 84
consciousness, body-mind 131, 135, 177, 224–5; states of 223
consciousness, states of 108, 134; body-mind 223; complementary 103
conventional 4, 89, 105, 111, 132, 168, 189, 201, 213, 223; body-mind predication 165, 194; body-mind question 130; conceptions 88; conceptual framework 112; disciplines 122; divisions in descriptions 92; dualistic fissure 103; living 158; metaphors we live by 70; mind over body 166; notion of substantiality 143; notions of subjectivity and selfhood 151; Occidental categorization 149; pillars of theory of reality 56; psychoanalytic know-how 195; psychoanalytic psychotherapy 162; psychology 136; suppositions 115; theoretical formulations 118; truths 129
conventional duality 174; between matter and spirit 145
conventional oppositions 150; language and action 228
Cook, F.H. 6, 137, 181, 189
Cooper, J.W. 18–19
Cooper, P.C. 38, 125, 126n4, 155
counter-culture 122, 231; 1960s 173
countertransference 15, 31–2, 120, 201; bodily 190; somatic 54, 76
Csordas, T.J. 69, 218

Damasio, A. 34, 91–2, 95, 98n1, 145, 179
dasein 34, 65
Dao/Tao 140–1, 147n15
Daoism 147n14
Daoist 183; based practices 173; conceptualizations 77; constant flux 143; constructs 147n14; doctrine 159; non-duality opposites 123; perspective 80; philosophy 37, 123, 140; potentiality and being interplay 223; presuppositions 121;

psychotherapeutic practice 189; sage 186; system of medicine 125; terms in psychoanalysis 232; texts 35, 147n16, 189; therapeutic systems 225; underpinning of Zen-Buddhism 115
deconstruction 64, 96, 115, 165; hermeneutic 76; of psyche-soma 58
deconstructive: challenge of empirico-transcendental selfhood 163; function of emptiness 131
dependent co-arising/dependent origination (*Pratītya samutpāda*) 14, 128, 136, 151, 165, 224
dependent co-origination 142, 225; reciprocal co-origination 180
dependent origination 128, 136, 151, 165, 224
Derrida, J. 71, 76–7
Descartes, R. 20–1, 23, 59n2, 91, 101, 201; *see also* Cartesian, Cartesianism
Deutsche, F. 24, 54
developmental 9, 113; approach in psychoanalysis 211; arrest 63; bias 19; evaluative sphere 221; pathway 166; perspective 91; position 119; psyche-soma fissures 8; presuppositions 143; pre-verbal stages 56, 63; psychoanalysts 175; psychological-mental step forward 25; psychological scheme 36; research 4, 68, 91, 94–5, 97, 164; standpoint 17; supremacy 39; theories 29–30, 32, 48; theorizing 219
developmental distinctions 39; body-mind 79, 166
developmental progress 87; epigenetic 48, 56; linear progressive models 141
developmental progression 140, 174; body-mind 220; linear 143; temporal 144

dharma 129, 166, 178, 210, 230; Buddha-dharma 137; teacher 167n2; true eye 11n2, 183
discursive 10; consciousness 180; discourse 178; discursive-linguistic awareness 146; knowledge 38, 172; knowledge-power relations 220; logic 218, 223; opposition 228; subjectivity 170; thinking 89, 162, 172, 177, 227, 230
discursive-embodied language 184
disposition (Samskara) 150, 168, 183, 186, 198, 230, 232; analyst's 211–12; analytical 205; attitudinal 209; awakened 199; body-mind 190, 193; compassionate 209; compound dispositional attitude 193; embodied-hermeneutic 34; embodied therapeutic 10; empathic 214; mental 112, 142, 205; non-discriminative 40, 177; non-tensional 204; positivistic 31; psyche-somatic 193; psychoanalytic 53; realist-mystical 228; somato-psychic 176; undifferentiated 198; *see also* predisposition
dispositional: body-mind-set mode 230; compound attitude 193; mindset 209
Drummond, M. 7, 196
dualism 23, 57, 90, 103, 139; Aristotle's 41; attempt to overcome 212; boundaries 110; Cartesian 7, 20–1, 50, 62–3, 91, 100, 188, 200; developmental failure in non-dualism 113; functional 28; grafted on to Greek thought 19; interactive 44; mind body 2, 20, 171, 220; pairing with monism 143; penchant for 44, 58; perceived as a hindrance 112; Platonic-Cartesian 50; Plato's 18; recalcitrant 109, 117, 220; seeming inevitability of 132; seeming intrinsic 217; shown to be

dualism *continued*
   nonexistent 222; substantial 26; surmounting 131; *see also* body-mind dualism
duality 11, 29, 40, 175; Cartesian mind-body 102; as complementary formulation 138; conventional 145, 174; inveterate 117; loosened 111; transient suspension of 145, 176, 211

Eigen, M. 4, 30, 81, 83, 96, 101, 114, 155, 182, 195, 221, 232
elements 92, 100, 105, 140, 164, 168; Buddhist Great Elements model 136; comprising body (rūpa) 150; difficult to convey in words 104, 169–70; of language 73; mental 151, 224; prosodic, of communication 73; relationally valid 195
Elisha, P. 28, 62, 71, 74
Ellman, S.J. 66, 76
embodied 86, 209; attunement 204; awareness 146, 196; capacities 232; cognition 52, 136, 144; cognizance 10, 227; consciousness 69; contemplation 197; empathic-compassionate role 11; empathic relating 203; epistemological claim 180; experiential undercurrent 186; expressive articulations 228; heart-mind 187; hermeneutic disposition 34; injunctions 156; interactions 175, 193, 227; intersubjectivity 119; intersubjective relationship 226; involvement 186; knowledge 172; language 40, 176, 184, 187; meaning 51, 174; mental posture 199; mindedness 121; mindfully 159; minds 8, 21, 23, 74, 121, 148, 180; mode of letting go 178; modes of being 36; non-dualistic epistemology 134; participation 137, 187; perceptual sphere 137; presence 185, 187, 210, 226; psychology 40; realism 180; relationality 189; resonance 61; responsiveness 167; semiotic sphere 182; sensational and emotive life 197; sense of understanding 66; subject 120, 145; subjectivity 35, 101, 120, 125, 145, 149, 170–1; transposition 201; unspoken dimensions 189; in upright sitting 184
embodied selfhoods 125, 227; spiritual aspects 226
embodiment 27, 33, 69, 81, 95, 104, 172, 187; of body-mind-one 198; of compassion 208; of mindfully-saturated reality 166; recognition of subject's 179; of truth 167; of understanding and cognition 75; Zen-Buddhist notions of 146
emergent 99; body-mind scheme 164; capacities 145; clinical situation 66; psyche-somatic process 93; quadruple matrix 50; self-hood 86, 164; selves 92; therapeutic disciplines 37
emergent features 105; consciousness 69, 165
emergent properties 93–4, 165, 221; of the body 27, 91; of gestural conjuncture 85; non-discriminate 10; of psyche and soma 111
emergent states: of consciousness 103; sensual-affective-somatic 91
empathic 67; attuned mindset of therapist 208; attunement 207; body-mind presence of analyst 190; bonds 62; capacity enhanced 214; compassionate role of therapist 11, 193; embodied relating 203; feeling-in 202; interpretations 211; involvement 209; linkage 193; presence-

attunement 214; psyche-somatic attunement 202; resonance 195, 213; sensibility 201; stance 164; understanding 188; verbal response 193
empathic-relational mindset 201
empathy 62, 65, 175, 201–2, 208, 230; attuned 203; enacted 211; feeling-in 212, 215n2; practice-wisdom of 204; role in psychoanalytic discourse 214; somatic 78n3; Zen-empathy 208
emptiness (śūnyatā) 10, 128, 130–1, 134, 146n2, 146n4, 146n6, 146n9, 147n14, 160, 177, 198, 229; of emptiness 129; emptiness-potentiality of experience and conceptualization 225; of essential nature 223; Nāgārjuna's notion of 143, 223
enactments 61, 73–5, 79, 85, 108, 169, 195, 209, 213, 233
energetic 57, 61; conduits 159; drive 92; economic meta-theory 39; Freudian proposition 43, 48; legacy 47; monistic 44; proposal 56
energetic models 8, 17; Freudian 47; monistic 45
energetic-sensual-perceptive-mental properties of patients 226
energy 17, 44, 51, 59n3, 93, 159, 161, 200, 225; animating 207; circulation 180; emotional 105; Ki- 198; lack of 46; matter-energy (qi) 160; mental 92; psychic 43, 47–8; repression of 45
Engler, J. 151, 166, 194
enlightened 180, 199
enlightenment 22, 172, 180, 196; European 19
epiphenomenal 43; mechanism 28
epiphenomenalism 26
epiphenomenalist 59n1
epistemology 3, 45, 57, 64, 68, 77, 79, 88, 90, 110, 182; body 70; body-mind 159, 180; Cartesian 211; conventional Occidental 58; of dialectics 102; of intersubjectivity 97; intuitive 178; non-dualistic embodied 134; rift with orthodox 96; unitary 80; Zen 178, 180
epistemology, psyche-somatic 76; experiential 223, 225
Epstein, M. 38, 94, 129, 143, 145
Eubanks, C. 186–7
events 10, 24; bodily 177; chain of continuous 151, 153; consolidate to pre-reflective unified gestalt 93; endless web of 128; interactive 164; mental 42, 97; psyche-somatic 197, 224; psychical 54–5, 171, 177; psychophysical 149, 151; verbal-metaphysical 31
extensa *see res extensa*

Fast, I. 107
flux/change 15, 76, 109, 139, 151; ambience 200; constant 5, 10, 38, 40, 143, 165, 176, 223–6; constant flux-becoming 190; continual 149; of disciplinary matrix 39; embracing, through non-attachment 225; fundamental nature of the world 140; immanent 140–1; inherent 147n14; in key Mahāyāna text 141; low speed 55, 104; originative source of 50; perspective of 225; process of 199, 209; of psycho-physical events 151; therapeutic 53; Zeitgeist 231
Foucault, M. 71, 101, 165, 173, 218
Freud, S. 1, 16–18, 20, 28–31, 33, 36, 39, 41n3, 42–5, 48, 52–4, 59n1, 59n2, 60–2, 74, 80, 88, 91–2, 95, 97, 100, 113, 128, 144, 146n2, 148, 197, 198–9, 216–17, 220, 230–1; death 47, 172; feeling-in empathy 201, 212, 215n2

Freudian 18, 30, 42, 49; analyst 216; depth psychology 93; meta-theory 42; orthodoxy 90; post-Freudian theorizing 56; theory 16, 43, 47–8; unconscious 47
Frie, R. 3, 75, 145
Friedman, L. 42–3, 55
Fromm, E. 35–6, 38, 121, 123–4, 126n4, 173, 176, 232
fusion 81, 195, 217, 221

Gabrieli-Rehavi, I. 89, 232
Gadamer, H.G. 66, 172, 217
Galton, G. 1–2
Garfield, J. 128–9, 131
Gates, F. 29, 31, 40, 54, 213, 219
Gellman, J.I. 83
Gill, M. 56, 59n3
Goenka, S.N. 196–7
Grotstein, J.S. 49, 53
Grunbaum, A. 43, 55

Hakeda, Y. 127, 141, 143
heart (*shin, kokoro*) 21, 51, 105, 161, 179, 220; attack 178; governs blood 160; at the-heart-of our-body (*hsin*) 37; heart-to-heart transmission 183; heart-mind 187; open-hearted 190; of the problem 144; think with the heart 69; warm 136
Heart Sūtra 130, 135, 146n4
Hegel, G. 49–50
Hegelian 57; framework 49; paradigm 32, 39
Heidegger, M. 64–5, 80, 85–6, 97, 99, 123, 157; Heideggerian underpinnings of Western phenomenology 222
Heine, S. 6, 186, 207, 228
hermeneutic 6, 48, 57, 86, 228; bodily-bound outlook 163; conceptualizations borrowed from Zen-Buddhist tradition 98; deconstruction 76; embodied disposition 34; embodied stance 40; explanatory models 143; investigation 79; meta-theories 8, 90; reconstruction 104; reconstructive theories 122; theoretical proposition 27
hermeneutically derived meta-theory 96
hermeneutical meta-theorizing 118; plea to a psychoanalytic meta-theory 86
hermeneutic-biologistic oppositions 97
hermeneutic-linguistic 76
hermeneutics 61, 74, 84, 86, 97, 115, 217; Gadamer's 66; modern 172
Herzog, B. 170, 209
hierarchical body to mind distinctions rebutted 166, 231; non-hierarchical distinction 154; positions 63; presuppositions 143; progression from body to mind 220
Holt, R.R. 23, 43, 56
Horney, K. 77, 194
Husserl, E. 62, 65, 69, 73, 98n3, 208; underpinnings of Western phenomenology 222
Hutten, E.H. 23, 99, 113

identity theory 28, 91
impermanence 198, 229
intentionality 48; actional 156, 167; de-tensionalized 156
interconnected 58, 135; language and phenomena 184; mesh 136; selfhood 176; sphere of experience 86
interconnectedness 98n4, 126, 151
interdependence 58, 102, 111, 115, 128
International Association for Relational Psychoanalysis and Psychotherapy 167n1
interpenetrations 6, 11, 16, 47, 60, 66, 72, 75, 87, 96–7, 115, 120, 137,

143, 183, 190, 193, 195, 201, 208, 233; analytic 87; body eludes 67; of body and mind 138; conducing non-dual subjectivity 165; divergent 157; embodied manner of delivery 125; empathic 97, 211; failure of verbal 118; genetic and dynamic 175; linguistic 9, 55; of patient communications 201; of phenomena 155; procedural 170, 173, 209, 215; psychoanalytic 189; psychoanalytic verbal 27; in psychodynamic psychotherapy 172; psychosomatically informed 76; of qi 160; replaced by transmutation 210; silent 170, 209, 233; something more than 107, 114; therapist's 195; total 211; traditional role of 202; truth of 33; of universality and particularity 186; verbal 32, 173; Zen 189, 202–4, 207, 209, 212, 214, 228
intersubjectivity 3, 30, 40, 84, 94, 96–7, 101, 119, 150, 165, 195, 201, 204, 219
introception 49, 69, 193; introspection-introception 204
introspection 100, 193; introspection-introception 204
Irwin, J.W. 40, 115, 163
Izutsu, T. 222

James, W. 81, 221
Japanese Soto-Zen 4
Johnson, M. 2, 7, 20–1, 70, 74, 100–1, 112, 149, 169, 171, 179–80, 220
Jones, J.W. 101–2
just sitting (*shikan taza*) 155–6, 165, 178, 180, 206

Kakar, S. 214
Kalupahana, D. 182, 184
Kant, I. 33, 41n4, 59n5, 65, 100
Kantian 39; analytic approach 57; subjectivism 33, 40, 49, 65; subjectivity 50, 63, 133
Kantians 100
Kasulis, T.P. 7, 36, 122, 134, 140–1, 143, 147n10, 181, 197–8, 208, 213, 223
Kavaler-Adler, S. 24–5
Kim, H.J. 6, 131, 137, 167, 177, 180, 184
Knoblauch, S.H. 3, 40, 93–4, 165, 202, 229
Kohut, H. 34, 43, 87, 89–90, 96, 102–4, 164, 166, 170–1, 190, 194, 210; post-Kohutian 103
Kuang-Ming, W. 22, 37, 77, 148, 163–4, 222, 226
Kuhn, T.S. 11, 17, 39, 99, 118, 218
Kulka, R. 6, 89, 103, 125, 144–5, 155, 174–5, 188, 194–5, 223, 232

Lacan, J. 77, 88–9, 170, 183
Lacanian 88, 183; notion of Real 67; psychoanalyst 60; reconstructive theories 122
Lachmann, F.M. 4, 30, 92–3, 95
Lakoff, G. 7, 21, 70, 74, 112, 149, 169, 179–80, 220
language 2, 7–8, 20, 24, 27, 33, 74–5, 87, 168, 174, 188, 199, 226–7, 229; appearance of 85; of becoming 184, 227; body 47, 68, 72; Buddhist 182; from Buddhist and Daoist texts 189; cohesive 58; constraints on 5, 38, 223; of continuous process 93; of a discipline 122; embodied 40, 176, 184; evocative 108, 214; inherent limitations of 10; linguistic elements of 73; logical-explanatory-scientific 66; non-discursive 218; ordinary 24, 171; other 171–2; philosophy of 66, 70, 79, 182, 220; primacy of 48; professional 23; of psychoanalysis 220; reformation of 40, 220; relations of 173, 186–7,

language *continued*
228; representational 121; specific 110; theoretical 121; therapeutic 171, 187; use of 23–4, 67, 170, 178, 220; Zen 177, 182–3, 190
Lash, S. 122, 173, 218
Lawner, P. 4, 56, 104, 114, 194
Leavy, S. 81, 87, 103, 213, 228
Leder, D. 62, 101, 160, 167n3
Leighton, D. 147n10, 199
Li, C.L. 140, 223
Little, M. 53, 56, 233
Lobel, T. 136, 144
Loewald, H.W. 29, 124
logos 20, 80
Lombardi, R. 54, 70, 72, 75, 212, 228
Loy, D. 131–2, 221

Mūlamadhyamakakārikā (MMK) 128–9, 131, 146n3
Mackay, N. 43–4, 48
Magid, B. 6, 37–8, 94, 113, 125, 142, 155, 163, 213, 225
Mahāyāna 127; doctrine of Hua-yen 137; Lankavatara sūtra 141; Prajñāpāramitā canonical texts 146n7; schools 128, 146n1; sūtras 186–7; tradition 146n5
Mancia, M. 57, 74
Masunaga, S. 22, 40, 217
McDougal, J. 50
medicine 2, 189; Chinese 159; Eastern 64, 159, 200; Eastern Daoist and Buddhist-informed systems 125, 159; Eastern mind-body 21, 29; history of 192; Oriental 109; social research 47; Zen philosophies 37; Western 125
meditation 64, 156, 175, 199, 230; Buddhist 194, 197, 229; Descartes's sixth 20; flux-change acquired 225; Mindfulness 196, 212; outcome of 81; practitioners 196; Zen (zazen) 147n11, 199, 204

meditative practice 10, 36, 125, 194; Buddhist 7, 11, 193; co-originative matrix of procedural relationships 184; furthers experiential mode 177; introspective body-mind 203; performed in the physical-mental posture of just sitting 165
Meissner, W. 17, 20, 26, 28–30, 33, 69–70, 76, 94, 168, 188, 194, 208, 217, 221, 229
mental states 96, 146n2, 153, 196, 198; inseparability from soma 231; interaction with bodily postures 163; physio-mental states 4, 206; primitive 180–1
Merleau-Ponty, M. 7–8, 34, 62–3, 66, 75–6, 78n3, 84–6, 93, 97, 98n3, 123, 149, 160, 173, 182, 218–19, 222
metaphysical 18, 87, 160, 180, 224, 226; argumentation 114; attainment of awakening 158; concepts 72; form 127; interventions 28; metaphysical-mystical 81; metaphysical-spiritual pole 114; perception 51; psyche 63; reality set apart 186; selfhood annulled 151; stance 189; truth 129; undercurrent 108; unity 93
metaphysical-verbal (verbal-metaphysical) event 31; interventions 28, 30; psychic-cognitive-intellectual-verbal-metaphysical attributes 38–9
metaphysics 115, 118; western, refuting 140
meta-theory/metatheory 17, 23, 118; alternative 114; body-mind 1, 8; energetic economic 39; Freudian 42–3; parsimonious 188; of psyche-soma 1, 122, 221; psyche-somatic 117; psychoanalytic 42–3, 55, 85–6, 121, 217; reconstructive 86; revised 76; theoretical re-evaluation 96

metonymic 20; portrayals 190; metonymical relationship 71
metonymy/metonymies 60; psyche-soma 79
Milner, M. 4, 81, 88–9, 126n1, 155, 201, 204, 214
mindfulness (Vipassanā) 9, 157, 196–8, 212, 229; body-mindfulness 148; practice 230
Molino, A. 35–6, 38, 94, 112, 123–4, 194
Moncayo, R. 77, 88, 98n5, 102, 177
monism 26–7, 44, 139, 143, 217
moulting 147n10, 190; of body and mind 10, 217
mysterious leap 8, 45, 50, 75; initial 31, 54; from mind to body 1, 16, 39, 83, 171; between psyche-somas 89
mysterious undercurrents 9, 100, 103–4, 113, 143
mystery 1, 39, 45, 101, 121, 127–8, 130; interpersonal 16; of intimacy 184; of psychical events affecting the body 54
mystical 89, 212; contributions 17; experiences 83, 90; feeling 82; instrumental-mystical aspiration 184; metaphysical-mystical 81; oceanic state 94, 113; perspectives 90; psyche-soma unity 88; spirituality 180; studies 81; underpinnings 103
mystical-religious 9, 96, 99; approaches within psychoanalysis 27, 211; experience 88; frame of reference 30; off-shoots of mainstream psychoanalysis 94; positions within psychoanalysis 90; propositions 97; psychoanalysis 88; strain 142, 219; strand of contemporary psychoanalysis 119; terminology 4; thinkers 175; trends within psychoanalysis 5, 39

Nāgārjuna 10, 128, 130–2, 143, 146n3, 173, 223
Nagatomo, S. 7, 155, 157, 162, 166, 180–1, 204, 206–7, 214, 222, 224
Nauriyal, D.K. 7, 29
Neo-Kantian proposition 65
neuro-psychoanalysis 91, 94, 119, 165
neuro-psychoanalytic 9, 91, 99, 109, 202, 211, 219; monistic resolutions 28; perspective 29, 142, 208; proposition of the mind 94; research 68, 92, 97; theories 4, 95–6; trends in psychoanalysis 5, 39
neuro-psychological 105; base for psycho-analytic theories 95; conceptualizations 107; nomenclature 195; psychoanalysis 91; research 30, 78n3, 94–5; state-of-the-art practice 196; unitary formulations 55
neuro-psychology 210, 220
neutrality 31, 52–3
Ng, M.L. 37, 125
non-Cartesian interpersonal psychotherapeutic endeavour 213; psychoanalysis 33
non-discursive communication 219; language 218
non-discursive corporeal involvement 218
non-dualism 113; psyche-soma in psychoanalysis 121
non-duality 6, 80, 83, 88, 115, 118, 134, 144, 154, 167n4, 170, 212, 221, 228; absence of substantiality 130; body-mind 155; Buddhist perspective 144, 151; Buddhist-psychoanalytic discourse 125; in contemporary psychoanalysis 96; Daoist 123; Eastern foundational 37; in Eastern medical models 21; forms of 132, 137; fundamental 143; of life and death 149; Mahayana roots 128; organizational

non-duality *continued*
  principles 120, 142; overarching 148; psyche-soma 8, 231; psyche-somatic 232; psychoanalytic conceptualizations of 37; of selfhood 165; spiritual acquisition of 188; theories of 9; Zen 176; Zen-Buddhist 10, 121, 127–8, 131
non-representational view of the mind 188

oceanic: experiences 96; feelings 36, 80, 91; state 94, 113
Ogden, T.H. 40, 52, 58, 85–6, 120, 231
Opatow, B. 4, 29, 48, 91, 97, 109–10, 114–15
Orange, D.M. 66, 101–3, 111

paradigm shifts 17, 38–9, 110, 118, 218, 228, 231; hypothesized 83; innovative 4; mind-body relations 125; in philosophy of language 79; in psychoanalysis 221; in scope and aims of psychoanalysis 88
paradox(es) 9, 11, 88, 100, 103, 111, 113, 121, 128, 130, 142–3, 183, 186, 195, 199, 229; conceptual 28; Freud's 16, 18; inherent 18, 71, 102, 216; resolution to 182, 223; Winnicottian 58, 101; Zen concept of 198
parallelism 27; linguistic 26–7
parallelist 59n1
parallelistic: divides 28; paradigms 168
Park, Y.J. 7, 77
phenomenology 7–8, 64–5, 84; of dasein 34; of perception 62, 75, 86; of perceptual-sensual states 52; of pre-reflective unitive experience 87; of psyche-soma participation 75; of psyche-somatic states 27; unified bodily-mental 26; of unmediated experience 72

phenomenology 97, 110, 123, 134, 218–19; of body-mind 155, 225; of body-mind experience 177; of Heidegger 157; psyche-somatic 118, 162; of unformulated experience 224; of unitive experience 96, 99; Western 156, 182, 222
physio-mental states 4, 206
Pickering, J. 176
Plato 7; allusions to the soul 20; dualism 18
Platonic 8; -Christian philosophical tradition 19; depictions of the soul 18; paradigms 38; presuppositions 222; views 19
Platonic-Cartesian dualism 50; presuppositions 220
Platonism 19
positivist 84; outlooks 87; routes 86; positivism 87
positivistic 43; -biologistic 76; conception of reality 49; conceptualizations 144; disposition 31; meta-theorizing 118; presuppositions in psychoanalysis 218; rejection of 173; study of unconscious as object 219
potentiality 11, 121, 127, 139, 141, 146n9, 226; of consciousness 91; Dao as endless 140; dynamic 142; emptiness 225; of existence 5, 10, 37, 40, 223; infinite 160; life 170; pre-representational 33; without thinking 224
practice 10, 81, 146n7, 180, 196, 227, 230; authentication 203; Buddhist 193, 225, 232; clinical 3, 16; of conferring meaning through enacted communication 183; contemporary 30, 60, 117, 195; decapsulated 203; deeper 184; dualistic 198; Eastern medical 159; embodied 125; indivisibility from realization 228;

intellectual, reversal of 156, 176; medical 13; mindful 197; mindfulness 230; oneness with awakening/realization 157, 187; practice-based orientation 181; of the psyche-soma, unitive 178; psyche-somatic form 199; of psyche-somatic integration 55; psychiatric 22; of psychoanalysis 59n4; psychoanalytic 3, 75, 80, 117, 142, 167, 180, 189–90, 202, 211; psychotherapeutic 162, 176, 189; radical changes 124; realization 158, 165–6, 199, 208, 224; therapeutic 22, 36, 64; therapeutic goal 225; wisdom of empathy 204; Zen 157, 198, 203, 213; Zen and Daoist-based 173; *see also* meditative practice

pre- 9, 87–8, 90, 97, 99, 139–41, 143, 223–4; *see* pre-conceptual, pre-dating, pre-determined, predisposition, pre-reflective, pre-symbolical, pre-verbal

pre-being 141;

pre-conceptual 141; conceptualization capacity 91; content of unthought-known 91; mode of consciousness 89; reality 88

pre-dating: Chan Buddhist paradigms 147n14; distinction of psyche-soma components 89; symbolical representation 63

pre-determined 33; behaviour 44; meaning 190

predisposition 119, 126n2; psyche-somatic 8; unitive 112

pre-ontology 127, 139, 143

prereflective/pre-reflective 9, 87–8, 119, 141, 181, 202, 208; ability to merge with an-other 201; building-blocks 84; ego 85; experience 134; interweaving 66, 85; meaning 190; psycho-mentation 145; selfhood 119; stance 181; unconscious 84; unified gestalt 93; unitive experience 87

presentation 74, 76, 86, 118, 152, 170, 190, 217; bodily 75; of the body 62; of the body-psyche 70; direct 8, 53, 56, 62, 233; distinction from representation refuted 177; primary 73; of reality 56; unarticulated 81; unmediated 187

pre-symbolical 165; aspects of psyche and soma 40; consciousness 85; function 192

pre-verbal/preverbal 188, 202; aspects of psyche and soma 40; communication 50; consciousness 85; developmental stages 63; experiences 170; forms of being 173; interactions 56; life 63; modes of awareness 211; psychic structures 32; relational paradigms 94; selfhoods 92

primary 59n5, 114, 124; bodily manifestations 74; bodily subjectivity 64; body-mind consciousness 135, 140; essentiality 130; existence 111; fusion 81, 221; maternal preoccupation 183; mental concepts 56; motivational and cultural forces 61; mystical perspectives 90; oceanic feelings 91; phenomenon 66, 76; presentation 73; progression to secondary 36; primitive aspect 119; role of body 40, 48, 62; sensations 36; somatic and mental-spiritual attributes 36; status 88, 96; symptoms 37, 125; transcendental-noumenal truth 90; unitive experiences 81, 88; unknowable element 89

primary processes 17, 34, 66, 81, 88, 119, 124; instinctual 62; untamed bodily forces 84

primitive 62; aspect of selfhood 17; body-aspect 119; bodymind proposition 217; mode of experience 87; object usage or self-object relationships 164
primitive states: emergent sensual-affective-somatic 91; mental 150, 180–1
proto 9, 90, 99, 143, 224; conversations 85, 175; dialogues 93; formation 89; mind 58, 89
proto-mental: capacities 33; phenomenon 90
proto-self/selves 91, 120; selfhood or predisposition 119
proto-states 140; of being 89
proto-type: psyche-soma 97; schemata 172
psyche-soma 1, 22, 28–9, 32, 34, 52, 76, 80, 104, 183, 211; bodily aspect of 69; co-joint unit 8; components 74, 89; compound 42; conceptualization in psychoanalysis 45; continuum 56; deconstruction of 58; divide 111; dual form of active attunement 208; duo 33, 39, 76; dyadic interaction 127; dyadic relationship 40; integrative theory 232; interaction 223; intuitive intimacy with 213; linguistic contributions of Zen-Buddhism 11; matrix 50; meta-theory 122, 221; metonymies 79; non-dualism 121; in object-relations 48; participation 75; proto type 97; quadruple interactions 33; regulatory loops 30; relations 4, 6, 17, 27, 35, 38, 43, 48, 64, 79, 88, 119, 122, 222; scientific study 98n1; unit 8, 39, 54, 224; unitive practice of 178; unity 176
psyche-somatic 8, 23, 75, 166, 178, 181, 231; agent 165; a-intellectual modus 37; body-mind interaction 39; Buddhist scheme of 156; clinical demeanour of analyst 57; cohesive unity 119; communions 208; continuum 51; convergence 1, 99; duo 36; emergent process 93; epistemology 76; expression, dual-track conceptualization 233; flow, arrest in 162; function of *alaya-vijñāna* 141; happenings, events 212, 224; heuristic 101; integration 55, 232; leaps 48, 54; life 164, 212; linkages 193; meta-theories 43, 117; non-differentiated system 159; non-duality 232; organizational patterns 84; patterns, shared 107; phenomenology 118; position of mutuality 164; pre-reflective structures and processes 9; presence 195, 211; sense of non-obstruction 161–2; split 34; subjectivities 171; subjects 213; substrate of un-differentiation 176; suffusion 214; unified manifestations 218; unitary ontological predication 119; unity 103
psyche-somatic attunement 112, 193, 210; empathic 202; expression and 233; mutual 11, 207
psyche-somatic being 49, 224; unfamiliar levels 207
psyche-somatic communications: interactive grid 52; non-verbal 201
psyche-somatic, compound 45; categories in language 220; interlaced relationality 201; mental-spiritual functional 159
psyche-somatic entities 90, 225; isolable 32; leaps between 54
psyche-somatic experience 219; experiential undertaking 223; subjective 58
psyche-somatic form 229; practice 199; transformation 211
psyche-somatic reality 168; non-dualistic 89; overarching 58; shared 112

psyche-somatic relations 42, 60, 112; interlaced-compounded relationality 201; in psychoanalysis 29–30
psyche-somatics 118
psyche-somatic states 206, 230; compound 45; continuity of self-states 153; of emergence 194; experience and phenomenology ignored 27; non-dualistic 5, 38, 223, 229; unconscious, empathic resonance with 213; unified 34
psyche-somatic theorizing 47; dualistic 142
psyche-somatic unitive experiences 4, 108; reciprocal 227
psychoanalytic-Buddhist 125, 176, 180; dialogue 10, 118, 121, 123, 125, 145, 155, 173, 187, 194–5, 221, 231–2; training 232; *see also* Buddhist-psychoanalytic
psychosomatic 45, 192; differentiation 4; life 73; models 8; psychoanalysis 46; relations 19, 118; symptoms 109; theory 36, 47; theorizing 50
psychosomatics 42, 44–5, 47, 56–8, 118; conventional 53; orthodox 50–1, 54
Pytell, T. 57, 142

qi (ch'i) 10, 159–60, 162–5, 225–6, 232–3

Rahula, W. 149
Rand, M.L. 202
Raz, J. 128, 141, 184, 227
Real, The 170
reality 27, 38, 64, 129, 137, 146, 158, 168–9, 172, 182–3, 229; all-inclusive nature 141, 154; attune to 222; body immersed in 164; body-mind 190; Buddhist configuration of 128–30; clinical 217; conceptual 226; corporal-concrete 177; dualistic approach 132; emotional 63; encountering 208; engaging with 166; experiential 102; external 184; facets of 174, 178, 203; indivisible nature 98n4, 189; inter-personal 32; intertwined with the mind 50; intimacy of psyche-soma 167; means of recognizing 181; non-dualistically inhabit 113; out there 49; of participative experience 66; physical 122, 180, 190; pleasure/reality principle 89; as present-presented 61, 79; psychic 54, 84, 172; relationship with language 186–8, 223, 228; relinquishing all views 131; shared psyche-somatic 112; social 62; suchness of 141, 182, 190, 203; ultimate 129, 212; unitive inter-connected 94; *see also* ultimate truth or reality
realization 133, 158, 166, 206, 228; awakening 157, 207; intellectual and spiritual 224; practice 165–6, 199, 208, 224; self- or other 205
reason 90, 116n1; versus emotions 20
reasoning 20; line of 58, 66, 128, 137, 176; of neo-revisionist epigone 43
Reich, W. 34, 74, 78n4
Reis, B. 3, 23, 49, 52, 54, 62, 66, 76, 85–6, 90, 98n3, 114, 201, 208, 211
relational 221; analysts 1, 90, 229; aspects of non-verbal responsiveness 211; awareness 155; conceptualizations 107; criticism 90; empathic-relational mindset 201; feminist-Buddhist stance 202; formulations 84, 188; formulations, non-dual 188; installations 60; integration of temporal and spatial cues 92; interpenetration 207; inter-personal sphere 50; knowing, implicit 93–4; matrix 183, 203, 227, 232; perspective 62, 105, 195, 208; perspective of pre-verbal

relational *continued*
  interactions 56; point of view 202; state, profound 164; system 57
relational interaction 198; pre-verbal perspective 56; psychoanalytic modes 73
relational intersubjectivity 150, 165, 219; embodied 118–19; perspective 142
relational paradigms, contemporary 149; pre-verbal and non-verbal 94
relational psychoanalysis 30, 94, 167n1, 219; IARPP 167n1; modes of psychoanalytic interaction 73; psychoanalyst 93–4, 108, 144, 169, 178, 213
relationality 163; dependent 51; embodied 189; interlaced-compounded psyche-somatic 201; intuitive intercorporeal 148
religious 81, 152; contributions repudiated 17; conventional forms 114; dogma 71; experience 83; mystico-religious writers 165; quasi-religious 89; sentiments 125; thought 173; traditions 4, 20, 220; *see also* mystical, mystical-religious
Rendon, M. 32–3, 49, 205
representational 66; aspects of the body 54; awareness 142; language 121; meaning, loss of 51; non-representational view of the mind 188; post-representational order 119; pre-representational potentiality 33; symbolic level 76
representations 10, 86; of the body 17; communicability of somatic intersubjectivity 33; mental 49, 63, 73; metaphorical 48; narrative 48; preconscious 92; of sensual-affective-somatic states 91; symbolical 8, 56, 63, 66, 74, 76; verbal 66; of the world-view 22
representations 170, 177, 190, 229; of external reality 184; mental formations 98n5; symbolical 118
*res cogitans* 21, 49–50, 55, 58, 59n2, 75, 91, 104, 158
*res extensa* 21, 50, 55, 58, 59n2, 91, 104, 158
reverie 53, 89, 120, 139, 145, 230, 232; analyst's 40, 85, 201; non-intellectual mode of 188, 203; sensual-affective 214; sensual and bodily 211–12
Rhys, D. 155, 223
rhythmic 51; rhythmicity 220
rhythm(s) 9, 73, 107–8, 111–13, 174, 192, 202, 229; body 93; of laughter and weeping 152; of psyche-somatic life 164; unfitting 106
Rick, M. 54, 231
Rorty, R. 66–7, 96, 169, 227
Rubin, J.B. 6, 23, 38, 126n4, 197, 199, 214, 229, 232

Safran, J. 6, 37, 125, 144
Sawyier, F.H. 2, 49, 122
Scalzone, F. 43, 55, 58, 104, 139, 158
Schafer, R. 44, 49, 56, 58
Scharff, D.E. 44, 50, 87, 92
Schore, A.N. 28, 30, 48, 53, 73, 91–2, 95, 120, 195, 205
secondary 219; primary-to-secondary progression 36; symptoms 37, 125
selfhoods 103, 134, 144, 148, 151, 176, 207, 212, 218; affirmed by suchness of reality 203; body-mind 10, 214; composite genetic and environmental 104; core and emergent 86; conceptualized as combination of physical and mental aggregates 77; embodied 227; embodied/spiritual 125, 226; empirico-transcendental 163; mental-physical 224; non-dual 166; pre-symbol-formation 92; primitive aspect of 17; proto 119; quantum

145; sense of emotional 152; sensual-perceptual-somatic aspects of 150; transcendental 89
Sella, Y. 25, 122, 149
semiotic approach 78n3; communication 4, 9; embodied sphere 182; significance 75; tools 75; transmission 73; vehicle 6
semiotics 68, 74, 118
sensations (*Vedanā*) 22, 52, 66, 82, 92, 136, 150–1, 161, 178, 196, 198, 212; background 34; binding 44; bodily 48, 67, 197; discontinuity of movement 46; focus on 152; giving rise to 34; paying attention to 74; physical 216; primary 36; psyche-soma's 76; sharing 162; somatic 197, 229; two as one-ness 22, 29, 217; valid for free association 41n3; visual 154
*Shōbōgenzō* 4, 6–7, 11, 133, 154, 191n2
Shaner, D.E. 7, 134–5, 147n10, 156, 166, 177, 222, 226–7
Shapiro, S.A. 62, 174
Sheets-Johnstone, M. 69, 231
sign 35, 67; linguistic 168; signifier 226
sign-signified 40, 85; breach 10; grid 71; matrices 120; reference-referent matrices 79; relations 190
skin 138, 146, 154–5, 202, 204, 216; get under another's 108, 221; brain-skin 71, 77; skin-ego 6, 71, 77, 79, 108, 119, 171
something more 100, 107, 113–14
soul 151, 160, 163; acting interdependently with sense-perception and imaginal capacities 41n1; Cartesian concept 21; immaterial 18–19; immortal 61; metaphors for 20; present in every part of the body 70; tripartite formation 20; Zen alternative 36

Sperry, L.E. 30, 88, 94
spirit 18, 86, 101, 105, 127, 130, 145, 163, 165, 174, 223; becoming a 81, 95, 104; of embodied presence 226; free 95; Romantic 172; spirit-psyche 217
spirituality 88; debut into psychoanalysis 219; mystical 180
Spotnitz, H. 170, 233
Stambough, J. 6, 203
Stcherbatsky, T. 151, 154, 224
Stern, D.B. 120, 188
Stern, D.N. 4, 6, 34, 40, 67–8, 86, 92–3, 95–6, 106–7, 114, 145, 164, 170, 195, 232–3
Stolorow, R.D. 2, 16, 30, 40, 41n4, 42, 73, 84, 219
Suler, J. 94, 124, 209, 227, 233
supra 9, 99; perceptual 83; positions 90
supra-ordinate 97, 181; order 119; order with transformative potential 89; organizing function 89; reality 88; self 104; stratum 83, 97; structures 171
Suzuki, D.T. 35, 121, 123–4, 138, 160, 173, 182
Suzuki, S. 215n1, 228
svabhāva 128
systems 30, 100, 104–5, 111, 113–14, 119, 142–3, 219, 225, 233; affected-affecting 107; body-mind 165, 2244; conceptual 2, 20, 171, 220; connectionist models 9; connectionist systems-oriented theorizing 106; Eastern and psychoanalytical 233; functional 159; medical 225; of medicine 125; psychic 52; shared conceptual 171, 220; somatic-mental relations 219; theorems 10

talking cure 16, 23, 28, 75, 171, 174, 217, 219

Tanahashi, K. 11, 11n2, 133–4, 137–8, 154–5, 157–8, 165–6, 178, 180, 183, 189, 199, 200, 204–5, 208, 210, 213, 216, 230
Tao *see* Dao
transcendence 80, 86, 152
Trevarthen, C. 4, 85, 93, 95
Twemlow, S. 31, 198–9, 214, 229, 232

Uchiyama, K. 213, 230
ultimate truth or reality 129, 131, 182, 196, 212
undifferentiation 9, 81, 195; undifferentiated 198; undifferentiating 112, 124
unitive experience 3, 6, 8–9, 54, 77, 79–81, 84, 91–2, 94–6, 99–100, 103, 111, 113, 120–1, 125, 136, 166–7, 175, 189, 203, 211, 213–14, 219, 226–7, 229; alternative scheme of 168; at odds with medical protocol 109; attempt at integrating 228; concepts springing from 171; conceptualization 90, 228, 230; demystification of 174; disavows substantiality 165; dual 217; embracing as primary human attribute 87–8, 119; non-divisible 164; patient's 109, 112; psyche-soma 83, 115, 230; psyche-somatic 4, 108; tool for furthering 193; Zen of 221

Van Buren, J. 58, 89
Varela, F.J. 7, 68, 94, 180
vitality 9, 93, 115, 119–21, 159, 164, 202, 216–17, 220, 226, 233; affects 92; body-mind 225; corporal 163; forms of 145; Forms of 6, 93, 107, 232; life 77
Voloshinov, V.N. 171–2, 226

Wachtel, P. 174
Wallace, E.R. 16, 23, 59n1

Watts, A. 2, 112, 121–2, 126n4, 182–3, 222
Way 154, 157, 177, 180; *see also* Dao/Tao
well-being 51; future 210; psychical 53; psychological 52
Weltanschauung (world-view) 6, 29, 37–8, 158
Wilhelm, R. 35, 74, 123
Winnicott, D.W. 1, 6, 51–5, 57, 59n4, 68, 70, 72, 88, 98n2, 101, 116n1, 122, 126n1, 145, 147n13, 170–1, 190, 192, 195, 211, 229
Winnicottian 183; direct presentation of reality 53; paradox 58, 101; tradition 88
without thinking/not thinking (*hishiryo*) 133–4, 146n9, 181, 188, 198, 208, 224
Wittgenstein, L. 24, 67, 96, 171
Woolf, V. 44, 56, 58
Wrye, H.K. 23, 72, 102, 104, 139, 141, 202

Yuasa, Y. 7, 36, 77, 147n10, 198

*Zazen* (Zen meditation) 137, 147n11, 199, 204; Zazen Shin fascicle 133
Zen 126n3, 131, 146n7, 146n8, 147n12, 168, 176, 178, 180–1, 186, 209, 221, 223, 232–3; adepts 132, 145; attunement 204; canon 135; clinic 149; clinical body 165; concepts 148; conceptualizations 163, 204; convergence of realization-practice 166; Dao influence on 140; Daoist critique 77; on dualistic thinking 138; eyes 189; freedom from thought 133; infrastructure 184; instructor 94, 113; interpenetration-attunement 202; language 172, 177, 182, 190; master 208; meditation 147n11; perspective 137, 206; practice 157,

173, 198, 203, 213; practitioner 176; psychoanalysis 121; psychoanalytic dialogue 36, 214, 227; scholar 122, 156; student 1; students' initiation 154; teachings 228; terminologies 37; texts 11, 181, 187; training 145, 198; *see also* Zazen

Zen approach 149; body 154; body-mind 122, 166, 222

Zen-Buddhism 4, 8, 35, 41, 77, 115, 123, 142, 146n1, 147n14, 160, 222; body-mind integration 213, 221; incorporated into 1960s counter-culture 173; linguistic contributions 11; non-duality 37, 121, 131; and Psychoanalysis 35; supports non-dualistic frameworks 189

Zen-Buddhist 140, 154, 167n2, 223; conceptualizations 77, 94, 98, 112, 118, 125, 171, 187; dialogue with psychoanalysis 4, 6, 9, 37, 58, 80, 100, 123–4, 146; formulations 142, 222; integrated psychoanalytic approach 210; medical models adopted 159; meditative mindsets 229; notions of non-duality 10, 121, 127–8, 137; teacher 228; teachings 36; texts 6; therapeutic systems 225

Zen non-dualistic approach 212; body-mind paradigms 193; perspective 197–8; undivided activity 188

Zen-shiatsu 67; classes 105; session 216; therapist 22

Zen teacher 131, 155, 177, 198, 200, 213, 229; teacher-disciple relationship 183; teacher-student dialogical relationship 207

# Taylor & Francis eBooks

## Helping you to choose the right eBooks for your Library

Add Routledge titles to your library's digital collection today. Taylor and Francis ebooks contains over 50,000 titles in the Humanities, Social Sciences, Behavioural Sciences, Built Environment and Law.

Choose from a range of subject packages or create your own!

**Benefits for you**
- Free MARC records
- COUNTER-compliant usage statistics
- Flexible purchase and pricing options
- All titles DRM-free.

**Benefits for your user**
- Off-site, anytime access via Athens or referring URL
- Print or copy pages or chapters
- Full content search
- Bookmark, highlight and annotate text
- Access to thousands of pages of quality research at the click of a button.

REQUEST YOUR **FREE** INSTITUTIONAL TRIAL TODAY

**Free Trials Available**
We offer free trials to qualifying academic, corporate and government customers.

## eCollections – Choose from over 30 subject eCollections, including:

| | |
|---|---|
| Archaeology | Language Learning |
| Architecture | Law |
| Asian Studies | Literature |
| Business & Management | Media & Communication |
| Classical Studies | Middle East Studies |
| Construction | Music |
| Creative & Media Arts | Philosophy |
| Criminology & Criminal Justice | Planning |
| Economics | Politics |
| Education | Psychology & Mental Health |
| Energy | Religion |
| Engineering | Security |
| English Language & Linguistics | Social Work |
| Environment & Sustainability | Sociology |
| Geography | Sport |
| Health Studies | Theatre & Performance |
| History | Tourism, Hospitality & Events |

For more information, pricing enquiries or to order a free trial, please contact your local sales team:
**www.tandfebooks.com/page/sales**

The home of
Routledge books

**www.tandfebooks.com**